habnf   HEB
364.138 CENZI

DISCARD

Cenziper, Debbie, author
Citizen 865
33410016487987   11/13/19

W9-CAA-523

Hebron Public Library
201 W. Sigler Street
Hebron, IN 46341

CITIZEN
865

MORE PRAISE FOR
CITIZEN 865

"In telling the story of a little-known Holocaust site called Trawniki and the people who dedicated themselves to bringing some of modern history's worst monsters to justice, Debbie Cenziper has honored the vanishing plea to never forget, first by breaking my heart with the worst of humanity, and then, with the best of us, stitching it back together."

—David Finkel, winner of the Pulitzer Prize and *New York Times* bestselling author of *The Good Soldiers*

ALSO BY DEBBIE CENZIPER

Love Wins: The Lovers and Lawyers
Who Fought the Landmark Case for Marriage Equality

CITIZEN 865

The Hunt for Hitler's
Hidden Soldiers in America

DEBBIE CENZIPER

 hachette
BOOKS

NEW YORK   BOSTON

Copyright © 2019 by Debbie Cenziper

Cover design by Jeff Miller/Faceout Studio
Cover images: Houses © Photo by H. Armstrong Roberts/ClassicStock/
Getty Images; Auschwitz-Birkenau concentration camp © Jonathan Noden-
Wilkinson/Shutterstock; Eagle © pne/Shutterstock; texture © Shutterstock
Cover copyright © 2019 by Hachette Book Group, Inc.

Map of Eastern Europe courtesy of Worth Chollar

Hachette Book Group supports the right to free expression and the value of copyright.
The purpose of copyright is to encourage writers and artists to produce the creative works
that enrich our culture.

The scanning, uploading, and distribution of this book without permission is a theft of the
author's intellectual property. If you would like permission to use material from the book
(other than for review purposes), please contact permissions@hbgusa.com. Thank you for
your support of the author's rights.

Hachette Books

Hachette Book Group

1290 Avenue of the Americas

New York, NY 10104

HachetteBooks.com
Twitter.com/HachetteBooks
Instagram.com/HachetteBooks

Printed in the United States of America

First Edition: November 2019

Hachette Books is a division of Hachette Book Group, Inc.

The Hachette Books name and logo are trademarks of Hachette Book Group, Inc.

The publisher is not responsible for websites (or their content) that are not owned by the
publisher.

The Hachette Speakers Bureau provides a wide range of authors for speaking events. To
find out more, go to www.hachettespeakersbureau.com or call (866) 376-6591.

Print book interior design by Tom Louie.

Library of Congress Cataloging-in-Publication Data has been applied for.

ISBNs: 978-0-316-44965-6 (hardcover), 978-0-316-44966-3 (ebook)

LSC-C

10 9 8 7 6 5 4 3 2 1

For Brett and Zack—
with love

CONTENTS

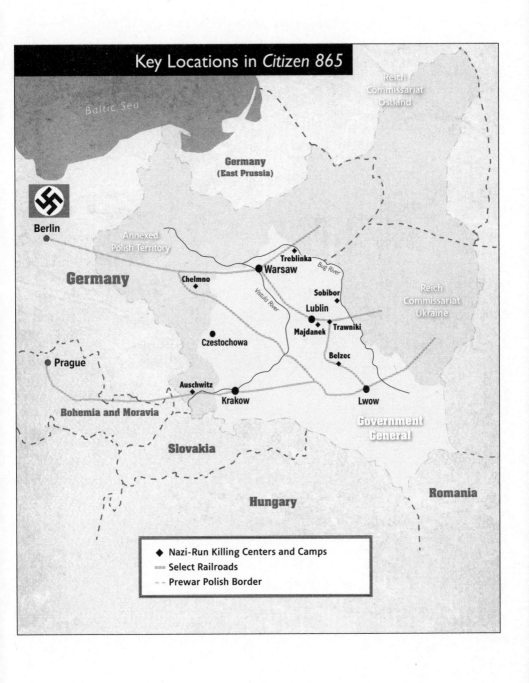

Key Locations in *Citizen 865*

Baltic Sea

Reich Commissariat Ostland

Germany (East Prussia)

Berlin

Germany

Annexed Polish Territory

Chelmno

Treblinka

Warsaw

Bug River

Vistula River

Sobibor

Lublin

Reich Commissariat Ukraine

Czestochowa

Majdanek

Trawniki

Belzec

Prague

Auschwitz

Krakow

Lwow

Bohemia and Moravia

Government General

Slovakia

Hungary

Romania

◆ Nazi-Run Killing Centers and Camps

▥ Select Railroads

- - Prewar Polish Border

AUTHOR'S NOTE

At a crowded holiday party in 2016, I met a lawyer from the US Department of Justice. Over a long conversation, Robin Gold described the history and mission of a unit deep inside the massive federal agency that had raced against time to track, identify, and bring to justice Nazi perpetrators found in America's cities and suburbs in the years after World War II. For three decades, the Office of Special Investigations (OSI) pursued a series of high-profile cases against concentration camp guards, police leaders, Nazi collaborators, and propagandists. I found one lesser-known investigation particularly compelling: the search for the men of Trawniki.

Citizen 865 is a story about darkness but also about light, the pursuit of truth by a team of American Nazi hunters that worked to expose the men behind the most lethal operation in the Holocaust. Year after year, the team scrambled to hold these collaborators accountable for their crimes, not only for those who had perished in the war but also for those who had survived, and for the benefit of a world that too often finds itself in the exact same place more than seventy years later, forced to explain bigotry, hate, and mass murder.

This book is a work of nonfiction based on hundreds of hours of interviews with historians and federal prosecutors and thousands of pages of government documents, Nazi rosters and records, scholarly research, trial transcripts, and court filings. Most of the documents came from the US Department of Justice and the archives of the United States Holocaust Memorial Museum in Washington, D.C., which provided access to several dozen boxes of papers, articles, and records donated in 2015 by former OSI historian Peter Black.

Additional research was conducted in the archives and museums of Prague, Warsaw, and Lublin, Poland. Court transcripts, records, and interviews with those who had direct knowledge of conversations allowed me to reconstruct the dialogue in this book.

At the request of family members, the Polish names of survivors Feliks Wojcik and Lucyna Stryjewska have been used. Taped interviews spanning a decade and on-the-ground research in Lublin, Warsaw, and Vienna allowed me to chronicle their wartime journeys.

I also traveled to Trawniki, Poland, where Nazi leaders in the early years of the war recruited a loyal army of foot soldiers. Some of these men would eventually make their way to the United States and live undetected for years, ordinary Americans with extraordinary secrets.

Their lies unraveled under the unflinching glare of history and through the work of men and women who refused to look away.

It speaks well of American justice that it will not close the books on bestiality until the last participant has felt a *frisson* of fear and is routed from the land of the free.

George F. Will, the *Washington Post*, 1998

PROLOGUE

THE DANCE

New York City
1992

Nazi recruit 865 ducked into the US Attorney's Office in the Southern District of New York, rode the elevator to the seventh floor, and sat down in a hushed conference room, where three federal prosecutors were waiting. He smiled, a practiced smile, the smile of an old friend. Tufts of silver hair were combed neatly over his ears, and a mustache grown long ago straddled a thin upper lip. He was lean from years of careful eating and late nights spent in the dance halls of Munich after the war, gliding across the floor to music that reminded him of home.

"Ready?" one of the lawyers asked.

He nodded, clear-eyed and steady, and raised his right hand. "I affirm to tell the truth."

His eastern European accent had softened over the years, and the words sounded lyrical, a light and mellow promise. He was an obliging helper who had come when he was called, traveling all this way from a modest frame house on the shoreline of Lake Carmel, sixty miles upstate, where retirement waited on a spit of a beach and in the faded blue dinghies that bobbed along the water.

Even his name was benign, shortened to three quick beats decades earlier when he had stood before an American flag and vowed to defend the Constitution. Jakob Reimer, the newest citizen of the United States, had given himself a new name. *Jack*.

"We could do this in another language, such as German, if you prefer," the lawyer offered.

"No, no," Reimer replied. Before these new friends, he would share a great secret. "To tell the truth, I used to read and write German.... Now I have forgotten."

From across the table, Eli Rosenbaum managed a slight smile. Years earlier, he had questioned a Polish man who once kept meticulous count of how many bullets he had used to kill Jews during a roundup in the war. At the start of the interview, Rosenbaum shook the man's hand and mused to himself that he had earned his annual government salary in that single moment, forced to make pleasantries with a murderer.

Rosenbaum had investigated and prosecuted dozens of Nazi perpetrators since then, concentration camp guards and police leaders who had slipped into the United States with bogus stories about war years spent on farms and in factories, far removed from the killing squads and annihilation centers of occupied Europe. But the case against Reimer was different.

Soon, the US Department of Justice would move to expose one of the most trusted and effective Nazi collaborators discovered on American soil, an elite member of a little-known SS killing force so skillfully deployed in occupied Poland that 1.7 million Jews had been murdered in less than twenty months, the span of two Polish summers.

It was midmorning in New York, and on the streets outside, city workers lingered in the sun. But inside the US Attorney's Office, in the shadows of the Brooklyn Bridge, Rosenbaum felt as if time had given way, stretching and shrinking, as he peered at the seventy-three-year-old retired potato chip salesman who had once vowed to bring Nazi racial order to the occupied East.

"I would like to have this go as smoothly as possible," Rosenbaum said. "But I will need the truth, Mr. Reimer, all right?"

"Look, Mr. Rosenbaum," Reimer replied. "Let me say this. My wife says to me, 'You always preach we should love the Jewish people and you are being picked on.' I say, 'You got to understand. If six million Polish people were innocently killed, you would feel the same way as the Jewish people feel.' Any way I can help, I will be glad to help."

It was a serene dance, and Rosenbaum decided to play along. "All you have to do is tell me exactly what happened. That is how you can help, and I think that is how you can help yourself as well."

Rosenbaum produced Reimer's visa application, stamped by US immigration authorities in Germany in 1952. Reimer was quiet as he studied the document, and Rosenbaum watched for flashes of fear or regret. But Reimer looked like a babysitter, not a killer.

He had lied with ease for years, hiding in plain sight in middle-class America, and now he had American sons and an American wife, a church, a Social Security card, a two-story house in the hamlet of Lake Carmel, population eight thousand. Time had been good to Reimer, every new year, every new decade, distance from a loaded rifle and a uniform bearing the stripes of a first sergeant.

But now Rosenbaum knew better. Seven stories above Manhattan, four thousand miles from Poland and forty-seven years after the end of the war, Rosenbaum was quite certain that the man sitting before him had once been part of one of the most diabolical operations in the Holocaust.

He studied Reimer.

"The Trawniki camp," Rosenbaum said carefully, "that was an SS training camp... right?"

PART ONE

OCCUPIED POLAND
1941–1943

CHAPTER ONE

THE SHTETL OF ZOLOCHIV

Eastern Poland
1941

Go east, his father had said, since there was no place left to run. Pass the synagogue on Jateczna Street and the candy shop in Old Town, pass the school buildings and the tenement buildings with windows of white lace. Pass the stone benches where old Polish men sit and whisper and the farms and fields that stretch for miles, slicked by winter's first frost.

Go east toward the foothills of the Carpathian Mountains. Go east and go far.

Nineteen-year-old Feliks Wojcik had fled on a bicycle with only a carton of cigarettes for trading and pedaled for ten days to Lwow, a medieval city of green-domed churches that in the fall of 1939 had fallen under Soviet occupation. In the historic region of Galicia, Feliks enrolled in medical school, busing tables for food and mingling with other Jewish students who had also escaped to eastern Poland, to a town without German soldiers, where it was supposed to be safe.

For many months, Feliks had thought of his mother, Sophie, who once fancied young Feliks a musical protégé, wedging cork between his fingers so that his tiny hands could span the octaves of his first violin. How long since he had slept in his rambling house in Lublin, filled with family and classical music and the smell of fresh onion rolls, nearly two decades without hunger or pain?

In the bustling city southeast of Warsaw, his father had gone to night school to become an architect, and the family settled into a grand apartment house outside the cramped Jewish quarter, where shoemakers and carpenters of more meager means squeezed into narrow houses, hauling water by the bucket from an old stone well. Other young Jews in Lublin grew up fearing flashes of antisemitism, homemade weapons fashioned from rocks or gnarled sticks, suitable for a serious beating.

But Feliks, at five foot nine, with a slender face, deep green eyes, and an impish half grin, had lived in a far more assimilated world, studying French and Latin in a Polish-Catholic high school that his father had helped build.

"What do you think of my son being considered as a student in your school?" his father, Samuel, had once asked the bishop. "Would it be possible for him?"

"Of course it would be possible," the bishop had replied and then arranged for a Jewish professor to visit weekly so that the school's only Jewish pupil would have the chance to learn his own history, the customs and teachings that had guided generations of families.

Feliks had spent long, happy evenings performing in a family quartet with his older sister, Sala, who played the piano, an uncle who played the cello, and a cousin who played the viola. He spent summer afternoons on a tennis court and winters on a sled in a park in the city center, near a teeming Jewish market that sold wheat-dough pancakes topped with onion and poppy seeds.

Once a year his father took him to a prayer house inside a stranger's living room, but it was stuffy and boring and Feliks wasn't allowed to eat until sundown. This, he knew, was his father's duty, a gentle way of showing Feliks what it meant to be a Jew.

Lublin had fallen early, just weeks after the Germans denounced a nonaggression pact with the Polish government and invaded from the north, south, and west, crushing Polish defense forces. It had been a stunning onslaught, watched across the world, and as tension mounted in Europe, Britain and France two days later declared war on Germany.

The Germans considered Lublin a strategic acquisition, with a railway that connected the east to the west and more than forty thousand Jews who could repair guns, clear forests, mend shoes, and build the forced-labor camps that under German rule would soon rise across the Polish countryside. There was much to do: Adolf Hitler was looking to create living space for the German people, and Poland provided a rich and bountiful expanse of farmland.

One night, Feliks's father had staggered home, beaten by a mob of Germans and Poles. His only son had to escape.

Jews had lived in Poland since the Middle Ages, but even in Lublin, with two Yiddish newspapers, a Jewish hospital and orphanage, three Jewish cemeteries, twelve synagogues, and the largest rabbinical school in the world, there was no place to hide. There were no friends to help.

Factories, businesses, and universities were shuttered. Jews had been made to give up their cameras, furs, radios. Gone was the violin that Feliks had once played until his fingers were raw. The Germans had issued a forced-labor decree, rounding up Jews from across the city for backbreaking work in labor camps.

It would be safer in the east, Feliks's parents had reasoned, in one of the Polish cities or towns annexed by the Soviets under a nonaggression pact that Hitler had struck with Joseph Stalin, containing a secret deal to divide up eastern Europe between Nazi Germany and the Soviet Union.

In the final months of 1939, Feliks had said good-bye to his parents and sister and left the so-called Government General of Poland—a German occupation zone of the newly defeated country, covering much of central, southern, and, eventually, southeastern Poland, including Warsaw and Lublin. He traveled 220 kilometers from home, sneaking across the demarcation line along the winding Bug River. He soon arrived in the Soviet-occupied city of Lwow, settled in the fifth century and home to several hundred thousand Poles, Ukrainians, and Jews.

He managed to complete nearly two years of medical school, getting by in student housing and dodging the Russian soldiers who were rounding up able-bodied men for work in faraway Soviet coal mines.

But as the summer of 1941 crept closer, the tenuous state of affairs in Poland was about to grow worse.

IN JUNE, HITLER directed the German army to carry out a surprise attack against the Soviet Union, his partner in the conquest of Poland. Operation Barbarossa would become one of the largest military operations in modern warfare, launched by Hitler to eliminate the threat of Communism and gain control of land within the Soviet Union.

In Poland, German soldiers crossed the demarcation line into territories controlled by the Soviets. They soon marched into Lwow, a terrifying sight, and in the bedlam that followed, motley gangs of students stalked the halls of Feliks's dormitory, searching for Jews. He was pushed to the ground and ordered to scrub the floor of a new pub for German officers.

The Germans tended to favor Ukrainians, unless they were Jews or Communists, and across the city local militants trolled the streets, stripping and beating Jewish men and women. Later, Feliks would learn that German soldiers had roused the crowds by spreading rumors that Jews were responsible for the mass killings of local prisoners under Soviet occupation.

The mobs forced Feliks into a sprawling labor camp set up in a factory on the outskirts of the city, desolate rows of brick buildings with barbed-wire fences and barracks with wooden boxes for beds. The prisoners worked on the pier at the River Poltva, which flowed through the city. Those who grew tired and slouched were kicked from all sides by German guards.

Don't go down, Feliks told himself as he joined the others. He pretended his body was numb. The work went on for hours, and when it was done the prisoners were made to run back to the barracks, past the bodies of men who had been shot and left for dead.

Feliks managed to slip past the guards several days later, running until he could no longer see the camp. Back in town, the Germans were looking for mechanics, and Feliks quickly decided that working in a garage commandeered by the German police seemed a far better option than the confines of a brutal forced-labor camp. He volunteered with a group of Jewish men.

"I have no blind idea about mechanics," Feliks confided to the Polish man who appeared to be in charge. It was a risky admission, but Feliks reasoned that the head mechanic would soon have seen for himself.

"Shhh," the man said. "Be quiet. We'll help you when we can. You do what I tell you to do."

Feliks tapped and tinkered and twisted, making a good show of it until a German officer pulled him into a quiet corner of the garage.

"Is it true you're a medical student?"

Feliks hesitated, studying the officer, a doctor in the German army who appeared to be in his late twenties.

"Yes," Feliks said softly.

"Look." The doctor's voice was urgent. "As of tonight, they're going to take all of you away. I don't know where."

The doctor pointed to a cluster of buildings just beyond the garage. "There's a stable on the left side of the building there. I'll give you something to carry for me to the stable and meet you there."

Feliks walked quickly, careful not to draw attention from the

German soldiers who were milling about the garage. In the stable, the doctor motioned to a secluded corner near some horses. "They will never find you there."

Feliks crouched low.

"Somehow, you have to get out of here and go to town," the doctor instructed and slipped away.

He returned once more, late in the night, to give Feliks a cooked chicken. It was a benevolent gesture in a world that had gone mad, and Feliks could scarcely find the words to thank him.

"That's all I can do for you," the doctor said. "I'm so sorry."

He frowned and disappeared.

The next morning, the garage was cleaned out, the Jewish workers whisked away, just as the doctor had promised. The only place Feliks knew to go was his dormitory, and he crept inside and made his way downstairs. In the basement, he discovered three Jewish medical students huddled on the floor, the shallow breathing of hunted men, waiting in the darkness.

LWOW WAS STILL overrun by mobs. Feliks and his three classmates decided to go farther east, through fields and forests that would provide cover under the night sky. They crept out of the dormitory and walked, kilometer after kilometer, the town giving way to farmland. Sometime in the night, a Russian truck rumbled past, and Feliks waved his hands over his head, frantic, hoping the soldiers might take them to Moscow. But the soldiers only pointed their guns and drove on.

Feliks and his companions kept walking, passing grain and sugar-beet farms, until they saw a small village in the distance. The shtetl of Zolochiv, once part of the dual monarchy of Austria-Hungary, was one of the oldest Jewish settlements in Galicia. They inched toward town in silence, taking slow, measured steps through thickets of birch and fir trees, unsure what they would find beyond the tree line.

The armed men seemed to come out of nowhere, from behind,

from the sides, guns drawn. Quickly, they forced Feliks and his class-mates into the town square. Bodies were everywhere, piled one on top of the other. At first glance, Feliks thought they were praying.

"Line up! Hands up!" someone shouted.

The square was a mass execution site.

Pushed to his knees on the cobblestone street strewn with the dead, Feliks looked straight ahead at the brick wall in front of him. German officers prepared to fire before a rapt crowd, hundreds of local farmers and shop owners who had poured into the village to welcome the Germans with bread and salt, certain that the Germans would be far less violent than the Soviets.

Feliks closed his eyes and waited, three seconds, five, ten, his mind and body still. This, he decided, must be what death feels like.

He thought about his father, who months earlier had managed to slip out of German-occupied Lublin and make his way to Lwow. Soviet soldiers caught him swimming across a narrow expanse of the Bug River and accused him of being a spy.

"I am a Jew looking for my son," he had pleaded.

The soldiers let him go, and he soon found the dormitory where Feliks was staying. He cried when he saw Feliks, who had nothing but a dirty overcoat with a missing button to keep warm at night.

Feliks had marveled at the sight of his father, familiar eyes and a familiar smile in a town of strangers. "Don't worry about me here," Feliks said. "At least nobody is going to kill me. Nobody is going to shoot me."

His father pointed to Feliks's coat. "If your mother would see that, she would be very unhappy," he admonished. In town, he found a needle, thread, and a new button.

"Stay with me," Feliks pleaded. They would look for ways to bring everyone else.

His father only shook his head. "There is no way. There is no way to do that."

Several days later, his father returned to Lublin.

Crouched in the execution line alongside the three other students, Feliks waited for the first bullet. He felt almost peaceful, as if he were floating underwater, no sound, no movement. Years later, he would come to believe that his body was defending itself in a final, agonizing moment of violence.

Twenty seconds. Thirty. Feliks figured that he must be dead already. Such a short life, Feliks decided, a mere twenty years.

Finally, he opened his eyes and blinked, taking in the scene around him. The German executioners and many of the spectators had been sprayed by bullets. He looked to his right and saw one of his classmates slumped over, shot dead in a puddle of blood. Then Feliks saw the shadows of two departing Soviet warplanes. They had fired into the town square just as the execution squad was taking aim, striking the German officers and the boy next to him.

It was a wicked twist of fate, life and death separated by inches, the air between bodies.

Run. Feliks and his two surviving classmates darted back through the trees toward a river on the outskirts of the village. There was no place to hide except in the cold, murky water, and they sunk in neck deep. Feliks pulled brush and sticks over his head for cover. He lost track of time, the rise of the sun and the moon. The water was relentless. It numbed his limbs until he was too miserable to care about dying. Several days passed. Finally, he pulled himself out of the river and inched back toward town with the others, passing a group of local men.

One of them laughed. "Three more Jews not killed?"

But the pogroms that had swept eastern Poland in the days after the German invasion were finally over. Up the road, they found a Jewish hospital that was still in operation, and the three boys stripped off their rotting clothes and sank into beds. Feliks couldn't bring himself to sleep. He wanted to get word to his father. He needed to tell his family that he was still alive.

Feliks and his classmates left the hospital and made their way back to Lwow, through the fields they had crossed only days earlier. In town, Feliks found a Polish man who was willing to smuggle a message to Lublin.

Feliks would never know exactly how his father had persuaded a Polish cab driver to help a Jewish boy in a country where such a gesture, if discovered, meant certain death. But three days later, under the cover of night, a driver from Lublin inched into Lwow. Feliks said good-bye to his classmates, slipped into the stranger's car, and closed his eyes.

He was going home.

CHAPTER TWO

THE COLOR OF BLOOD

Lublin, Poland
1942

The rolling hills of the Lublin countryside turned yellow and green in the springtime, acre upon acre of rapeseed flowers that sweetened the wind with scents of musk and honey. Lucyna Stryjewska had once waited for spring because after spring came summer, and summer meant meandering walks to the community swimming pool, barefoot and sweaty, and lazy nights spent at home with her younger brother, a pudgy-faced boy named David. Lucyna had been fourteen and David only six during that last, mellow summer, when their beds were soft and dinner was served on china.

Three summers had come and gone since then, and on a bleak morning in November 1942, a few hours before dawn, Lucyna woke to the sounds of shouting.

Come out to the square.

She bolted upright and peered into the darkness, blinking at the unfamiliar shapes and shadows in the stranger's shack where her family now lived. She hated the place, the never-ending stench of sweat and rot, the barbed wire and armed guards that kept them locked up like farm animals. But at least she still had her parents and brother, a miracle really. They were among the last Jews in the last Jewish ghetto of Lublin.

All Jews will be deported east.

Lucyna turned to her father, who stood motionless as he listened to the instructions shouted in Yiddish and Polish. His face was ashen. So many had already been taken, neighbors, friends, cousins, grandparents, sent away with only a bar of soap or a few scraps of silver tucked inside their knapsacks.

The Germans had talked of Jewish settlements in the east, but there were whispers inside the ghetto, tidbits of information from Polish friends about a Nazi-run camp called Majdanek, in plain sight from the main road to Lublin. "They are building something there," the Poles had warned, "something very suspicious."

Lucyna's family and a few thousand others had been told that they would get to stay in Lublin on a permanent Jewish settlement, set up on a tired stretch of farmland once occupied by Polish peasants. But now the shouting.

There is no more Jewish settlement.

Should they go or hide? Did they have a day or an hour? In the early-morning darkness, it seemed to Lucyna that time was passing too quickly, a flurry of urgent whispers between her mother and father that she couldn't bear to hear. And then another announcement, bleaker than the rest.

Come out to the square. You have three days. Anyone found hiding will be shot.

WAR HAD COME to Lublin from an angry night sky. Lucyna huddled in the cellar as the bombs fell, a crackling, shrieking assault that lasted until dawn, more terrifying than any sound she could remember. And then came a sight she would never forget, German soldiers with machine guns marching in the streets and town square, heavy boots crunching on the remains of fallen buildings. They had marched into a synagogue on the sacred holiday of Rosh Hashanah, the Jewish new year, but then turned around and left without uttering a word, as if they were sizing up the task at hand.

"This might be worse than any other war," her father said that first night, stunned at the collapse of the Polish government, whose leaders had fled to London.

It was September 1939, and Lucyna had just finished her first year in a private Jewish high school with dozens of other girls, the city's Gitlas and Chavas and Helenas and Reginas. But now much of the neighborhood lay in ruins, a bombed-out heap of concrete and glass. In their apartment house, Lucyna's parents stockpiled food and hid jewelry.

The grown-ups talked around the kitchen table, trading hearsay more than news since both of Lublin's Yiddish newspapers, the *Lublin Daily* and the *Lublin Voice,* had stopped publishing. Some families were fleeing east to parts of Poland that had fallen under Soviet occupation. Others were making plans to hide in attics, cellars, closets, back rooms of the local slaughterhouse.

Lucyna's neighbors planned to escape on a bus to the Soviet Union. There was room for Lucyna's family, but to her parents the prospect of a new life in the remote interior of a strange country was out of the question, and so they had dutifully turned in their radios and furs and worn armbands with the Star of David.

In 1939, there were 122,000 people in Lublin. One in three was Jewish. Jews had representation on the town council, controlled hundreds of commercial and social organizations, owned silver workshops and leather factories. This will pass, some of the elders said, convinced that the German occupiers and their rules were only a temporary problem, a political setback rather than a permanent shift in Polish-Jewish life.

But soon, SS and German civil administrators commandeered buildings. The street signs were changed to German, the Park Litewski, sprawled along Lublin's main thoroughfare, renamed in honor of Adolf Hitler. Lucyna had watched soldiers in white gloves round up Jewish men for forced labor, taking sons, husbands, and fathers in a matter of seconds. She hid inside with her parents and brother, but one afternoon three soldiers burst into the apartment, demanded to see the contents of the library cabinet, and stole the watch that Lucyna's mother was wearing.

Signs appeared around town: *For reasons of public interest, an enclosed Jewish residential district is hereby established with immediate effect.*

In this new Jewish district, Lucyna's parents would make themselves indispensable. Her father, Leon, spoke five languages and had been a court interpreter before the war. He would help run the Jewish administration in the ghetto. Lucyna's mother, Leah, had put herself through school to become a dentist. She would treat Germans and Poles in the hospital. Lucyna would get a permit to work in a bank in the city.

The Germans had called that first ghetto the "Jewish quarter," but to Lucyna it had been a short stretch of hell along Lubartowska and Franciszkanska Streets, in the oldest and poorest part of Lublin. The place was filthy, tens of thousands of bodies squeezed onto streets covered with a thick layer of mud, near a grand synagogue that had been built by Lublin's Jews in 1567.

Lucyna, her parents, and her brother had crowded into an apartment with three other families. Lucyna was grateful for the work permit that allowed her to leave, past the miserable houses packed tight with miserable people. The walk to the bank gave Lucyna a few moments of peace, a chance to lose herself in the familiar streets of the city, where she had once been a schoolgirl in fresh white tights and leather shoes, brown hair curled into a bob.

Inside the ghetto, German soldiers ripped the beards off Jewish men. Mothers hawked wedding rings for a day's supply of coal. Typhus had wiped out entire families. But Lucyna had been careful to avoid trouble and, for one summer and one winter, the chronic gurgling in her stomach had seemed only a temporary problem, a bad memory that would go away once Europe came to its senses.

THE MEN IN black uniforms and black caps seemed to appear out of nowhere. The Ukrainians, the elders called them, though by the sound of their accents there were also Latvians, Belarusians, Estonians, Lithuanians, and Russians.

Late one night in March 1942, they had surrounded the perimeter of the ghetto and lighted the street lamps, forcing sleepy, startled families outside. Then came a grim announcement: one thousand five hundred Jews a day would be taken away and resettled in the east.

Lucyna's family had been given an exemption by German security forces, a special stamp on their identity cards for Jews with critical jobs. When the ghetto was empty they would be moved along with several thousand others to a smaller ghetto on farmland once occupied by the poorest Polish peasants. The peasants had been resettled in city apartments owned by Jewish families. On her walks to the bank Lucyna had spotted pigs and ducks languishing on third-floor balconies. An absurd sight.

Jews selected for deportation were ordered to report to the ancient synagogue, for as long as Lucyna could remember a solemn site to mark births, marriages, deaths, to pray to God during the High Holy Days. But in those early days of March 1942, the synagogue teemed with the men in black uniforms, some not much older than boys.

Where had these violent jailers come from? They were surely more terrifying than the dreaded SS officers milling around the city.

The men in black stormed every apartment building in the ghetto, forcing Jews outside and using their rifle butts to bash the heads of stragglers and resisters. They killed with abandon, callously and randomly, creating chaotic, bloody scenes on the streets. The ghetto shook with the crackle of gunfire, the wails of children, shouting from the men who raced up and down the steps of apartment houses, guns cocked and ready.

Lucyna, huddled inside with her parents and brother, had tried very hard not to listen. She was sixteen, and she had met a boy.

The promise of something sweet and new kept Lucyna awake at night, filled with hope even when reason screamed that there was no place for love in the ghetto. Feliks Wojcik had seen so much more of the war already, moments that he could scarcely bring himself to talk about. Still, he was kind and warm and, to Lucyna, a badly needed distraction from the violence all around her. Feliks worked as a medic on the Lublin railway alongside his father. His family had also been spared from deportation, their work for the Germans considered too essential.

When the big ghetto was empty, the two families had moved together to the newer, smaller ghetto, clusters of thatched-roof shacks squeezed behind barbed wire. A summer place for Jews, the Germans had said, and then insisted that every family plant a garden. The soldiers had been rather cordial about it, offering prizes to anyone who could till the soil.

"I never believed that Jews could even plant flowers," a grinning Gestapo officer told Feliks, who had managed to grow blossoms the color of blood. Later, Feliks would say that he feared his reward would be a bullet to the head.

Lucyna heard talk about the new place becoming a permanent Jewish settlement. Jewish leaders were tasked with official assignments: housing, nutrition, finance, registration, lice control. But the deportations had continued, Jewish police officers and ghetto leaders who thought they had found a way to stay in Lublin taken away with their families. Lucyna dreaded the bloody, brutal process. *Is it only a matter of time?* she thought grimly.

THE SHOUTING BEFORE dawn in November 1942 had drawn Lucyna out of a sound sleep. There would be no more Jewish settlement. In the dank shack where her family had been staying, she watched her parents whisper.

Suddenly, Feliks appeared, pacing in front of them. "Why don't I take her?" he asked.

Together, Feliks and Lucyna would hide. Feliks's father had fashioned a secret space behind a wall that was just large enough for standing, and there was room inside for Lucyna. She looked at her father.

"Go," he said sternly. Her mother would head to the hospital, where doctors and dentists might be spared. Lucyna's father would hide in the attic of his office in the ghetto, and David would hide with family friends. Lucyna looked at her parents one last time, shadows in the early-morning light.

"Go, honey," her father repeated. "I'm going to try to take care of your brother and see what we can do."

There was no time to protest. Lucyna followed Feliks to his family's quarters and climbed inside the black, jagged hole next to his parents and sister. Lucyna could barely see her fingers. The air was thick, but coughing or sneezing would surely lead to their capture. She felt trapped, desperate to escape.

They stood there for eight hours, squeezed tight in the darkness, until someone knocked on the wall and whispered, "You might as well come out now. This is the end of the ghetto."

Lucyna climbed out of the hole, blinking in the light. The streets were unnaturally still as she raced back to her family's shack. She found her father hunched over, sobbing. The Jewish doctors and dentists had been taken to the camp down the road, the terrifying place called Majdanek.

For the rest of her life, Lucyna would imagine what it might have been like to say good-bye to her mother, what they would have said in that bleak, desperate moment, forced to decide whether to die together or separate for the sake of survival.

There was more shouting outside.

Meet in the main square for deportation. You have three days.

Feliks's father was frantic. "You are so young," he told Lucyna and Feliks later that night. "Run away through the barbed wire. At least the two of you will survive."

The next morning, under a weak winter sun, Lucyna and Feliks crawled through the fence, hoping to slip past the Ukrainian guards who patrolled the ghetto day and night. Before them lay open fields, the landscape that Lucyna had always known, the comfort of hills and trees. But as they ran she could hear the cries of guard dogs growing closer. Bullets pierced the air beside her ears. She ran faster, ignoring the burning in her lungs.

She felt the guards closing in before she saw them. Lucyna watched helplessly as a dog mauled Feliks's calf. Surely, she thought, they would die right there, alone in a barren field now covered with fresh blood. But one of the guards bellowed, "Back to the ghetto! Back to the ghetto!"

Someone started swinging a leather strap with a spiked metal ball affixed to the end. Feliks tried to shield his face, but he would permanently lose some of the vision in his left eye. They made it back to the ghetto, climbed inside the fence, and found Feliks's parents and sister, preparing to go to the square for deportation with all the others. Feliks, bruised and bloodied, begged them to reconsider.

"We don't want to fight anymore," Feliks's father said. After many months in the ghetto, he was skinny and exhausted, no longer the man who had once swum across the Bug River to see his son.

Lucyna and Feliks went to find Lucyna's father. He was crouched with David, and Feliks and Lucyna collapsed beside them. From a hole in the wall, Feliks watched his parents and sister walking toward the deportation point, heads bowed, mourners in the November snow.

Lucyna's father had one last plan. "I'm going to try to arrange, in the middle of the night, when it's dark, for you to get through the barbed wire."

The first escape had failed, but Lucyna's father was adamant that they try again. The only other option was deportation. Hours passed. At four a.m., Lucyna's father crept outside, motioning for Lucyna, David, and Feliks to follow.

The night was still. Nearly everyone in the ghetto was already deported or dead, and two Ukrainian guards watched them warily as they approached the fence. Lucyna's father dug into his pockets and pulled out wristwatches, a fountain pen, and a bottle of vodka. Lucyna could scarcely believe he had anything of value left.

"I have two watches here, and I have three people," he told the guards. "I want you to look the other way. I want to get my family out."

The guards paused. No one moved. Finally, one of the guards nodded. It occurred to Lucyna that the guards could have taken the watches and shot them anyway, but in that moment she could only think about her father.

"Please," she begged, pulling on her father's arm. "Come with us."

He shook his head. "I can't. I have to be with your mother."

He pushed Lucyna, David, and Feliks through the barbed wire.

"Go," he said firmly. "Go and see what you can do for yourself."

Lucyna took one last look at her father, and for the second time in three days, she took off running. She ran a mad zigzag through the fields with her brother and Feliks, ran in the darkness over frozen earth, expecting the dogs and gunshots but finding only quiet, a frigid dawn in the Lublin countryside.

A few kilometers up the road, she spotted a Polish farmer on a horse and buggy and asked for a ride into town. The farmer nodded silently. It was an act of great kindness, Lucyna knew, since the Germans were giving away a bag of sugar to anyone who turned in a Jew.

In the city, Lucyna, Feliks, and David crept toward the home of a Polish woman who knew Lucyna's mother. "Dear," the woman sighed after she opened the door and looked at Lucyna. "If you need money, we will help you. But we cannot keep you overnight."

Feliks knew a gardener who had worked for his family before the war. Feliks, Lucyna, and David walked in the shadows, knowing that every second spent on the street came with great risk. Feliks knocked softly on the gardener's door. His wife answered and made the sign of a cross when she saw Feliks, pale and rail thin.

"My God. Where are your Mom and Dad? What are you doing here?"

"Can you help me?" Feliks asked.

The gardener's wife rushed Feliks, Lucyna, and David into the greenhouse, and Lucyna breathed deeply because the room was warm. They could stay the night, but men who worked in the greenhouse would return the next morning.

"They would denounce you to the Gestapo," the woman said, wrapping Feliks in one of her husband's old winter coats. "They would kill us all."

Later, Feliks would ask himself whether he would have done the same, risked his own life to help others, resisting the pull of self-preservation. The night passed quickly. The next morning Feliks called on another family friend, a Polish man who had promised to keep tools and machinery for Feliks's father. The man slipped Feliks the names of several people who were working in the Polish Underground.

Back on the street with nowhere to go, Lucyna heard that her father had been shot dead, one of the last Jews in the doomed Jewish ghetto of Lublin.

CHAPTER THREE

THE WEDDING

Warsaw, Poland
1942–1943

Feliks, Lucyna, and David ducked out of the railway station in Warsaw a few hours after midnight, chins down, shoulders hunched, praying they could pass for Aryans in a city on the hunt for Jews. The streets were nearly deserted, lighted only by the moody, orange glow of street lamps. Feliks was grateful for the darkness. They made a suspicious trio, a man of twenty-two traveling with a sixteen-year-old girl and a boy of only nine, no luggage, no parents.

Feliks flagged down a rickshaw driver. There was a hotel in the city center where Feliks had heard that Jewish families were hiding from the Gestapo. Would there be space for the three of them? The possibility of being turned away was terrifying. They were 180 kilometers from home, and Feliks barely knew his way around Warsaw.

He glanced at Lucyna and David, shivering in the night air. How brave Lucyna had been, sitting with her brother on the train as it sped into the night, away from everything she had ever known.

They had made their way to Warsaw with a few coins that Lucyna's father had tucked into the pocket of her coat as he urged her to flee the ghetto with David and Feliks. Only a few days had passed, but to Feliks it felt like a lifetime, when he had a mother, father, and sister, and the dull hope that they would somehow survive together in the last Jewish settlement of Lublin.

After a single night in the gardener's basement, Feliks, Lucyna, and David had trudged along icy streets to Lucyna's old apartment building in the center of Lublin, where a Polish neighbor who ran a laundry business had agreed to hide the family's silver and artwork. Before the war, the neighborhood had been one of Lublin's poshest, with grand apartment houses painted pink and green and yellow, bouquets of poppy flowers in window boxes and doorways. The area had suffered heavy bombing during the German invasion, targeted for its concentration of government offices, and Feliks, Lucyna, and David walked slowly on streets strewn with concrete and glass.

Lucyna slipped inside the building while Feliks and David watched from the street.

"My God," her old neighbor said, gaping at Lucyna from the doorway. "Where are your parents?"

Lucyna struggled to find the words to describe all that had happened, why her cheeks were hollow and her insides felt numb, why she was suddenly terrified to ask for help from a neighbor who had known Lucyna since she was a four-year-old in knee socks and hair ribbons. She pushed out the words.

"Can I please have one of the candelabras so that I can sell it and find my way to Warsaw?"

"It's all in the attic," her neighbor had answered quickly. "Come back at two o'clock and I'll have everything ready."

Lucyna saw a flash of hesitation on the woman's face. It was there and then gone, like the faintest crackle of fallen leaves under footsteps that send hunted animals running. Something didn't feel right. Lucyna raced outside, breathless, and hid with Feliks and David behind a nearby building with a clear view of the apartment house. Soon, two Gestapo officers drove up and rushed inside. They emerged moments later, pointing and yelling, and split up to search the street.

There was another apartment house nearby, a place where Feliks knew a shoemaker. German bombs had taken half the building, but Feliks, Lucyna, and David ducked inside and tapped lightly on the shoemaker's door. His wife answered.

"The Gestapo is looking for us," Feliks whispered.

Since only Lucyna had been seen, the shoemaker's wife pointed to a curtain in the corner of the kitchen. Lucyna slipped behind it, and Feliks and David sat down at the kitchen table where in better times there had been veal and blueberry dumplings and tea. Feliks could hear the officers bounding up the steps. The shoemaker's wife stepped into the hallway to shake the dust from a blanket, as if she were busy with a mundane morning of chores.

"Did you see a Jewish woman running around here?" one of the officers asked.

"There are no Jews here," the shoemaker's wife answered, sounding bored. "They're all dead."

"There was a Jewish lady that we just lost sight of."

"You're welcome to come in. There's nobody here."

The two officers stepped inside the apartment. Feliks stiffened. He could see the tips of Lucyna's leather shoes peeking out from beneath the curtain.

A split second later, the officers left. Once again, Feliks, Lucyna, and David had dodged capture. Feliks thanked the shoemaker's wife, and the three slipped outside, heading north to a railway station in the next town, where they likely wouldn't be recognized. They needed to get out of Lublin.

THE CENTRAL RAILWAY station in Warsaw had been partially destroyed by fire and bombs, but Feliks barely noticed the haphazard piles of fallen brick and rocks as he guided Lucyna and David outside. The sleeping city seemed huge and unfamiliar, and he had been grateful when the rickshaw driver pulled up along the side of the road and nodded.

Feliks gave him the name of the hotel. The driver was quiet, and when he turned off the main road and onto a dark side street, Feliks at first failed to notice. He was settled back in his seat, allowing himself to feel safe under the cover of night. Lucyna sat next to him, bundled in a coat with fur lining. Soon, however, an instinct honed since the start of the war kicked in, a twitching deep in his gut, and Feliks sat forward.

"Where are you going?" he asked the driver.

"You know where I'm going. I'm going to the Gestapo."

It took Feliks a few seconds to take in the words. "Why would you take us there?"

"You filthy Jews," the driver said. "I am going to be paid for you very well."

If he had been alone, Feliks might have given up. His parents and sister were probably dead, and the thought of begging for his life seemed altogether exhausting when his bones ached and his head throbbed, too many months of hunger and hard labor, the minute-by-minute threat of violence. But he had Lucyna and David with him, so he thought quickly.

"How much can you get paid? Look, take whatever we have. We don't have much, but whatever we have is yours."

"No," the driver said. "You have to go."

"What do you care whether we live or not?"

The longest pause.

"You can take my rings," Lucyna pleaded. "You can take my watch, whatever we have."

The driver maneuvered the rickshaw to an abandoned shack on the side of the road. Feliks stripped off his coat and boots. He handed over his fountain pen. Lucyna turned over her watch, ring, and purse. She took off the coat with fur lining.

"Please," Lucyna said, "leave us here."

The driver took everything and slipped away, leaving Feliks, Lucyna, and David on the side of the street in the middle of the night in occupied Warsaw. The safest place to go was the Jewish ghetto, where Lucyna had an uncle.

At least we'll die among Jews, Feliks thought as they crept toward the center of the city, the night air closing around them.

THE WARSAW GHETTO sat behind ten-foot walls topped with barbed wire and broken glass. As they inched toward it, Feliks decided that sneaking in seemed just as dangerous as sneaking out. A group of Jewish men passed by, bound for a long day's work somewhere in the city. Among them was a familiar face. A friend of Feliks's father.

This way, he motioned, and Feliks, Lucyna, and David followed him inside the massive gates.

After Warsaw's four hundred thousand Jews were forced into the ghetto in the winter of 1940, Jewish leaders created underground schools, newspapers, libraries, youth movements, a symphony orchestra. Rabbis delivered weekly sermons about faith and suffering. A clandestine network of Jewish organizers documented births and deaths, going about the business of life in fastidious fashion. But soon the Germans slashed rations to less than two hundred calories a day, and the black market for potatoes and cabbage dried up.

The ghetto had grown crowded with filthy children who huddled under blankets, bare feet sticky from mud. They waited in line with spoons and bowls for a ladle of soup made from radish scraps. Orphaned girls carried orphaned babies. The streets stunk of the dead, whose bodies had been stripped naked for their clothing and covered with newspaper.

By the time Feliks, Lucyna, and David arrived, hundreds of thousands of the ghetto's inhabitants were already gone, deported by the Germans. Looking around the three square kilometers of misery that made up the largest Jewish ghetto in German-occupied Poland, Feliks decided it might have been better to have been shot.

They found Lucyna's uncle easily enough. He wasn't short on money, and while other families slept twenty to a room, he was living in a house with only his wife and infant daughter. He offered Lucyna the attic and Feliks and David the kitchen floor. There was no offer of food, and on the first night in the ghetto, Feliks went to bed hungry.

The next morning, Lucyna's uncle announced that Lucyna and Feliks would be married.

Feliks was drawn to Lucyna, who had a heart-shaped face and a smile that softened ever so slightly when she whispered to her brother or tugged on the beige wool scarf that her mother had given her in the last days of the Lublin ghetto. On mornings without deportations, Feliks and Lucyna had even teased each other and laughed together, nurturing the heady beginnings of a crush.

Now all they had was each other and the powerful pull of shared memory, of Feliks's family marching to the deportation point in the Lublin ghetto, of Lucyna's father standing in the snow at the gates, urging his children to run. But to Feliks, talk of love and marriage seemed altogether frivolous in a place where sewage overflowed into squalid streets and bellies churned from hunger.

Lucyna pleaded with her uncle. "I just lost my parents."

"If you are going to be together," her uncle replied firmly, "you have to get married."

"Just to think about marriage," Lucyna said, "is the last thing on my mind."

Her uncle was adamant. The nearest rabbi had typhus, but her uncle found another rabbi and borrowed a dress from a neighbor. The impromptu wedding ceremony of the young couple from Lublin drew a small crowd, and after Lucyna and Feliks toasted with a mouthful of wine that seemed to appear out of nowhere, a woman came up to Lucyna. She had been a friend of Lucyna's mother. She took Lucyna's bare hand.

"Here," the woman said, pulling the wedding ring off her finger. "Why don't you take mine? Maybe it will bring you luck." She pressed the ring into Lucyna's palm.

A group of refugees from Lublin were living on nearby Mila Street, once a lively hub of Jewish life in prewar Warsaw. Though a dozen families were squeezed into a single apartment, Lucyna, Feliks, and David were offered a spot in a corner of a room. There had been no offer of shelter from Lucyna's uncle, and they quickly accepted. The first night as a married couple, Lucyna and Feliks shivered on a canvas sack that Feliks covered with straw and topped with towels.

Feliks joined a work detail that left the ghetto every morning to haul coal at the train station. He returned at night with as much coal as he could carry, stooped over from the weight of it, and traded what he had on the black market for bits of carrots or cabbage, favoring calories over heat. Still, they were constantly hungry and suffered from miserable bouts of gastritis and fever. Feliks worried most about David, who wore a dazed expression whenever someone mentioned his parents.

"Just let me die like all the other Jews," Lucyna whispered to Feliks late one night. "You get shot and it's all over with."

Feliks understood. It was the dead of winter, and the apartment was frigid.

"*Kot kotek,*" he whispered to his young wife, using the Polish phrase for kitty cat. "*Kot kotek.*"

IN THE GHETTO, rumors had spread about the fate of the Jews, leaks from a place called Treblinka.

Vernichtungslager. Annihilation camp.

Even after the violence in the ghettos, the thought of mass murder took Feliks's breath away. It seemed surreal, impossible. During deportations, the Germans had been telling families to take their clothing and keepsakes, letters and photos and scrapbooks tucked inside satchels.

Still, the rumors persisted.

In the frigid early months of 1943, the ghetto's young Jewish leaders were forging plans to fight back. The Polish Underground had smuggled in guns and ammunition, and bunkers were being built beneath apartment houses, a subterranean maze connecting sewers to alleyways. Already, Jewish fighters had staged a daring resistance, attacking German soldiers when they had entered the ghetto in January for another round of deportations.

Feliks just wanted to get out. Lucyna and David needed light and fresh air, the chance to see ordinary people again. One afternoon on his work detail in the train depot, Feliks spotted a familiar face, a Jewish friend in a uniform who was working on the tracks.

"Aren't you from Lublin?" Feliks asked carefully.

"Pretend we don't know each other," his friend whispered.

The man had false papers and was living with his family on the Aryan side of Warsaw.

"I want to get out," Feliks pleaded. "What can I do to get out?"

"Come back again tomorrow, same time."

In the station the next day, Feliks's friend said, "I can get you out of the ghetto, but it will cost a lot of money."

All Feliks had was a few scraps of coal. He thought quickly. Once, back in the Lublin ghetto, his father had pointed to the ground near his office. Deep in the earth, he had buried a metal box with the family's jewelry and gold. "Whoever survives," he told Feliks, "can live the rest of their life on it."

Feliks hadn't thought much about his father's promise in the awful months that followed, but now he studied his friend. Feliks described the metal box. They could go look for it together.

"If you are willing to talk to your people and they are willing to take a chance, whatever they find, half is theirs. I only need a little to survive." Feliks paused. "Who *are* your people?"

"Polish Underground," his friend answered and disappeared into the bowels of the station.

A few days later, as a work detail left the ghetto, three Polish men whisked Feliks, Lucyna, and David outside the gates and into the city. They rode together in one streetcar and then another and were eventually shown into an apartment house where members of the Polish Home Army were meeting. It was the first time in months that Feliks had been in a house outside the ghetto, and when he heard rapid banter in Yiddish, he was momentarily disoriented. He peered into the next room, where a dozen Jewish people were hiding.

Lucyna and David would stay in the house while Feliks traveled back to Lublin with two members of the resistance, disguised in railway uniforms.

The city of his birth was bustling when Feliks arrived the next day. Work crews crowded the old Jewish ghetto, searching empty apartment houses for jewelry and valuables hidden away by the families who once lived there. Feliks quickly recognized the place where his father said he had buried the metal box. The spot had been a grassy clearing, but now it sat in the middle of a busy street.

He pointed.

"But that's a street," one of the men said.

Feliks was certain.

They stayed overnight in the home of a local member of the Polish Underground. The next morning, Feliks watched, astonished, as men wearing fake work-crew helmets set up a tent and detour signs and started digging in the street. Worried about being recognized, Feliks watched from inside a nearby building. The men promised to light a torch if they found anything.

Please, Feliks thought. His new friends needed money for weapons and ammunition, and Feliks, Lucyna, and David needed to find a way to stay out of the ghetto. An hour passed and then another. Finally, one of the men lighted the torch. Feliks slipped outside and watched as they pulled the box from the ground, just where Feliks's father had promised it would be. They lifted the lid.

Feliks sucked in his breath. The box was empty. Everyone in town knew that Lublin's Jews had buried gold and jewelry, and someone had clearly gotten there first. Feliks cursed his bad luck. He looked at his keepers, but they were silent.

"I guess we can't afford to be outside the ghetto," he said on the train back to Warsaw. "We cannot pay."

"What would you do in the ghetto?" one of the men replied. "You would perish in the ghetto. Maybe you can help us. . . . You can work for your upkeep."

Feliks nodded. He would do anything. Back in Warsaw, the Polish Underground helped Lucyna, with fair skin and a command of proper Polish, secure false identity papers and rent a one-room apartment, where Feliks and David would remain hidden.

Feliks fashioned a hiding space behind a toilet that led to the snarled, concrete guts of the building, which had been struck by a bomb during the German invasion of Warsaw. Feliks and David would come out only after dark, when their footsteps would be hushed by the bustle of day's end, doors opening, pots clinking, wooden chairs pushed back from dinner tables. It was bound to be a miserable existence, but at least they were no longer living in the ghetto.

A few weeks later, the sky over Warsaw turned red. The Jewish uprising, months in the making, had begun.

Night after night, Feliks and Lucyna stood on a hilltop overlooking the burning ghetto, knowing that all that separated them from certain death was a single piece of paper that had turned seventeen-year-old Lucyna into a Christian and not a Jew.

LUCYNA AND FELIKS couldn't see inside the ghetto's charred walls, where members of the same brutal unit that had liquidated the ghetto in Lublin months earlier were now assisting the Germans, throwing tear gas into cellars where Jewish families were hiding, and standing over the bodies of the dead.

The German commander in charge of the operation would soon send a detailed report to SS chief Heinrich Himmler, pronouncing the destruction of the Jews and "bandits" and praising his loyal forces: SS staff, police leaders, engineers, and the members of the unit from Lublin.

They were called the Trawniki men.

PART TWO

UNITED STATES
1978–1992

CHAPTER FOUR

PROPER WORK

New York City and Washington, D.C.
1978–1980

On a bustling corner in Brooklyn, in a ground-floor apartment with a view of the back alley, Peter Black turned over in bed and reached for the telephone. He had been tempted to ignore the ringing, content to stay under a blanket, cursing the kidney stone that was languishing in the lower half of his body and the inertia that had so far vexed his early career as a World War II historian.

It was just after Labor Day in 1978, and city streets hummed under a late summer sun. Brooklyn was recovering from a parade and a party, boisterous crowds of revelers who had danced down Eastern Parkway in rhinestones and feathers to celebrate Caribbean culture. In a fit of self-pity, wracked by waves of pain, Black decided that he had simply been born too late.

Stuck in bed, he had imagined himself at the Nuremberg trials in the mid-1940s, casting light into shadows alongside a generation of pre-eminent historians whom he would never come to know. Instead, he was working for five dollars an hour at a data-entry job in a warehouse the size of a football field and struggling in an overheated cubicle at Columbia University's library to finish the first chapter of his doctoral dissertation about the director of the Reich Main Security Office, Ernst Kaltenbrunner, who had succeeded the notorious Reinhard Heydrich.

Half of Black's 150-page first chapter was unusable, a tangle of extraneous facts.

"Are you Peter Black?" the voice on the other end of the line inquired.

Black squinted, cocked his head closer to the phone. "Yes, this is Peter Black."

"Have you heard of Boleslavs Maikovskis?"

Black instantly recalled the name. In 1942, Maikovskis, a police precinct commander in German-occupied Latvia, had carried out orders to arrest and slaughter more than two hundred villagers and burn their houses to the ground. Black had watched a *60 Minutes* report on Maikovskis, who had been discovered on Long Island, a resident of three decades. Active in Latvian organizations, Maikovskis had once served on a committee to help reelect President Richard Nixon.

The voice of the man on the phone was clipped and efficient. The US Attorney's Office in the Southern District of New York wanted Maikovskis removed from the United States, and federal prosecutors needed a temporary historian who spoke German to help pursue the deportation case.

"Would you be willing to come in for an interview?"

FOR A WORLD WAR II historian, Peter Black was on the young side, not yet thirty, with a mop of brown hair, a Boston accent, and eyeglasses that in moments of deep concentration slipped down to the middle of his nose, near a neatly clipped mustache that he had started to grow back in college. His parents had wanted him to study economics, but Black was consumed by the past, by the inhumanity that seemed to seize even reasonable people during times of war.

He had been something of a loner growing up in Newtonville, Massachusetts, content to spend long afternoons in his bedroom reading about the movement of armies, the slow, plaintive notes of the Five Satins playing on a suitcase turntable and a dog-eared copy of *The Rise and Fall of the Third Reich* sitting on his nightstand. Black played Wiffle ball in the driveway and pickup football games in a field behind the high school, but it was history that moved him, kept him awake at night in a bedroom filled with *Mad* magazines and comic books that at times seemed silly, given how war could turn ordinary people into murderers.

One day, Black decided in middle school, he would study the history of Nazi Germany. By the time he enrolled at the University of Wisconsin in 1968, Adolf Hitler had been dead for twenty-three years. But to Black, the need to understand the decisions of national leaders bent on mass murder seemed more urgent than ever in a world that had stumbled into a nuclear age.

Black was drinking his first legal beer at a college bar on a cold night in January 1969 when a sandy-haired girl in a wool sweater walked by with a friend. Her hair was cut to the line of her jaw, and Black found himself gazing at the prettiest eyes he had ever seen, shaped like a new moon when she raised her lower lids into a squint. Mary Mattson had grown up in a small Wisconsin town along the Mississippi River, the youngest of three sisters and a voracious reader who had often recited her favorite stories to the patient family mutt, Jenta.

Over long conversations with Mary, Black often talked about his studies in German history. At times of war and conflict, were human beings capable of deciding that it would be better to die a good person than to live as a killer? Mary listened in earnest, pointing to similar themes about human behavior in the writings of William Shakespeare.

Black studied in Bonn, Germany, during his junior year of college. But the relationship with Mary thrived, and they married before a local judge just before graduation in 1972. Black enrolled in Columbia University to study history.

With a doctorate degree, he figured he would one day become a history professor. But good positions were hard to come by in the late 1970s, and after a year in Germany researching his dissertation,

Black took the data-entry job instead, writing his thesis at night and living with Mary in a freezing railroad flat in Park Slope, Brooklyn. In 1978 they upgraded to a $275-a-month apartment that faced an alleyway, occupied on most afternoons by the superintendent's snarling German shepherd.

The call from the federal prosecutor was an unexpected break. Later, Black would thank the history professor at Columbia who had recommended him to the US Attorney's Office.

"I would love to come in for an interview," Black told the lawyer on the line. "But I'm lying here with a kidney stone. Can you wait a few days?"

Black had heard whispers for years about Nazi perpetrators who had made their way to the United States alongside great masses of European war refugees. In the 1960s, a *New York Times* reporter working off a tip from famed Nazi hunter Simon Wiesenthal identified a housewife in Queens who had used the soles of her jackboots to beat and torment prisoners at the Majdanek concentration camp in Lublin, Poland.

In the mid-1970s, a journalist who wrote for a Ukrainian-American newspaper exposed a factory worker in Waterbury, Connecticut, who had forced Jews down a narrow alley known as the *Schlauch,* or tube, to the gas chambers of the Treblinka killing center, built in a pine forest northeast of Warsaw. Nine hundred thousand Jews had perished in thirteen months.

A Cleveland autoworker stood accused of terrorizing and torturing doomed prisoners as they walked naked to their deaths at Treblinka.

All hiding in plain sight, Black thought, in America's cities and suburbs.

In college, he had studied the proceedings of the Nuremberg trials, in which twenty-two top Nazi leaders were tried by Allied prosecutors. Twelve were sentenced to death. Police officials, civilian collaborators, and concentration camp personnel at all levels were taken to court at subsequent trials that were held in both sides of divided Germany, the Eastern European Communist Bloc, and the Soviet Union.

Still, Black knew that thousands of Nazi perpetrators had gotten away in the chaos that consumed Europe after the war, slipping into Brazil, Chile, Argentina, the Middle East, Australia, and the United States. Some simply went back to their native countries to resume their lives. Simon Wiesenthal and a few other prominent proponents of justice spent decades tracking them, but as the Cold War raged, Communism became the greater threat and the search for Nazi perpetrators all but ended in most of the world.

Nazi hunting in the United States had for years fallen under the jurisdiction of the Immigration and Naturalization Service, but the agency drew criticism for showing little interest in pursuing immigrants from European towns that few Americans had ever heard of. "Half-hearted, dilatory investigations," berated Brooklyn congresswoman Elizabeth Holtzman, who had pressed in 1977 for congressional hearings on the matter.

When Black got the call from the US Attorney's Office in New York, Holtzman had helped pass legislation that made it easier for the federal government to deport anyone found to have participated in Nazi persecution, striking down a series of exemptions long provided under immigration law. She had also pushed to create a new unit within INS singularly focused on Nazi investigations and would soon convince the federal government to take its most significant step yet, one that would change the course of Nazi hunting in the United States.

The operation would be moved to the powerful Criminal Division of the US Department of Justice, expanded to include dozens of lawyers and investigators, and given a new name: the Office of Special Investigations.

On the cusp of a new decade, more than thirty years after the war's end, the United States government was promising to track, expose, and deport Nazi war criminals who had found refuge in America. A breathtaking mission.

Black thanked the lawyer on the phone, hung up, and went back to bed. Two weeks later, he passed the kidney stone and accepted the job, quite certain that he had just become the luckiest guy in Brooklyn.

ON A LATE summer morning in 1979, Black stood before the headquarters of the fledgling Office of Special Investigations.

He had spent the better part of a year hunched over a Selectric typewriter in the prosecutors' offices in New York, forming thoughts in German and English about the Latvian police commander under investigation for war crimes. And now, rather suddenly, Black found himself in Washington, called to town to interview for a permanent job at OSI.

The city still had the feel of summer, lush and green. Paddleboats bobbed in the tidal basin, and tourists in tank tops and denim lingered at the base of the Washington Monument, which soared more than five hundred feet over the National Mall. Schoolchildren milled about the National Archives, a sprawling building located halfway between the White House and the Capitol, with seventy-two Corinthian columns and a statue of a gazing old man holding a book that paraphrased Confucius. *Study the past.*

Black had often thought of the marble halls of the Justice Department along Pennsylvania Avenue, looming over one of the most famous streets in the world, with lawyers and investigators eager to step back in history to bring Nazi criminals to account.

But the Office of Special Investigations was set up in a dusty, noisy outpost of the Justice Department on the edge of Washington's red-light district, across the street from a public square that had drawn the nickname "Needle Park" for the dopers and dealers who milled about the trees and benches. Once, the building had been a grand, Beaux Arts–style hotel designed by a local French architect, but by

1979 the guest rooms had been converted into drab government offices that smelled of fried food and antiseptic.

Despite the nature of the work ahead, OSI had opened with little
fanfare. "Agency Studying Nazis Is Upgraded," the *New York Times*
had reported on page eighteen after Elizabeth Holtzman persuaded
the federal government to give the unit a new home inside the Justice Department's Criminal Division.

None of that mattered to Black as he ducked inside the building,
eager for the day ahead and anxious to make a good impression. He
was led to a small room with a dropped ceiling and cheap wooden
bookshelves. The head of investigations was waiting, and he frowned
as he studied Black.

The investigator was a classic gun-and-badge man, blunt, beefy,
twenty years older than Black, and clearly put off by the thought of
a pensive intellectual on the hunt for Nazi war criminals. He peered
at Black, no patience for pleasantries.

"Why would you want to come work here?" he asked, his voice
flat. "You'll never write any books here."

It seemed a scolding, not a question, and Black hesitated. He
could analyze source material, place facts into historical context,
hunt down records that had long ago been lost, but those skills
seemed unlikely to mollify the man in front of him.

"I can contribute to making solid cases based on my training,"
Black said carefully.

On the train back to New York, Black was all but certain that his
brief stint as a Nazi hunter had abruptly come to an end. When the
office manager at OSI called a few months later with a job offer,
Black could scarcely believe his good fortune.

For $23,000 a year he would become OSI's first formally trained
historian, working under a dozen investigators, who were working
under a dozen lawyers, who were struggling under the weight of
more than three hundred investigations that had long ago turned

cold. Alleged Nazi war criminals were living in New York, Chicago, Los Angeles, Philadelphia, Pittsburgh, Miami, Buffalo, Newark, Houston, San Diego, and Seattle.

Black told Mary the news and made plans to move to a rented apartment across from the Potomac River in Virginia, a few miles from OSI's headquarters. On the new job, there would be much to do, and the years were passing quickly. America had fought two major wars since the collapse of Nazi Germany. Suspects were growing older. Eyewitnesses were dying. Most people at OSI gave the unit a year or two, just enough time to investigate and prosecute with the goodwill and funding of the American public behind them.

Black would have to dig in quickly.

SITTING ON A southbound plane to Charleston in 1980, Black could not have known that the work of the historians at the Office of Special Investigations would one day help expose a group of Nazi collaborators behind the most lethal mass-murder operation in the Holocaust. He had been on the job in Washington for only a handful of months, and Black was frustrated.

Though some OSI attorneys had turned to Black for guidance, he felt pegged at times as something of an office misfit, a high-browed scholar rather than a tenacious investigator essential to the unit's mounting caseload. He was often excluded from interviews with defendants and witnesses, kept from meetings about critical cases.

Black spent long afternoons in the National Archives and the Library of Congress, studying captured German documents for evidence about the auxiliary police officials, concentration camp guards, propagandists, and civil servants under investigation at OSI. He rarely found the names of suspects, but he could dig up information about their units, duties, commanders, and ties to agencies of the German occupation.

Black had found an ally in another historian, a Brandeis University graduate brought on to OSI a few months after Black. On Fridays after work, Black and David Marwell took to commiserating in a pub that served cheap burgers to government workers and journalists from the *Washington Post,* which was headquartered just down the street.

"What the hell are we doing at this office if we're not taken seriously?" Marwell would grouse.

He joined Black in the archives. Once, amid horrific descriptions of war and bloodshed, they came upon a plan by Heinrich Himmler, one of the most feared men in the Third Reich, to use migrating storks to drop Nazi propaganda from the skies of eastern Europe. Nazis, Black and Marwell decided in a rare moment of levity, said the darnedest things.

What else was out there? They had no way of knowing. Tens of thousands of German documents were stashed behind the Iron Curtain, seized by the Red Army at the end of the war and deposited in Soviet and Eastern European archives. The Communist governments—in Prague, East Berlin, Kiev, Moscow, Budapest, Bucharest—had for years denied access to Western scholars. It was a monumental obstacle for the lawyers and historians at OSI, who worried that critical evidence was just out of reach.

Though there wasn't much money for travel, Black and Marwell had been given permission to attend a conference at the Citadel, in South Carolina, where a generation of prominent scholars was gathering to talk about the state of research on Hitler and Nazi Germany. OSI needed expert witnesses to successfully prosecute Nazi perpetrators in court, and Black knew the conference would be filled with qualified historians.

As the plane made its way south, Black settled back in his seat. He was too new at OSI to raise concerns about the role of the unit's historians, but something had to change. History needed to have a place in the deliberations, and the hodgepodge group of investigators he reported to were simply not experts on the strategies and practices of the Third Reich.

They had been pulled from agencies across the federal government: one from the Fish and Wildlife Service, another from the Internal Revenue Service, a third from the US Marshals Service. Some had applied to be part of the operation even though they had little training in Nazi war crimes. Black had begun to suspect that others had simply been assigned to the unit.

In Charleston, Black and Marwell dropped their bags at the hotel and set out for the conference. Finally, Black thought, he would be among like-minded thinkers, scholars and researchers who had mined the most abominable moments in world history to gain a better, deeper understanding of human behavior.

Dozens of people milled about the conference room, but Black found himself captivated by a speaker with a disarming Southern drawl. Charlie Sydnor, a history professor from Virginia, had authored a best-selling book about the work of the SS Death's Head Division, formed from SS guard units in prewar concentration camps. Black listened to him deliver appalling details about genocide in simple, striking prose.

On the second day of the conference, Black and Marwell followed Sydnor into the men's room.

"Don't be nervous," Marwell quipped, flashing his Department of Justice credentials as Sydnor stood at a urinal. "We're not here to arrest you."

Sydnor didn't flinch. "You didn't get that wet, did you?"

Black laughed, straight from the belly. For years afterward, Sydnor would take great pride in eliciting laughs from the younger historian, who considered distinguishing between right and wrong no less than a moral imperative for a sober student of history.

Black and Marwell described the mission of OSI. "We're going to bring cases against people who got into the country through fraud, by not revealing their true backgrounds," Marwell said. "These are people who were auxiliary policemen and local collaborators."

"What the hell are they doing here?" Sydnor asked.

"They lied about their backgrounds," Marwell said. "They were very good at posing as victims."

"We think there are hundreds of these people," Black added.

The Office of Special Investigations needed help. Federal law prohibited the government from waging criminal cases against defendants who had committed crimes on foreign soil during the war. But in civil court, under the rules introduced by Elizabeth Holtzman, OSI could seek to denaturalize and then deport anyone who had assisted in persecution and then concealed their activities during the immigration process.

It wasn't the toughest, most dramatic solution, but pursuing criminal cases against alleged Nazi perpetrators in the United States would have likely required a Constitutional amendment and new federal criminal laws. And potential sponsors in Congress had decided that there was simply no time for a state-by-state ratification process, given the advanced age of suspects.

OSI, Black and Marwell told Sydnor, needed a seasoned, likable historian who could serve as an expert witness at civil court hearings, explaining the origins of mass murder to American judges who generally knew very little about the sweeping network of collaborators involved in Nazi crimes. It was an uncharted field involving an entirely new set of legal issues and questions that would be aired not only before the courts but before the entire world since no other country in 1980 was actively and aggressively pursuing Nazi criminals.

Sydnor, a Southerner and a Christian, would be a charming, frank, and unlikely spokesman.

"If American citizenship is to have any meaning at all," Marwell said, "we have to take it back."

Sydnor moved to the sink and studied the two men. He nodded and grinned.

"You two," he said, "have become gumshoes."

CHAPTER FIVE

DARKNESS COMES MY WAY

Detroit
1982

The defendant swept into the federal courtroom wearing a cleric's cassock that brushed the floor. His hair was white and his face was round, fixed with a thick right eyebrow that lurched upward, as if he held a great secret.

Some men blamed for inciting the murders of hundreds of Jews might have appeared indignant, but the sixty-eight-year-old Romanian Orthodox archbishop remained still and inscrutable as he sat between three defense attorneys in the federal building that stretched across a full city block in downtown Detroit.

From behind the prosecutor's table, Peter Black studied the man he had come to know only through what history had left behind: a trail of clues, decades old and long forgotten, scattered across two continents.

Finally, the Office of Special Investigations had turned to Black to play a major role in what would become one of its most infamous cases. For most of 1981, Black had retraced the steps of Archbishop Valerian Trifa from more than forty years earlier, when he had been a prominent leader of the Romanian Iron Guard, a violent, fascist, and antisemitic movement whose members greeted each other with the Roman salute—arms extended and palms down.

As editor of an Iron Guard newspaper, Trifa in January 1941 had printed a call to arms against the regime of Romanian military dictator Ion Antonescu, whom the Iron Guard believed was moving too slowly against so-called enemies of the state.

A group of Jews and Jew-lovers are ruling everything.

In the streets, Jews were stabbed, beaten, shot, doused with gasoline, and set on fire. In a Bucharest slaughterhouse, they were murdered in a fashion intended to mock kosher butchering techniques, then left to hang on meat hooks. Others were assembled before a burning synagogue and forced to dance to the sound of gunfire. Afterward, Trifa fled to the Reich to avoid capture by Romanian authorities, who tried him in absentia and sentenced him to life in prison.

He had spent four years as a guest of Reich authorities before fleeing to Vienna and eventually to Paris. In 1950, he made his way to the United States and quickly rose in the church, settling into a sprawling farmhouse in the suburbs of Michigan.

There had been talk since the early 1950s about Trifa's Nazi past, and the federal government eventually filed a complaint against him, repeatedly pressed by a Jewish Holocaust survivor from Romania who had emigrated to the United States after the war. OSI took over the prosecution, and Black had helped prepare for a hearing, organizing Trifa's articles and speeches as well as German Foreign Office and police documents found in Bonn, Vienna, Bucharest, and other cities. Black had discovered the original leaflet written by Trifa and dispersed to a crowd in Bucharest on the night before the rioting.

All told, OSI prosecutors had a trove of 750 documents, along with a five-hundred-page report written by Black that chronicled Trifa's activities during the war. "Trifa's speeches, articles and newspaper editorials," Black had concluded, "had pounded home the themes of hatred towards Jews and foreigners."

The deportation hearing for an archbishop who had once

delivered the benediction before Congress had drawn intense interest, and journalists, Jewish leaders, and lawyers packed the courtroom. The diocese had hired its own attorney, who sat at the defense table alongside Trifa.

Black wondered whether the archbishop would take the stand, a tantalizing thought after so many months of research, burrowing inside the mind of a stranger. Black often wished he could talk to the dead, and now he found himself sitting only a few feet away from a historical subject.

The OSI prosecutor on the case was Kathleen Coleman, a meticulous lawyer who had joined the unit after working as an assistant attorney general in the US Virgin Islands. Months earlier, Black and Coleman had traveled to Israel together to prepare for another case, sharing the short highway between Tel Aviv and Haifa with Israeli troop convoys that were headed to and from the battle inside Lebanon, which had been invaded by Israeli forces a week earlier.

On a break, Black visited Yad Vashem, Israel's Holocaust remembrance center, lingering before an exhibit that showcased a postcard written by a Hungarian Jewish boy. In 1944, the boy had been deported to Auschwitz, the largest and deadliest concentration camp complex, about sixty kilometers west of German-occupied Krakow.

"I'm okay," the boy had written to family in Hungary. "They are putting us to work."

He had used big, looping letters, the careful cursive of a grade-school child. Black stood there for a long while, thinking about his own son, Aaron, born just two months earlier, and knowing that the Hungarian boy was likely already dead by the time his note reached home.

Immigration judge Bellino D'Ambrosio called the Trifa hearing to order, and Coleman stood up. She would summon a leading expert on Romanian history and several historical witnesses to the stand, but the heart of the case rested on Trifa's speeches, newspaper editorials, and articles.

Looking at the archbishop, who had once proclaimed that "Yid" blood was vile, Black wondered what had moved the son of a Transylvanian schoolteacher to such a hateful place. Coleman turned to the judge.

"Had the truth been known about Viorel Trifa," Coleman said, using Trifa's given name, "he would have been excluded from the United States."

"I think the government has vastly overstated what the evidence will show," Trifa's defense attorney countered. "The government's characterizations are historically incorrect."

Black knew with absolute certainty that wasn't the case. He had documented every stage of Trifa's life, and the work had been grueling. At home at night, he often sat with Mary watching *Perry Mason* reruns, trying to free his mind from grim, dark spaces.

TWO DAYS IN federal court passed quickly. On the morning of the third day, Black glanced across the room at Trifa, whose eyes were hidden behind horn-rimmed glasses. Coleman had spent hours probing Trifa's involvement in the Iron Guard, and overnight there was talk among the lawyers about a settlement in the case.

From the prosecutor's table, Allan Ryan stood up. Though some members of the Jewish community had balked at the idea of an Irish Catholic leading the new Office of Special Investigations, Black considered the thirty-seven-year-old former assistant to the solicitor general a fierce advocate for the unit. Broad shouldered, with a thick mustache and beard, the ex–Marine Corps captain had gathered the OSI staff together a few months after Black moved to Washington.

No federal judge, Ryan warned, was going to revoke the citizenship of an older, law-abiding immigrant simply because of falsified information on a visa application.

"These are war-crimes cases. These are not immigration cases," Ryan had insisted. "What we have to do is show the judge and whoever else is watching that this sixty-five-year-old guy who works in a factory or who owns a motel in Florida, we've got to show what this guy did in 1941, '42, '43, '44, and '45. We need the witnesses. We need the evidence. We need the documents. We need to paint the whole picture for the judge, and we're going to have to start at the beginning."

Ryan had decided that historians needed to play a central role in the investigative process. He gradually reduced the number of criminal investigators and hired more historians. "I want all the historians to think like lawyers," Ryan said, "and I want all the lawyers to think like historians. That's the only way we're going to make progress here."

Black had been grateful for the focus on context and history.

For two days in federal court, Ryan had sat quietly next to Coleman. Now he turned to face the judge. "We have agreed to a settlement of the case."

The archbishop, Ryan said, would admit that he had been a member of the Iron Guard and had perjured himself to come to America. He would leave the United States within sixty days of obtaining travel documents from a country willing to accept him. In exchange, the Justice Department would no longer pursue the case.

The judge turned to Trifa, and Black leaned forward in his chair, eager, for the record of history, to hear the man's voice and even the briefest explanation about his work and mindset during the war. Trifa stood up and made his way to the lectern in the middle of the courtroom.

"Sir, will you state your name for the record?" the judge asked.

"My name is Valerian D. Trifa." His eastern European accent hadn't faded after three decades in America.

"How old are you?"

"I am sixty-eight."

"Are you at this time under the influence of any type of alcohol, drugs or medication?"

"No."

"Do you suffer from any types of illness which would in any way affect your ability to understand the nature and purpose of these proceedings, why you are here, and what could happen to you?"

"I am not fully healthy, but I am aware of why I am here, yes."

"Do you understand the agreement which you heard read at this time and which has been signed by you?"

"I do."

"Did you enter this agreement at your own free will and of your own decision?"

"Yes."

"All right, thank you, Mr. Trifa."

"Thank you," Trifa said and sat back down.

Black knew that he would likely never again hear from Trifa, who was hoping to leave for Switzerland. Under federal law, deportable aliens had the right to choose a destination.

"All right," the judge said. "I enter an order that he be deported to the country of designation."

Coleman and Ryan started packing up, and Black watched months of research disappear inside boxes and briefcases. Ryan paused and turned to Black.

"Do you want to call the press on this?"

It was an unusually magnanimous offer. The Justice Department typically put only top lawyers before the media, not a historian who was earning less money and had less experience than some veteran government secretaries and paralegals. Black nodded and walked to a nearby office in the courthouse to make the call.

The next morning, the *Chicago Tribune* reported, "The deportation order was disclosed by Peter Black, historian for the Office of Special Investigations in the Justice Department."

THERE WAS NO time to dwell on the government's victory. Hundreds of clues and leads were waiting back in Washington. Some came from West Berlin, which had a central repository of Nazi rosters and records with names that could be vetted and potentially matched to those of men living in the United States. Other leads came from tips and media accounts.

One case was particularly compelling.

Years earlier, an article in a Soviet Lithuanian newspaper had alerted the Justice Department to a sixty-two-year-old Chicago man named Liudas Kairys, who had emigrated to the United States in 1949. He found work at the Cracker Jack Company, married another Lithuanian immigrant, and had two daughters.

The Soviets, responding to a request from US investigators, had produced a personnel file that showed that Kairys lied about his whereabouts during the war. On his visa application, Kairys claimed that he had worked on his father's farm.

The records, however, showed that he had been a guard in 1943 and 1944 at the notorious Treblinka labor camp in German-occupied Poland, where Jewish prisoners were forced to haul great piles of coal and stone and load sand from the banks of a river. The labor camp was about two kilometers from the Treblinka gas chambers, and prisoners considered too weak to work were simply dumped overnight between the fences on the perimeter of the labor camp and sent to their deaths the next morning.

The Office of Special Investigations had gone to court to strip Kairys of his US citizenship, the first step toward deportation. Prosecutors had largely focused on his service at Treblinka, but his personnel file had also listed the name of a Polish village, southeast of Lublin, where Kairys had spent time in 1942 and 1943 before he went to Treblinka.

Trawniki.

In history books, in transcripts from the trials at Nuremberg, and in some captured German documents, Black had seen scattered references to Trawniki, where, on the grounds of an old sugar factory, the SS had trained and deployed guards for deportation operations in Jewish ghettos and for work in occupied Poland's Nazi-run labor camps and killing centers. But historians had uncovered relatively little about the training camp itself or the extent of its role in the destruction of Poland's Jews, a conspicuous gap in the history of the war.

There had to be something more, Black thought. The idea was intriguing, an unexplored sliver of history.

Poland had once been home to one of the largest Jewish populations in the world, 3.3 million people, second only to that of the United States. But in less than twenty months, the Germans had wiped out 1.7 million Jews in a mass-murder spree that had been code-named Operation Reinhard, after the SS general Reinhard Heydrich, chief of the Reich Security Main Office and an architect of the Holocaust.

It had been an unprecedented and comprehensive operation: rounding up Jews from ghettos across German-occupied Poland and sending them on trucks, on freight-train cars, and on foot to three killing centers established solely for death. Belzec, Sobibor, and Treblinka had no need for holding cells because prisoners were killed upon entry in gas chambers within a few hundred yards of the train tracks.

The Jews of Lublin had been among the first to die. The village of Trawniki was forty kilometers away.

References to Trawniki, Black knew, had appeared in four other American court cases. In records connected to the Kairys case, OSI had identified Massachusetts resident Vladas Zajanckauskas, who told investigators in 1981 that he had been deployed merely as a server in the canteen at Trawniki. Since OSI had no records to contradict his story, lawyers agreed to set aside a case, at least until any new information emerged.

Back in the 1970s, federal prosecutors in Florida had pursued another man, a retired brass-factory worker named Feodor Fedorenko, who had served at the Treblinka killing center. Fedorenko had helped force trainloads of Jewish victims from the so-called reception area through the undressing barracks to the gas chambers, which were fed by a diesel engine removed from a captured Soviet tank. "Dante's Inferno," Treblinka's commandant had called it. Before Treblinka, Fedorenko had also been stationed in the camp at Trawniki.

And so had another man, a Ford Motor Company worker found in the suburbs of Cleveland. Jewish survivors had identified John "Ivan" Demjanjuk as a sadistic guard who beat prisoners with a gas pipe on the final march to the gas chambers at Treblinka. The capture of the notorious "Ivan the Terrible" on American soil had drawn international headlines. Demjanjuk, too, had spent months during the war at Trawniki.

Records in the Demjanjuk case had revealed the name of yet another Trawniki alumnus, living in New York since 1952. Under questioning in 1980, Jakob Reimer had maintained that he worked only as an accountant and paymaster in the administrative offices at Trawniki, and no case was brought against him.

What had taken place in the little-known village in southeastern Poland? The answers, Black suspected, likely sat behind lock and key in Soviet and Eastern European archives.

In the busy months after the Trifa hearing, Black filed the information away, a mystery for another day.

CHAPTER SIX

LIGHT AT LONG LAST

Warsaw, Poland
1984

On a frigid February morning in Warsaw, Peter Black set out for the Main Commission for the Investigation of Nazi Crimes in Poland, headquartered in a sprawling behemoth of stone and brick that stretched along Karola Świerczewskiego Street. The building was near one of the oldest and most prestigious avenues in the Polish capital, flanked by grand castles and manor houses dating back to the seventeenth century.

Black had come to accept an extraordinary offer, the chance to probe captured German records that no American investigator had ever seen.

For the first time since the war's end, the Communist government in Poland had offered to open its archives to historians at the Office of Special Investigations. Black and David Marwell had traveled to Warsaw on research trips months earlier, and now Black was back to hunt for clues about three men in the United States suspected to have ties to an ethnic German auxiliary police unit that had operated in the early part of the war.

The Main Commission was set up in a courthouse that bordered the old Jewish ghetto; the building had once been a meeting place for people on both sides of the ghetto wall. Black was eager to get to work, mining the thousands of war records collected by the commission since its founding by the Polish government in 1945.

He ducked inside the building with Jim Halmo, the chief of US consular affairs in Warsaw, who would accompany Black to a meeting with the commission's director.

Black had never met Czeslaw Pilichowski, a noted scholar and author who had fought in the Polish Communist underground during the war and had gone on to chronicle the impact of German occupation on Polish life. Shown inside Pilichowski's office, Black offered a polite nod.

The sixty-nine-year-old director was in no mood for pleasantries. He scowled in grand fashion at the two Americans, pacing and shaking his head. Black spoke German, not Polish, but he quickly picked up the message.

You Americans send spies into Poland, criticize our country in the press, and refuse to help us when we need it. Why should I help you?

It was the last thing Black expected, an emphatic, official lecture about the tumultuous state of affairs between the United States and the military dictatorship of Polish general Wojciech Jaruzelski. Studying the frowning director, Black had a terrible suspicion that the goodwill extended by Polish authorities had, quite suddenly, vanished.

BLACK HAD BEEN to Poland once before, six months earlier, to review war records in Warsaw, Poznan, and Radom, a city on the banks of the Mleczna River that was once home to thirty-three thousand Jews. Jim Halmo had offered a warm greeting as well as a series of instructions.

Don't exchange money on the black market. Don't take packages from strangers. Don't accept unsolicited invitations. Assume that your hotel room is bugged.

Threatened by prodemocracy activists, the authoritarian Communist government led by General Jaruzelski had drastically restricted normal life and imprisoned hundreds of people. Twenty-two months earlier, Poland's first postwar semi-independent trade union had been destroyed.

Black could see signs of the country's economic and political struggles everywhere. He had dined in restaurants with ten-page menus but nothing much to offer except duck back or fried brains, which he washed down with vodka because it was the only safe thing to drink. On a ride back to Warsaw one night, a truck driver pulled over to help Black change a flat tire. Black gave the man five dollars for his kindness, knowing that its value on the black market equaled roughly three month's wages. How sad, Black lamented, that finding money for basic comforts depended on such chance encounters.

For seven days during that first trip, Black had traveled along bumpy roads between Warsaw and Radom with a Polish lawyer and interpreter who worked as a paralegal in the US embassy. Squeezed next to Black inside a car the size of a Volkswagen Beetle, Danuta Antoszewska talked about growing up in the country's eastern borderlands a generation before Black was born. As a teenager during the war, she had watched Germans march Jewish families into the woods. Moments later, gunshots pierced the air.

"I knew many of those people," she said softly.

Black was touched that she talked so openly about her wounded country. Few other countries, Black knew, suffered more under German occupation than Poland, where the three death factories established by the SS had wiped out a people and a culture that had influenced Polish life for nearly six hundred years. Two other killing centers went up on territory annexed to Germany from western Poland: Chelmno, for the Jews of Lodz, Poznan, and the surrounding regions; and Auschwitz-Birkenau, where Jews from all over northern, western, central, and southeastern Europe were sent to die.

Over the course of the Holocaust, three million Polish Jews were murdered. Nearly two million non-Jewish Polish civilians were also slaughtered, some after they were caught trying to help or hide Jews. Punishment by death often extended to the rescuer's family, neighbors, and entire village.

Black was quiet as he listened to Danuta's story, knowing there was nothing he could say. "That's a burden to carry around," he offered. "I can't imagine."

Once during that first trip, a research specialist at the Main Commission archives in Warsaw had pulled Black aside. It was late afternoon, and Black was heading back to a stuffy hotel room with nothing much to do except consolidate his notes and watch Polish police dramas on a black-and-white television.

"Do you have plans tonight?" the researcher asked, smiling. "Would you like to come meet some friends of mine?"

Black suspected that he had just been invited to a meeting of Poles sympathetic to the underground movement, Solidarity, an independent labor union launched in the late 1970s after factory, shipyard, and coal workers grew frustrated by the shortages that vexed the country under Communist rule. Over time, the movement would trigger an end to Communism throughout eastern and central Europe and ultimately reach all the way to the Soviet Union itself, but in Warsaw in 1983, Black knew only that police were arresting Solidarity supporters during late-night raids.

He paused, tempted to see history unfold in real time. The Solidarity movement had drawn support from a broad range of international leaders, including Ronald Reagan, Margaret Thatcher, and Pope John Paul II. But Halmo had been adamant. "You're not a reporter. You're not a private historian. You are the United States government."

Given the tension between the Reagan administration and the Polish dictatorship, Black couldn't exclude the possibility that he might walk into a trap, accused of spying or engaging in sedition against the Polish government. He declined the invitation.

"*Nie, dziękuję,*" he mumbled in butchered Polish. No thank you.

He left Warsaw on a prop jet flanked by a soldier with a pistol holstered on his hip to deter hijackers. *It's in the Lord's hands,* Black told himself as the engine roared to life.

HE HAD DONE everything by the book during that first visit, and when the Polish government agreed to let him return in 1984 for another look at the country's war records, this time at the Provincial State Archives in Lublin, he planned to stay for five weeks. What might he find buried in a forgotten storage room in a city where fewer than two hundred Jews had survived the war? Though some records had likely been lost or destroyed, Black imagined stacks of boxes filled with identity cards, interview transcripts, and Nazi rosters.

Broad access to the Polish archives gave the Office of Special Investigations a remarkable new way to improve its research methods. To gain access to documents controlled by Communist governments, the unit had always sent specific requests for records to a liaison at the US Department of State. The request would be edited and dispatched in a secure pouch to the US embassy in the country where the records were held.

In Poland, the Ministry of Foreign Affairs would forward the request to the Federal Procurator's Office, the Federal Archives Administration, and the security agencies, which would transmit the message to the local legal or archival authorities.

OSI had often waited months, sometimes years, for a reply, and even when copies of records were provided, they often lacked context—a note from one file, a roster from another—distinct puzzle pieces from disparate time periods and locations, having in common only a mention of the target of the OSI investigation.

But the government of Poland, more than any other Soviet

Bloc country in the early 1980s, appeared inclined to grant un-
fettered access to its records. Black knew that thousands of Poles
had fought on the Allied side during the war and that Polish Underground organizations had provided critical intelligence to the
British and US governments. Exiled Polish leaders, in the early
years of the war, had been among the first to reveal details of the
mass killing of Jews, often in the form of eyewitness reports from
a handful of survivors who had escaped the deportation trains or
the killing centers.

Black had no way of knowing exactly what motivated the relative
goodwill on the part of the Polish archival authorities or how long he
might gain access to the records. He would move swiftly and carefully on his second research trip to Poland, gathering what he could.

He was looking forward to working again with Danuta, who had
written to him over Christmas: "We all are waiting to the new year
to come. What will it bring to all of us? Let's hope peace and friend-
ship."

Now, standing in the Main Commission, Czeslaw Pilichowski was
delivering a stern speech about US interference in Poland's affairs.
He glared at Jim Halmo. Danuta Antoszewska would not be es-
corting Black to the archives in Lublin. This time, the Communist
government would provide a car, a driver, and its own interpreter.

The tirade lasted a good ten minutes, and just when Black
thought he would be shown the door, Pilichowski appeared to cut
himself off. He turned to Black, smiled as if greeting a longtime colleague, and said in German, "Would you like some tea?"

Surprised, Black could only stammer, "*Ja, gerne.*"

Sipping his tea, Black tried to reassure Pilichowski. "I'm not the
CIA."

Pilichowski just shrugged, but his face softened as he studied
Black. "So what are you looking for?" he asked, scholar to scholar.

Black knew then that the tantrum had been theater, an exaggerated and intentional protest of alleged US intervention in internal Polish affairs. Black had been cleared to do his research.

AFTER SEVERAL DAYS in the archives of Warsaw, Black left the Polish capital, with block after block of squat, gray apartment buildings that had been built by the Soviets in the years after the war. He traveled south to Lublin, accompanied by a driver and the government's interpreter.

Black had never been to Lublin, and he wandered the cobblestone alleyways of the old Jewish ghetto, covered in ice and snow. How difficult it must have been to live here, he imagined, in houses without heat, shut away behind gates and guards. There had been no running water and very little food, but just beyond the western border of the ghetto, Polish farmers and traders from the Lublin countryside had hawked fresh buns and meat in a teeming market that had functioned since the nineteenth century.

Black knew that the ghetto had been nearly emptied in March 1942, when fifteen hundred people a day were forced from a gathering point at the oldest synagogue in Lublin onto freight trains that were waiting at a station just outside the ghetto. Though the Jews of Lublin didn't know it, they would be taken 130 kilometers southeast to the railway station in Belzec. It had been the first killing center constructed under Operation Reinhard, the Nazi plan to murder the Jews in the Government General.

At Belzec, signs in German, Polish, and Yiddish read: *Please undress. Go the bath area. Shower. Relax on the straw.* Struck by whips and rifle butts, the stunned prisoners were forced along a narrow pathway from the barracks into a gas chamber that would soon fill with exhaust fumes from a diesel engine.

Black left the area and moved along to the Lublin neighborhood where, in 1939, SS leaders had commandeered a middle school painted buttercup yellow and soon began to craft plans for mass murder. The man in charge was Odilo Globocnik, a one-time hot-head in the Austrian Nazi Party who had enjoyed the confidence of top Nazi officials, including Heinrich Himmler, Reich Marshal Hermann Göring, and Reinhard Heydrich, the chief of security police and a top deputy to Himmler.

Lublin was a blood-stained city, and during Black's second week on the road, with three more left, he wanted to call Mary at home in Virginia. From behind the Iron Curtain, that meant waiting by the phone for a day or more with no guarantee of a connection. Black missed his wife and young son, Aaron, who had said a few words when he was a year old and then stopped talking altogether.

"Kids develop in different ways," David Marwell offered when Black mentioned that Aaron had been diagnosed with developmental delays. "They have their own timelines."

Black had always been a bit of a worrier. He had fretted about American engagement in Southeast Asia and about the pushback against civil and equal rights at home. When Ronald Reagan was elected president in 1980, Black worried about a country that seemed bound to become less tolerant, which affected not only his sense of morality but also his family since Aaron would one day rely on federal law that banned discrimination against people with disabilities.

What kind of world, Black wondered, would his young son inherit?

LUBLIN WAS FRIGID and night came early, but Black needed every bit of three weeks to finish his research. Early each morning, he trudged to the archives on streets covered with ice and mud and settled in for a long afternoon of reading, working through lunch so that he didn't lose time.

One afternoon, Black was studying an inventory of records, making notes about the files he wanted to review. He stopped on one of the entries: Trawniki.

There it was again.

Black thought of the men found on US soil. Though OSI had opted not to file cases against Jakob Reimer or Vladas Zajanck-auskas, Feodor Fedorenko had been ordered deported to the Soviet Union. Liudas Kairys was facing the loss of US citizenship, and Israel had issued an extradition request for John Demjanjuk, identified as "Ivan the Terrible" of the Treblinka killing center.

In each of the three cases, the training camp at Trawniki had been a supporting fact, an essential tool linking the men to Treblinka. In the Demjanjuk and Kairys cases, service at Trawniki had even been part of the allegations filed in court by OSI. But the focus of the prosecution was largely on the Treblinka killing center and forced-labor camp, where daily horrors had been documented by scholars worldwide.

Black wanted more information about the operation and scope of Trawniki, particularly in the case against John Demjanjuk. Black was a documents man, and something didn't fit.

Holocaust survivors had placed Demjanjuk at the gas chambers of Treblinka, but Black had studied Demjanjuk's SS-issued identification card, with a picture of the twenty-three-year-old ethnic Ukrainian dressed in an earth-brown uniform, his identification number—1393—pinned just above the gold button on his breast pocket. Two work assignments were recorded near the bottom of the card, one in September 1942 at a so-called SS and police estate about two dozen kilometers east of Lublin, and a second at the Sobibor killing center in March 1943.

There was no reference to Treblinka.

On a flight to Chicago to interview a witness in another case, Black mentioned the discrepancy to OSI lawyer Bruce Einhorn. The son of a chemist, Einhorn often ate his tuna-salad sandwich in the historians' offices at lunch, chatting about cases that he couldn't bring himself to discuss at home. Sharing the awful details with his wife, Einhorn had concluded, would be like passing along the flu.

When early-morning fog diverted the flight from Chicago to Detroit, Black leaned over in his seat. "How do you reconcile what these witnesses say and what stands on the document?"

"The witness testimony is very, very strong," Einhorn had replied.

But Black knew that human memory could be frail, distorted within minutes of an experience or shaken and changed by the passage of time. Black also knew that no historian had been heavily involved in the Demjanjuk investigation, which had been launched before the Office of Special Investigations was established.

Later, Black decided to approach historian Charlie Sydnor, who had agreed at the conference in Charleston to work with OSI as an expert witness. "How do we explain the discrepancy between the card and the survivors?" Black asked.

Sydnor shrugged, impressed by Black's persistence. Ruthless objectivity, Sydnor would come to call it.

"If this man is not Ivan the Terrible of Treblinka," the older historian said in a Southern drawl, "if all these survivors are wrong, then he's Ivan the slightly less terrible of Sobibor. So who really gives a shit?"

Clearly, Demjanjuk was not an innocent man. Though OSI had no documentary evidence establishing that he had served at Treblinka, Demjanjuk's identification card placed him at the killing center Sobibor, where at least 167,000 Jews had perished.

Still, a finding of guilt based on faulty or missing facts would compromise the credibility of the legal case and the ongoing work at the Office of Special Investigations.

Black hoped to get the details straight for the record of history and to establish, unequivocally, where and how Demjanjuk had served the Reich. Too many questions lingered.

One came from a stamp on the back of Demjanjuk's identification card:

Dienstsitz Lublin
Ausbildungslager Trawniki

Service Location Lublin. Trawniki Training Camp.

What had happened there, on the site of an abandoned sugar factory that long before the war had delivered a living wage to Polish families? What had brought together five strangers—Kairys and Zajanckauskas from Lithuania, Demjanjuk and Reimer from the Soviet Ukraine, and Fedorenko from the Sivash region of Crimea—to the exact same place as the Germans launched the deadliest part of the Holocaust?

Sitting in the archives of Lublin, not far from Trawniki, Black asked to see all the files on the training camp. The director nodded and sent his archivist to search for the records. He returned some time later, shaking his head. The Trawniki files had been sent to another archive in Poland. He did not say where.

In the matter of Trawniki, Black would go home empty-handed after all. But OSI in 1984 had no active Trawniki case, and Black had plenty of other work to do in Lublin.

CHAPTER SEVEN

BREACH OF POWER

Washington, D.C.
1987

Just before Easter on a breezy night in Washington, OSI director Neal Sher sat alone at his desk, thinking about the dozens of Nazi war criminals pursued by the Office of Special Investigations over eight years and the single, high-profile case that could permanently undermine the operation.

The place was empty. The lawyers and historians had long wrapped up for the day, and Sher was grateful for the time alone. He had a decision to make.

One wrong move and it could all be over, the Office of Special Investigations shut down long before the work was done. For OSI's newest leader, it was an intolerable thought, given that Peter Black and the historians were poring over thousands of Nazi records from Warsaw, Lublin, West Berlin, and Israel, and OSI prosecutors were scrambling to remove Nazi perpetrators who had been found in nearly every corner of the United States.

One of them was a sixty-seven-year-old land surveyor in Long Island.

In 1981, a federal court had stripped Karl Linnas of his citizenship after OSI found that he was once the commandant of a Nazi concentration camp in Soviet Estonia, where women and children had been bound by their hands, forced to kneel at the edge of a ditch, and shot by a firing squad. After Linnas appealed the ruling, Sher had asked Rudolph W. Giuliani, the US attorney in Manhattan, to argue the case on appeal before the US Court of Appeals for the Second Circuit.

Sher had read the court's damning assessment so often that he had committed key passages to memory: *"Karl Linnas' appeal to humanity, a humanity which he has grossly, callously and monstrously offended, truly offends this court's sense of decency."*

Linnas was ordered deported to his native Soviet Estonia, where a court in 1962 had tried him in absentia and found him a traitor and a murderer. But an alliance of Eastern European émigré groups had rallied to block the deportation, arguing that no one in the United States should be delivered into the hands of the Soviet government, a totalitarian regime responsible for the deaths of millions.

The groups secured a powerful ally with ties to the White House, Patrick Buchanan, who weeks earlier had reached out to the attorney general of the United States. Buchanan's intervention seemed outrageous to Sher, a significant breach of power by a man who had just stepped down as the director of communications for President Ronald Reagan. For years, Sher had scoffed when Buchanan criticized OSI, lambasting the unit for "running down 70-year-old camp guards."

"If not now, when?" former OSI director Allan Ryan had regularly shot back.

Ryan had gone on to become an attorney for Harvard University, passing the reins of the unit to Sher, a thirty-nine-year-old OSI prosecutor who had listened to an avalanche of confessions, denials, regrets, and excuses, elderly witnesses who bowed their heads and cried, "Those poor Jews," survivors who brought their children to interviews because they could only bear to tell their stories one time before they died.

Both Ryan and Sher had tried to keep the politics of Nazi hunting away from the unit's twenty-three lawyers and historians, fearing that constant threats about OSI's demise would distract from necessary investigations. Most of the threats had been little more than rhetoric, but in the Linnas case rhetoric had grown into something far more menacing, and its pull had reached the most powerful law enforcement agent in the country.

US Attorney General Edwin Meese was said to be seriously considering a last-minute agreement with Panama to provide refuge to Linnas.

Sher was angry and agitated. So much was at stake.

Sending Linnas to the beaches of Central America would show the world that White House politics could easily undercut measured judicial rulings, crippling the Office of Special Investigations at a time when the unit was investigating five hundred suspected Nazi perpetrators in the United States. Sher wanted to plead his case directly to the attorney general, to urge him not to dismantle a series of unequivocal court rulings and the steadfast work of one of his own units inside the Justice Department.

Instead, alone in his office, Sher made a quick decision. He tracked down the address for the residence of the Panamanian ambassador to the United States, slipped outside, and headed to Northwest Washington. It was dark when the taxi pulled up in front of the house.

"Your ambassador should read this," Sher said, thrusting a copy of the court ruling, with critical passages highlighted, at the aide who answered the door.

At the relentlessly discreet Justice Department, Sher knew that behind-the-scenes maneuvering was broadly discouraged. But he had never been one to back down from a fight. With slicked, black hair and a jawline that some of his colleagues decided could have come straight from a Hollywood movie, Sher was a fretting, cursing, no-nonsense champion of the Office of Special Investigations.

He had traveled to the Soviet Union in 1980 just after President Jimmy Carter announced that the United States would boycott the Olympic games in Moscow as punishment for the Soviet invasion of Afghanistan. Sher had interviewed witnesses for OSI's first trial, coolly ignoring the men dispatched by the Communist government to trail twenty yards behind everywhere he went.

Two years later, as Peter Black sunk into the case against Archbishop Valerian Trifa, Sher had asked to meet with officials at the West German embassy in Washington.

"We'd like you to accept him as a deportee," Sher pressed, hoping Germany would not only take back Trifa but put him on trial for war crimes.

"Why should we take back your garbage?" an embassy official asked.

Sher, more drill sergeant than diplomat, was quick with a reply. "We're just returning the garbage that you created."

Over time, Sher's supervisors at the Justice Department had learned to anticipate the combativeness, but until the Karl Linnas case, it had never been directed squarely at the attorney general of the United States.

Screw it, Sher thought as he headed home, hoping his clandestine visit to the ambassador's residence would convince Panama to turn Linnas away, no matter what the attorney general had to say about the matter.

AT THE OFFICE the next morning, two top advisors summoned Sher to a meeting. Meese had decided to send Linnas to Panama, and the attorney general wanted Sher to prepare a new deportation order for sign-off by an immigration judge.

Sher studied the advisors, wondering how he could possibly say no to what amounted to a direct order. Sher was fairly certain that William Weld, who would go on to become the governor of Massachusetts, and Stephen Trott, who would soon accept President Reagan's nomination for a seat on the US Court of Appeals for the Ninth Circuit, were on his side, wanting to see Linnas deported to his native Soviet Estonia. Not a single US court had objected. But the attorney general's decision trumped all, and in this case the decision was Panama.

Sher paused. He imagined Linnas living out his days on the resort island of Contadora in the Gulf of Panama, where the shah of Iran had found balmy refuge in 1979 when the Carter administration forced him to leave the United States. Slowly, Sher shook his head. In a level voice, he told Meese's deputies that he wouldn't revise the immigration order.

Weld and Trott went to see the attorney general. Sher asked if he could go with them and wasn't particularly surprised when he was turned down.

Sher considered his next move. He walked to the offices of the attorney general and, within earshot of Meese's secretary, picked up a phone and called Elizabeth Holtzman, the former congresswoman from New York who had pushed to create the Office of Special Investigations in the late 1970s. Sher needed support, a political powerhouse with strong ties to the Jewish community.

"Is Liz there?"

"Is it important?" Holtzman was now the district attorney in Brooklyn, and her secretary sounded rushed.

Sher whispered, "Could not be more important."

Moments later, Holtzman came on the line.

"It's Linnas," Sher said. "They want to send him to Panama."

"When?"

"This afternoon."

Sher hung up, knowing there was little more he could do. For the third time in twenty-four hours he had defied his supervisors at the Justice Department. He started drafting a letter of resignation. He thought about Karl Linnas, waiting in a detention center in lower Manhattan, and Pat Buchanan, who several years later would argue that the diesel engines that pumped carbon monoxide into the gas chambers of Treblinka were not capable of killing.

All Sher could do now was wait.

IT WAS THE dark little details that wouldn't fade away, that clawed back into the light and settled there, stubbornly, even after jokes or drinks or time away with family. The lawyers and historians of OSI had come to recognize the symptoms, the sudden silences among colleagues in the middle of a gruesome discussion about war, the urgent need for a taste of something mundane. For air.

For Peter Black, there was the enduring memory of a concentration camp survivor in Niagara Falls, Canada, who had paused for the briefest, loneliest moment when he realized that the face in one of the faded photographs that Black presented was familiar, a vicious German dog handler whom the survivor hadn't seen in forty years.

"This man shot a prisoner," he said, pointing to the photo, and then excused himself, stumbled into the kitchen, and drank a swig of schnapps.

For David Marwell, there was the young Jewish girl murdered by a high-ranking member of a Ukrainian militia group established by the Germans after they invaded eastern Poland in 1941.

An eyewitness was asked about the girl's murder. Did the man shoot at close range?

The witness replied, "He was holding her hand."

For Eli Rosenbaum, there were late-night images of powerless parents forced with their children to the edge of a killing pit. "You try to imagine these things," Rosenbaum often told friends and colleagues, "and then you try real hard not to imagine them. Or else you're too paralyzed to do the work."

When Elizabeth Holtzman called after her conversation with Neal Sher, furious about the plan to send Karl Linnas to Panama, Rosenbaum quickly stepped in. They had only hours, or less, to try to stop the deportation.

As the general counsel for the World Jewish Congress, Rosenbaum made a formidable partner. He had become a trial lawyer at OSI only months out of Harvard Law School, just as Baltic and Ukrainian émigré groups were mobilizing against the unit. In native-language newspapers, the groups called on Congress to impose a statute of limitations on war-crime prosecutions and accused OSI leaders of collaborating with the KGB.

"We are getting evidence wherever it can be found," Allan Ryan said early on as he stood before the Ukrainian American Bar Association during its annual convention in New Jersey.

FBI analysts would forensically examine fingerprints on Nazi records sent by the Soviets. Document examiners would study handwriting samples and confirm that the paper was used during the war. Chemists would use hypodermic needles to withdraw and analyze the age of the ink. Still, Ryan received death threats, a handful of anonymous letters with a map to his house in northern Virginia that he had turned over to the FBI.

Frustrated by the pushback and drained by a succession of wrenching interviews with survivors, Rosenbaum left OSI for a New York City law firm and, later, the World Jewish Congress. From his new offices in New York, he had often wondered why Pat Buchanan and others had taken such a contemptuous, public stance against OSI.

Rosenbaum could at least in part understand the resistance from émigré groups. Many OSI defendants came from the Baltic States and Ukraine, and some of the evidence against them had been sent by the Soviets, who after the war had imposed hard-line Commu-nism throughout much of Eastern Europe. But Buchanan, who had once chastised the Justice Department for "wallowing in the atroci-ties of a dead regime," was another matter entirely. His words made Rosenbaum cringe.

ELI ROSENBAUM'S MOTHER had been born in Berlin and his father in Dresden. They had both fled Germany as teenagers in the 1930s when anti-Jewish hysteria mounted across the region.

His father returned five years later to fight with the US Army's Third Infantry Division but was transferred to a psychological-warfare unit in the Seventh Army when his supervisors discovered that he spoke fluent German. He questioned high-value prisoners and monitored German radio broadcasts, including some transmit-ted from Dresden on the night Allied warplanes leveled the city of his birth.

In New York after the war, he had regaled his young son with light stories about the army—how his comrades once convinced him to drink too much and climb into a boxing ring even though he wasn't a fighter, how he had changed his name from Rosenbaum to Rowe in case he was captured by the Germans.

But talk about the fate of the Jews was decidedly off-limits, even in a dining room with an oil-burning menorah that the family had managed to take out of Germany. In a split-level house humming with the lyrical voice of WQXR-FM classical-radio host Duncan Pirnie—"Tonight, we wake up to *Sleeping Beauty*, by Tchaikovsky"—Irving and Hanni Rosenbaum monitored the radio for news from Israel, where Hanni's family lived during the war.

Rosenbaum desperately wanted to understand his father's si-lences. But his boyhood marched on, a blur of five-cent baseball-card packs with bubble gum that cracked when Rosenbaum chewed it, of fingers smudged by the fresh ink of the Friday afternoon paper, with Gimbels department store ads and comics that appeared in glorious full color.

One winter day in 1970, Rosenbaum and his father were inching up a snow-covered highway in the family's Cadillac, heading north to a ski outing. Irving Rosenbaum had lapsed into one of his silences.

Finally, he spoke. "You know I was sent to Dachau the day after its liberation?"

The question came suddenly, and Rosenbaum was quick with a reply. "What did you see?"

He waited for an answer, but there was only more silence. He looked at his father, whose eyes were wet. His mouth was open as if he was about to explain, but the question hung in the air. Rosenbaum would never get his father to talk about Dachau, with thirty railroad cars filled with corpses.

At OSI, Rosenbaum had been a measured, meticulous prosecutor, brown hair parted down the side, mustache neatly clipped. He had spent hours strategizing with Neal Sher, who began to call the younger lawyer "Roosevelt" after a telephone operator once botched his last name.

Rosenbaum had launched and led the development of OSI's case against NASA scientist Arthur L. H. Rudolph, who was accused of overseeing slave laborers at a factory that produced rockets for the German war machine. Rudolph, one of more than a hundred German rocket engineers who were secretly brought to the United States after the war, had agreed in 1984 to give up his citizenship and move back to Germany.

That year, Rosenbaum left the Justice Department and found himself free to publicly denounce OSI's detractors. He had maintained a high profile, directing the World Jewish Congress investigation that in 1986 helped unearth the Nazi past of United Nations secretary general Kurt Waldheim.

Rosenbaum had already heard about the plan to deport Karl Linnas to Panama when Elizabeth Holtzman called in April 1987. It occurred to Rosenbaum that the decision had been made on the first day of the Jewish holiday of Passover, when Jewish organizations that would surely oppose the plan were closed.

"The Passover plot," Holtzman said wryly.

Before dawn the next morning, Holtzman and Rosenbaum caught a flight to Washington and took a cab to the Panamanian embassy. Rosenbaum hoped they weren't too late. Reporters were set up outside the building when they got there, alerted by the Jewish groups that Rosenbaum and Holtzman had scrambled to call the night before.

Rosenbaum reached for his leather briefcase, tightened the belt of his camel-colored overcoat, and climbed the stone steps to the embassy's front door. A flustered aide showed them inside, where senior embassy officials were waiting. There was no need for discussion. Panama was withdrawing its offer to provide refuge to Linnas. The aide shook his head, glancing outside.

"Embarrassing," he muttered, adding that the embassy hadn't seen so much media attention since the negotiations over the Panama Canal in the 1970s.

Rosenbaum thanked the aide and left. He went to find a pay phone. "Chief," Rosenbaum sighed when Sher came on the line.

Linnas would not be leaving for Panama.

ROSENBAUM WANTED TO catch the first flight home to New York, to banish all thoughts of Linnas and his killing pits. But in a matter of hours, Pat Buchanan planned to appear live on national television, and Neal Sher needed Rosenbaum to defend the unit.

The *New York Times*, the *Washington Post*, and the major television networks had extensively covered the Linnas case, and two months earlier Rosenbaum had appeared on CNN's nightly live debate show, *Crossfire*, to square off with a member of an Estonian émigré group lobbying to keep Linnas out of the Soviet Union.

Sher wanted Rosenbaum to appear again, opposite Buchanan. Rosenbaum tried to say no, but officials at the Department of Justice had declined CNN's invitation. Rosenbaum took a cab to the CNN studios in Washington and sat down on the set, pressing his palms to his pant legs to straighten the wrinkles from the suit he had put on before dawn that morning.

Rosenbaum shifted in his seat, squeezed between Buchanan and conservative commentator Robert Novak, who would make a last-minute pitch to keep Linnas out of the Soviet Union. *Why did I let Neal talk me into this?* Rosenbaum thought as he waited. He was about to be doubled-teamed by two of Washington's most experienced debaters.

The cameras started rolling. "Mr. Rosenbaum, Mr. Rosenbaum," Novak said when the show began. "How would you feel if you had a client, or if you yourself were stuck in a position where you were placed by the instrumentalities of the US government on the tender mercies of the Soviet Union? Do you trust Soviet justice? Isn't it an oxymoron—Soviet justice?"

"It's not a matter of trusting Soviet justice," Rosenbaum quickly replied. "Karl Linnas has been tried.... The important thing to remember about Karl Linnas is that...he admitted...that he had been at the Tartu Nazi concentration camp, that he served in a supervisory capacity, that he had the guard detail...under his command. What would you have the viewers think that Mr. Linnas was doing...while people were dying?"

"To be a guard at that camp," Buchanan interrupted, "is not an offense for which you should be hanged, which is what would happen to him in the Soviet Union. What is your objection to sending him to Panama? He loses his citizenship. He's out of the country."

"In Panama, he will spend the rest of his days living very comfortably under palm trees," Rosenbaum shot back.

"And the Soviet Union will hang him."

"Mr. Linnas was found by an American court to be responsible for these crimes."

"Being a supervisor in a concentration camp is not a hanging offense," Buchanan countered.

Later, Rosenbaum would think about the parents and children torn apart at the gates of Nazi-run camps.

"What I want to know," Buchanan said, "is why the World Jewish Congress is collaborating with an antisemitic regime like the Soviet Union."

"If we are collaborating with anyone, it is with the US judicial system, which you obviously don't trust. It's with the United States Department of Justice."

"Look," Buchanan said. "...Do you want this guy hanged without a trial?"

"We want him sent to—"

"To the Soviet Union," Buchanan said flatly.

"Any country that will do something other than to allow him to live in peace for the rest of [his] life. He committed a capital offense."

Rosenbaum went on. "This man has been before at least ten courts in seven years in the United States. He's had more due process than any person in American history, at least that I can think of. The court found specifically that he had committed acts of mass murder, time and again."

"You can sleep well at night," Novak asked, "knowing you are sending a man into a Soviet execution chamber?"

"The only thing that keeps me up at night is reading the district court's account of what Karl Linnas did, the atrocities that he perpetuated."

Buchanan interrupted. "Because you hate him so much you would send him to Moscow...to be executed? Okay. I think you ought to examine your conscience."

Rosenbaum left the studio certain that no other unit in the history of the Department of Justice would face a more sustained, intensive, and public attack than the Office of Special Investigations.

LATER THAT NIGHT, Neal Sher called the immigration office at John F. Kennedy International Airport. Though Linnas was preparing an emergency appeal to the US Supreme Court, Sher wanted to be ready with travel plans. Unless the court stepped in or another country agreed to provide refuge, Linnas would be deported to the Soviet Union as planned.

Sher needed to identify an airline that flew directly to an Eastern Bloc country so that Linnas would have no chance of claiming political asylum when he stepped off the plane. Sher found a direct flight to Czechoslovakia. The next morning Sher called the Czech embassy in Washington to alert local officials.

Four days passed. Finally, Sher's phone rang. The Supreme Court had declined to hear the final appeal, clearing the way for deportation.

Sher raced to call immigration officials at the airport. "It's a go."

Less than an hour later, Linnas, in a gray suit and brown cap, with a thick white beard that stretched from ear to ear, was taken to the plane. Linnas struggled at the door of the aircraft, yelling, "Murder! Kidnapping!" before federal agents pushed him inside.

Sher stayed in his office late, until the plane was well over the Atlantic Ocean. After thirty-six years in the United States, Linnas was finally going home to answer for his crimes.

CHAPTER EIGHT

GOD'S GRACE

Washington, D.C.
1988

Michael Bernstein weighed 155 pounds on a full belly, but at thirty-six he was a storied prosecutor at the Office of Special Investigations who spent long afternoons in the records room, a lone figure hunched under the fuzzy glow of fluorescent lights, files from cold cases spread across the table.

No one was much surprised to find him there, searching for clues that may have been missed and then wandering back to his office, where he had taped an adage from a fortune cookie to the door: *The law sometimes sleeps but it never dies.*

After particularly grueling days interviewing indignant old men who had once been armed and eager to kill, Bernstein would tell his wife, "This is not what I imagined doing as an attorney."

But his work consumed him, and Stephanie Bernstein learned to forgive the heap of yesterday's clothes on the side of the bed or the day she had to catch a taxi to her job as a clinical social worker because the Chrysler sedan that she shared with her husband was still sitting in the OSI parking lot. Bernstein forgot he had it and rode the bus home.

"I'm sure one day I'll find this amusing, Mickey," she said, eyeing her contrite husband, whose brown hair was slicked back and parted down the side. "But right now, I am pissed off."

Bernstein would have been a history professor if law school hadn't seemed more practical, and at OSI he spent hours with the historians, who were almost always mired in some dark mystery, fitting together clues—a roster from West Berlin, an identity card from Warsaw, a confession sent from Moscow—with a kind of deliberate order often missing from the frenetic pace of prosecutorial law. OSI had long relied on tips from outside sources, but now the historians were copying massive batches of archival records and cross-checking them against records of immigrants who had come to the United States after the war.

Bernstein and Peter Black had worked on investigations of former guards from the Mauthausen concentration camp, built on the bank of the Danube River near a stone quarry outside Linz, Austria. The only massive concentration camp on Austrian territory, it had been a horrid place where starving prisoners were forced to heave granite blocks up uneven steps to the top of the quarry.

Other lawyers thrived inside the courtroom, but bluster made Bernstein cringe. Methodical and excessively patient, he had convinced every OSI defendant on his roster to voluntarily relinquish US citizenship, avoiding the hassle and expense of trials.

At the chilly start of December 1988, Bernstein agreed to fly to Vienna on behalf of OSI. He would be home in time to celebrate Chanukah with his seven-year-old daughter and four-year-old son.

IN AUSTRIA, BERNSTEIN would see about a matter that had been thwarting the mission of the Office of Special Investigations for years. In Bonn in 1954, the Foreign Office of West Germany had signed a critical commitment, neatly typed and bearing the coat of arms for the Federal Republic of Germany, a black eagle, wings extended wide against a golden field.

*The Foreign Office has the honor to inform the Office
of the United States High Commissioner for Germany . . .*

The country had agreed to take back Nazi perpetrators discovered in the United States after the war. American diplomats also secured a nearly identical guarantee from neighboring Austria, which promised that Nazi criminals would be readmitted "upon demand of the American authorities."

US officials had tucked copies of the guarantees inside the immigration files of thousands of European refugees who entered the country in the mid-1950s, and no one thought much about it—a rather technical agreement between friendly nations—until the Office of Special Investigations discovered dozens of Nazi collaborators guarding ugly secrets in America's cities and suburbs.

In the early 1980s, juggling a growing roster of OSI defendants, Eli Rosenbaum and Neal Sher had pressed the matter at the German embassy in Washington. Without countries willing to readmit Nazi perpetrators, OSI could not enforce deportation orders.

"We can't find a copy of that guaranty in our files," the German Consul General told Sher and Rosenbaum, frowning at the two men. Rosenbaum, fresh out of law school, watched his boss cringe.

"It's in US government immigration files," Sher had replied sternly. *Thousands of them.*

More than two hundred thousand refugees were admitted into the United States under the Refugee Relief Act of 1953, a sweeping immigration law passed by Congress to assist displaced eastern Europeans in the years after the war. Sher produced a copy of the agreement, but the German Consul General was indignant.

"My government questions its authenticity."

The text, she pointed out, didn't contain the umlaut, a character that appears over several vowels in the German alphabet. Rosenbaum frowned. "You can't seriously suggest that this isn't authentic."

She shrugged, and Rosenbaum knew that the conversation was over. He thought of the concentration camp guards and police commanders who had committed crimes in the name of the German state and then escaped justice by fleeing to the shores of America, home to tens of thousands of Jewish survivors and the veterans who had crossed an ocean to free them. How many Nazi collaborators would get to grow old in comfort while OSI pleaded with Germany to take them back? Unlike the US government, Germany possessed the legal authority to criminally prosecute Nazi perpetrators.

The Austrians had resisted, too, arguing that the readmission guarantee was nearly three decades old and no longer valid. In truth, the agreements applied only to refugees who came to the United States in the mid-1950s. Hundreds of thousands had emigrated earlier in the tumultuous postwar years when Communism was advancing across Eastern Europe.

Rosenbaum and Sher believed that Germany and Austria bore an ethical obligation to take back the criminals that the Third Reich had created, empowered, and armed, no matter when they had slipped out of Europe and crossed the Atlantic.

Turned down by the West Germans and Austrians, OSI started encouraging Nazi defendants to leave voluntarily for West Germany, where they could step off the plane, renounce their American citizenship, and potentially continue to receive Social Security benefits. Rosenbaum also proposed sending defendants to the US occupation sector of West Berlin.

But the plan raised concerns inside the Justice Department, and the US State Department balked at the idea of agitating the Germans, a bulwark in NATO and an ally against Communism.

"Serious adverse foreign policy consequences," European-affairs chief Richard Burt wrote in a 1984 memo to the State Department's deputy secretary.

It had been clear to Sher and Rosenbaum then that no help was coming. From its obscure outpost at the Department of Justice, under the critical eye of pundits and émigré groups, and with resistance from the diplomats who represented the United States in foreign affairs, OSI would have to find a way to remove Nazi defendants on its own.

Later, Rosenbaum would imagine himself standing on the rooftop of the Justice Department, shouting into a megaphone, "My fellow Americans, you will not believe this, but Germany WILL NOT TAKE THEIR NAZIS BACK."

The lack of cooperation from Germany and Austria was a significant threat, the most critical in the short history of OSI, and when the Austrian government appeared to be reconsidering its position in the final months of 1988, Rosenbaum and the staff of OSI could scarcely believe the turn of events. After years of pushback, the Austrians were willing to come to the table to talk about readmitting Nazi criminals. It was an olive branch, Rosenbaum thought, a potential step toward real cooperation.

Michael Bernstein and an official from the US State Department had attended a first round of talks in Washington, but the meeting ended without an agreement. The Austrians insisted on a meeting in Vienna.

Sher was traveling in Budapest. Rosenbaum, who had decided to return to OSI to become Sher's deputy director, was busy overseeing the office. Both men had disqualified themselves from the Vienna assignment since they had worked on the high-profile Nazi war-crimes investigation that, one year earlier, barred Kurt Waldheim from entering the United States. The former United Nations secretary was now the president of Austria.

Bernstein would go. He was one of the best negotiators in the office. It promised to be a plum assignment, the chance to bring home a badly needed diplomatic win for the beleaguered unit.

Finally, OSI might catch a break.

EVEN IN THE bustling offices of the Justice Department, the sound of a breaking-news bulletin, rushed and urgent, was unmistakable. Pan

Am flight 103, just thirty-eight minutes into its route from London to New York, had lost contact with air traffic controllers in the skies over Lockerbie, Scotland, and gone down in a ball of flames. There were 259 people on board. All were believed to be dead.

Eli Rosenbaum sucked in his breath. After four days in Vienna, Michael Bernstein was on his way home, a copy of the freshly signed deportation agreement tucked inside his briefcase. The Austrian government had agreed to take back its Nazi criminals, an extraordinary victory for OSI.

Rosenbaum didn't have Bernstein's flight information, so he went to look for attorney Bruce Einhorn.

"Don't panic," Einhorn said. The details of Bernstein's travel plans were unclear.

Rosenbaum drove home, kissed his infant daughter, and settled into the family's two-story townhouse near Dupont Circle, in a historic district in Northwest Washington. His phone rang later that night.

Bernstein's original flight had been canceled, and no one was entirely sure which plane he had rebooked on since multiple flights a day flew between London and New York or Washington. Stephanie Bernstein was calling the airlines, but she couldn't get a firm answer.

Frantic, Rosenbaum started making calls. In the early-morning hours, the phone rang again. It was official: Bernstein had been on the doomed flight.

Rosenbaum couldn't reach Neal Sher, who was still abroad. Instead, he called the Justice Department Command Center and asked to be patched through to Deputy Assistant Attorney General Mark Richard. Richard asked a question that Rosenbaum would remember years later.

"Tell me that Mike had a signed travel authorization."

"He did," Rosenbaum answered, knowing that with the authorization, the family would receive employee death benefits.

Rosenbaum steadied himself for the day ahead.

THERE BUT FOR the grace of God go I.

The words looped round and round in Rosenbaum's head as he parked his car near Michael Bernstein's house later that morning and made his way inside. He thought about his own family, the daughter who had been born only two months earlier, and wondered what he might say to Bernstein's children, Sara and Joe.

Rosenbaum went to look for Stephanie Bernstein. She had been using her exercise bike in the basement the night before when news of the crash flashed on television. She raced to make calls and knew that her husband was dead when she was finally transferred to a phone line for relatives of passengers on the Pan Am flight.

She peeked in on her children and decided to let them sleep through the night, a few more hours without knowing, steady breaths under warm blankets, in tiny bedrooms with views of the wildflowers that bloomed every spring in the family's backyard. She wandered to her own bedroom, past the haphazard pile of issues of the *New York Review of Books* that her husband stacked on the floor by the side of the bed for some time later when there would surely be time for reading. She started making phone calls.

Looking at Stephanie, a widow at thirty-seven, Rosenbaum felt sick. The Pan Am Boeing 747 jetliner, once dubbed the Clipper Morning Light, had left a wreckage that spread across one nautical mile.

He imagined Bernstein in seat 47D, heading home to his family, the signed agreement with the Austrian government in the overhead bin. Later, the world would learn that a terrorist bomb had punched a twenty-inch hole on the left side of the plane's fuselage.

Rosenbaum hugged Stephanie and wandered upstairs, where four-year-old Joe was playing in his bedroom, oblivious to the somber gathering.

Rosenbaum would help send FBI agents to Scotland to try to persuade authorities to release Bernstein's remains so that he could be buried quickly, according to Jewish custom. He would call the *New York Times* to request an obituary and ask famed Nazi hunter Simon Wiesenthal to write a letter of condolence to the Bernstein family. He would deliver remarks at the memorial service on behalf of the Department of Justice and recite the Mourner's Kaddish alongside hundreds of people.

Yitgadal v'yitkadash sh'mei raba.

He would tell journalists that Bernstein was responsible for deporting seven of the twenty-four Nazi defendants that had been removed from the United States since OSI had been in operation. He would help write the Justice Department announcement, three months later, declaring that a California man who was once an armed SS guard at Auschwitz had been deported to his native Austria, thanks to the agreement that Bernstein helped negotiate.

He would keep a picture of Bernstein in his office for as long as he stayed at OSI, a daily reminder of the man who had died in the line of duty more than forty years after the war's end.

But sitting beside young Joe Bernstein, who would grow up with only a dim memory of being scooped up like a football and settled into his father's lap, Rosenbaum could do absolutely nothing at all.

NEAL SHER PUBLICLY blamed the Austrian government for Michael Bernstein's death, pointing out that the young lawyer would not have flown to Vienna if the Austrians had honored the deportation agreement in the first place. Sher suspected that the meeting had been called to create an artificial crisis, retribution for OSI's effort to bar Austrian president Waldheim from entering the United States.

Peter Black considered the loss of his friend and colleague more a matter of extraordinary bad fortune than international politics, a sequence of ill-fated events that had placed a good man on a plane with a bomb wrapped in baby clothes and tucked inside a suitcase.

CHAPTER NINE

SECRETS AND LIES

Washington, D.C.
1988–1989

In the mid-1980s, two members of the Estonian émigré community secretly arranged to collect the trash from a dumpster used by the Office of Special Investigations in downtown Washington. For two years, they took heaping bags of garbage to a local garage and dumped the contents onto the floor for sorting. Amid the crushed cigarette butts and scraps of yesterday's lunches, they found documents and notes that OSI had thrown away, which they surreptitiously packaged and mailed to accused Nazi collaborators.

Two envelopes were sent to the family of defendant John Demjanjuk in Cleveland. After living in the United States for thirty-two years, Demjanjuk had been stripped of his US citizenship and extradited to Israel to stand trial as Ivan the Terrible, the notoriously violent gas-chamber operator at the Treblinka killing center.

Inside the packages, which were sent anonymously, the Demjanjuk family found material that appeared to undermine OSI's case, including leads to another Ukrainian man who had been identified by former Treblinka guards as the reviled Ivan.

At first, Demjanjuk's family thought that someone inside OSI was leaking information. But Edward Nishnic, Demjanjuk's son-in-law, told a journalist at the *New York Times* that he was later invited to

Washington, where he found a woman picking through garbage in a stinking garage filled with plastic bags. Nishnic had pulled on rubber gloves and coveralls to help.

Demjanjuk's family accused the government of withholding critical evidence in the case, and a federal judge ordered OSI, under the Freedom of Information Act, to provide a listing of documents related to the Demjanjuk case.

In the wrenching days after Michael Bernstein's death in December 1988, OSI was still consumed by the judge's demand, and teetering piles of legal folders, years old and pulled from the depths of a storage room, were rising around the office.

Peter Black found the whole matter deeply troubling. Though the attorneys who had first prosecuted Demjanjuk in Cleveland in 1981 had long since left OSI, the revelations would surely provide fodder for those who wanted to see the unit closed for good. There was also the disturbing matter of the legal case itself.

Black had expected the District Court in Jerusalem to sort out the discrepancies in the case, but only seven months earlier, the Israeli court had found Demjanjuk guilty for his service at Treblinka and sentenced him to death by hanging. Black opposed the death penalty on principle and worried about a serious miscarriage of justice, regardless of how guilty Demjanjuk might have been for crimes committed elsewhere in occupied Poland.

On a late December afternoon, Black sat alone at his desk. It was a dreary month in Washington, with frigid winds and nights that fell long before dinner. A few blocks away, the green and gold lights from the national Christmas tree twinkled along Pennsylvania Avenue as Washington celebrated the winter holidays. But grief had settled over OSI, along with the very real possibility that the unit would struggle with the Demjanjuk case for months or even years.

Black was lost in thought when OSI attorney Bruce Einhorn knocked on the door, clutching a slip of paper.

"Take a look at this," he said to Black. "Something came in."

Black studied the single page from top to bottom, once and then twice, a surgeon's precision. While searching for documents to turn over to the Demjanjuk defense team, Einhorn had found cable traffic between the US Department of State and the Soviet Foreign Ministry.

Back in 1980, someone at OSI had asked the Soviets for records relating to New York businessman Jakob Reimer, whose name had turned up during the Demjanjuk investigation, placing both men at the Trawniki training camp. Two OSI lawyers went to question Reimer about it, but the matter was quickly closed after Reimer insisted that he had never known Demjanjuk and had only served in Trawniki's administrative offices.

Now Black was intrigued. The cable traffic indicated that the Soviets had complied and sent documents on Reimer in 1981, a year after his interview with OSI. Since the case had been closed by then, Black wondered, had anyone bothered to read the records?

"What did the file say?" Einhorn asked.

Black held up his hands. "What the hell did we *do* with the file?"

There was no easy way to look for it since OSI had no computers. Black and Einhorn started with the investigative file that OSI had put together on Reimer years earlier. They dug through boxes and cabinets. Nothing.

Black decided to ask the Soviets to resend the file, which meant following standard, tedious channels: a request from the State Department to the US Embassy in Moscow and then on to Soviet agencies and archives.

Black had no idea how long it might take, if the file was even sent at all. But Trawniki had come up too many times, a pattern too suspicious to ignore. Fedorenko, Kairys, Demjanjuk, Zajanckauskas, Reimer—five men on US soil.

In the village near Lublin, whose Jewish population had been nearly wiped out during the war, the SS had set up a training camp for police auxiliaries. Scholarly references had made clear that the men were Ukrainian and Polish civilian recruits and captured Red Army soldiers pulled from German prisoner-of-war camps.

But so much about Trawniki was not yet understood: the mission, the strategy, the training process, the scope of its role in Operation Reinhard, the secret plan to exploit and murder the Jews of occupied Poland.

Did some men staff the killing centers while others stayed behind? Were some men exclusively cooks, paymasters, or waiters, and others guards or killers? Black wasn't certain. What was clear was that five men who had spent months or years at Trawniki had spent decades trying to hide it from US authorities.

Black had read an infamous 1944 report about the murder of Poland's Jews that Odilo Globocnik, the SS and police leader in Lublin District, had submitted to Heinrich Himmler. The content was horrifying, but the words were as a sterile as a bank ledger's.

"The evacuation of Jews," Globocnik reported, "has been carried out and completed. The requirement here was to seize the people by means of a methodically correct procedure, with the weak forces available, reducing to a minimum economic damage to war production. In general, the operation was successful."

The report included an accounting of the assets collected from the dead, worth 180 billion reichsmark. Grand larceny on a massive scale, Black thought as he studied the numbers:

236 gold bars
Nearly 400,000 gold coins
2,134 silver bars
More than 60,000 watches
1,900 freight-car loads of textiles
Nearly 16,000 gold and diamond rings

1,716 pairs of gold earrings studded with diamonds

3,240 coin purses

627 pairs of sunglasses

350 electric razors

41 silver cigarette cases

Paper foreign currency from the United States, Canada, France, Brazil, Turkey, Switzerland, South Africa, Egypt, Argentina, Paraguay, Sweden, Palestine, Cuba, and Albania

The mass murder of 1.7 million Jews and an untold number of Roma, Soviet prisoners of war, and Polish civilians, along with the sorting and cataloguing of their assets, would have required a highly organized operation and the participation of thousands of personnel.

In early January 1989, Black wrote up a buck slip, a yellow five-by-eight-inch slip of paper with notes, and attached the Soviet cable that Bruce Einhorn had found. Black sent it to Eli Rosenbaum, requesting to reopen the investigation against the mysterious Jakob Reimer.

IT HAD BEEN 500 deutschmark cheaper to fly out of the airport in East Berlin in 1971 when twenty-year-old Peter Black and two friends studying at the university in Bonn decided to travel to the Middle East on a winter break. As night fell, they caught a train to West Berlin and then a transit bus to the Berlin Schönefeld Airport. The bus rumbled to a stop at the border, and a guard who looked no older than Black climbed inside.

"*Ihr Pass ist nicht gültig*," the guard said, studying Black. Your passport is not valid.

Black's three-year-old passport had expired the previous summer, but a State Department official in Wisconsin had assured him that a new US law extended the life of his passport by two years and that all foreign governments were aware of the change. Black pulled out a printed copy of the law.

"We are aware of this regulation," the guard said politely, "but as your government didn't bother to officially inform us of the change, we see no obligation to recognize it."

"What can I do?" Black asked in German.

"You should probably get off the bus and go back to West Berlin."

"But I have a plane to catch."

"Well, I can let you in, but I can't guarantee what will happen."

If Black had been an older man, he probably would have turned back. But fear at twenty was fleeting, outweighed by grand travel plans that included a visit to Turkey, Israel, and Ethiopia. He decided to take his chances.

At the airport, Black dutifully reported to the border police. He watched as an officer studied the passport and grew red in the face.

"You have entered the German Democratic Republic illegally," the officer declared. "The penalty for that is five years in prison."

Taking Black by the scruff of his collar, the officer frog-marched him to another office and shouted at a police officer wearing the greenish-gray uniform of the People's Police. The second officer reminded Black of a cross between Reinhard Heydrich and a blond-haired bully that Black remembered from middle school.

The officer took his time studying Black and then the passport, in no hurry to deal with the young, fretting American.

"Why did you enter the German Democratic Republic?" he finally asked.

Black tried to explain. Five hundred deutschmark. A trip to the Middle East.

"The fact remains that you entered the German Democratic Republic illegally. We can arrest you now and turn you over to the prosecutor for indictment." The officer paused. "But I don't think you would want this."

The officer offered another option, deportation back to West

Berlin. As Black jumped up to agree, the officer interrupted. "But you have a plane to catch."

Black, who had been contemplating life inside a Communist prison, suddenly found himself with a temporary transit visa and permission to board the flight with his friends.

Sitting stiffly in a US military car as it inched toward a checkpoint that crossed into East Germany in October 1989, nineteen years after his first visit, Black eyed the grim-faced border guards pacing before a thick gate. They moved with deliberate precision, and Black felt a flash of unease, as if something unexpected might happen at any moment, a diplomatic snafu that would send him back to West Germany.

This time, however, Black was with OSI attorney Bruce Einhorn on official business, representing the government of the United States. The car passed into East Berlin without incident.

On the fortieth anniversary of the founding of the German Democratic Republic, Black and Einhorn could see the stirrings of revolution everywhere, in a generation of denim-clad young people who favored Bruce Springsteen and David Bowie, in the thousands of demonstrators who had lined the city's grandest boulevard to greet Mikhail Gorbachev, the secretary general of the Soviet Communist Party. "Gorbi, help us!" they shouted again and again.

Soon, the Berlin Wall would fall at the feet of jubilant crowds, and the head of the East German Communist Party would announce that citizens could cross freely into the West. The movement apparently had not been lost on the East German Ministry of Culture, which, for the first time since the end of the war, had extended an invitation to discuss broad access to its archives.

Already, historians from Canada and Australia, in newly opened Nazi-hunting units largely modeled after OSI, had made a first pass through some of the collections. "You guys have to get over here," one Canadian historian told Black.

OSI historians had for years dug through the archives in the West and in Poland. Cases were growing cold, suspects and witnesses dying. Now, finally, East Germany seemed willing to cooperate, offering access to one of the world's largest collections of documents on the Nazi regime.

For the better part of a week, Black and Einhorn traveled from archive to archive, taking careful note of collections and files that OSI historians would soon return to study, stashed away for decades by the Communist government.

THE BRIEF TRIP to East Germany had produced hundreds of research opportunities, and as Black scrambled to coordinate the unit's next steps, he received word that the Soviets were also relenting. One month after his visit to East Berlin, on the last day of November 1989, Black joined Eli Rosenbaum in Moscow.

It was nineteen degrees below zero when Black checked into the Intourist Hotel at the center of the city, a towering, box-shaped building designed in classic Stalinist style, stark, drab, and likely bugged. The hotel was stifling, heated by an overzealous furnace, and though the journey had been exhausting, Black and Rosenbaum ducked outside to cool off and explore nearby Red Square.

The frigid air reminded Black of the coldest Wisconsin winters. Droplets of icy water froze on the lens of his camera, and he couldn't advance the film. Black imagined what German soldiers, clad in summer uniforms, must have endured as they reached the suburbs of Moscow in the first freezing days of December 1941.

Peering across the square, he marveled at the remarkable turn of events that would soon place him before top officials at the archives in Moscow, negotiating for access to war records. The revolution that had gripped Poland had spread to the Soviet Union, where an elected Congress of People's Deputies had been set up. CNN for the first time was transmitting its programs to Moscow, and in the

Soviet legislature reformers openly criticized the Communist government.

How quickly things changed. Black had searched the archives of Poland, the most amenable Communist state, on three research trips. David Marwell had gone to Poland twice before he left OSI in 1988 to become the head of the Berlin Document Center, which housed troves of Nazi records.

Both historians had found tidbits of information spread across various records and rosters indicating the involvement of thousands of German and non-German participants in the Nazi killing machine. But, too often, the evidence needed to win a case had been just out of reach, kept in the Soviet archives.

Now, Rosenbaum and Black had a meeting set up with the Soviet Federal Archival Administration. For the first time since the war's end, the Soviets seemed willing to open their archives for a wholesale, general inspection. Access to the archives in Moscow, Black knew, would likely also lead to access to the archives in the Baltic States, Belarus, and Ukraine, where more than two million Jews had perished during the war.

Black could scarcely imagine what he might find, how lost Nazi records might deepen and reshape his understanding of the Holocaust. Though émigré groups continued to call for OSI's closing, the collapse of Communism had given OSI—one of the few agencies in the world still actively investigating Nazi offenders—more options and resources to do its work.

A lease on life, Black would say later.

SHORTLY AFTER BLACK returned from Moscow, Jakob Reimer's personnel file arrived from an archive in southern Ukraine, with a round seal and a Soviet stamp. A photo of a young Reimer, with cropped black hair, an oval face, and a smile that could have passed for a scowl, was attached to the three-page file. Black scanned the heading: *Personalbogen Nr. 865.*

He paused. From Reimer's immigration paperwork, Black knew that Reimer had been born in 1918 in a Mennonite settlement in the Ukrainian countryside, north of the Black Sea, where thousands of ethnic Germans known as *Volksdeutsche* had settled in the eighteenth and nineteenth centuries. Reimer had been drafted into the Red Army at the start of the war and received a commission as a second lieutenant before his platoon was captured by German soldiers in July 1941 near Minsk, Belarus, not far from the interwar eastern Polish border.

Three million Soviet soldiers died in German POW camps. But the Germans considered *Volksdeutsche* valuable racial stock and Baltic nationals and Ukrainians, perceived to hold strong anti-Soviet sentiments, reliable recruits for managing land that the Germans planned to conquer. In the late summer of 1941, the SS selected Reimer from among the camp's captured Soviet soldiers and sent him to Trawniki.

The personnel sheet sent by the Soviets was dated September 3, 1941. Black noted that Reimer had been stationed at Trawniki for at least three years and had been promoted to the level of a noncommissioned officer, part of the Trawniki elite, likely because of his German-language skills. Only one other Trawniki man found on US soil had attained such an exalted position.

Black had seen the details before. Near the end of the war, Reimer had applied for citizenship in Nazi Germany and had mentioned his service at Trawniki on the application. OSI had received a copy from the Berlin Document Center.

Black moved on, reviewing the back of the personnel sheet sent by the Soviets. It contained a service oath that Reimer had pledged to the SS and police.

I herewith declare that I am obligating myself for service in the guard detachments of the Commissioner of the Reichsführer-SS and Chief of the German Police for the Establishment of SS and Police Bases in the Newly Occupied Eastern Territory.

The oath did not surprise Black either. Trawniki man Liudas Kairys, already investigated by OSI, had signed the same pledge.

Black scanned the dates and deployments listed in the file. Two entries immediately caught his eye.

Reimer, the self-styled "paymaster" at Trawniki, had been deployed on at least two critical missions. In September 1942, according to the file, Reimer was assigned to Detachment Czestochowa. Black paused, remembering. That month, SS and police units in the Polish city deported forty thousand Jews to their deaths in the Treblinka gas chambers.

Reimer had returned to Trawniki, but on April 19, 1943, he left again, this time deployed to Warsaw. On that day, desperate Jewish residents rose in armed resistance against German forces brought in to liquidate the ghetto.

If Reimer had played an innocuous role during his service at Trawniki, Black saw no sign of it.

He pulled out Reimer's immigration file, compiled by US authorities before Reimer settled in New York City in 1952. Black scanned the visa application, searching for a mention of Trawniki.

But Reimer had said nothing about the camp. Instead, he had told US officials that he had been drafted into the Soviet armed forces, captured by the Germans, and made to work as an interpreter at a sawmill and then in work camps along Poland's Vistula River.

It had been a plausible story until investigators from the US Army Counterintelligence Corps found that Reimer had been granted citizenship in Nazi Germany in 1944. US investigators called him for an interview and, for the first time, asked about Trawniki since Reimer had listed the camp on his citizenship application. He had easily brushed aside the reference.

SUBJECT stated that he had been assigned to a guard company near TRAWNIKI and that his supervisor officer was a member of the SS. He claimed that he was never integrated into an SS unit, but was assigned as a paymaster in the guard company.

Reimer had added his own statement about his work at the camp. "We were told that we were civilians," he wrote. "I never was taken over by SS."

He was approved for entry in the United States, in part, Black knew, because an American Red Cross supervisor in Germany had described Reimer as an "honest and dependable" person who would "make a good American citizen," and in part because US immigration authorities in 1951 had little information about the Nazi-run camp in the village of Trawniki.

Now OSI could refute Reimer's claim that he had served only in the Trawniki administration. Reimer, it appeared, had been deployed to at least two ghettos at the exact same time that tens of thousands of Jews were being rounded up for deportation to the Treblinka killing center or shot on the spot.

"Oh my," Black told Einhorn as he recounted Reimer's lies. "We have a case."

CHAPTER TEN

SUNRISE IN PRAGUE

Washington, D.C., and Prague
1990

Elizabeth "Barry" White ran her fingertips over a fat stack of paper piled high on the desk in front of her. The only female historian in the Office of Special Investigations was chasing down hundreds of leads against a clock that delivered never-ending grief, another day coming to an end, a new one creeping closer.

There were fugitive lists from foreign countries and tips called in by strangers, wartime documents of SS units that had routinely carried out mass murder and immigration files on men, long settled in America, whose names had turned up on Nazi personnel records half a world away.

Suspects were growing older—there was so little time—and on some days it seemed to White that the work of OSI drew only questions and contempt. Once, on a park bench in northern Virginia, another mother had asked White about her job.

"Oh," the woman declared when White explained the leads, the clock, the mission. "I don't want my government doing *that*."

Fifty years from now, White thought, if we were to catch the people who blew up Pan Am flight 103 and they were living in the United States, would we choose to ignore them?

Even from inside the Justice Department, OSI faced unusual

scrutiny. The majority of criminal cases were settled before trial, often after defendants pleaded guilty to lesser charges. But OSI had no room to compromise. The only course of action in the American court system was denaturalization and deportation, and 40 percent of OSI's cases went to court.

OSI almost always won, but denaturalization rulings could take months and were regularly appealed, then appealed again. After that, the deportation process began—another trial, another wait for a decision, another appeal, a second appeal.

"Aren't you done yet?" other prosecutors would often ask.

WHITE HAD BEEN a girl of six in 1961 when someone stuck a burning cross on the front lawn of her family's colonial-style home in Norfolk, Virginia, near a trim patch of dogwood trees that bloomed pink and white in the springtime. Her father raced for a garden hose and doused the flames, but a black scar in the grass nearly reached the house. It was the year that she realized her family was different.

On the surface, the Whites were like many other Southerners in the stately neighborhood along the shores of the James River: white, Protestant, and relatively affluent. White's father was a pediatrician who tended to Norfolk's children, her mother a Vassar graduate who had broken Japanese naval codes during the war and then moved to the South to be with her husband.

The river was just across the street, and on steamy afternoons with her best friend and her standard poodle, Pooh, White would wade into the water in tennis shoes, careful to avoid the oyster shells and stinging nettles underfoot. There were crabs to catch and sticks and weeds that could be twined together for rafts to float on. She would walk home slowly, bare feet sticky with mud, cropped blond hair still wet from the water.

On Sundays, there was church, creaking pews filled with girls in frilly dresses and shiny Mary Janes. When White took her first communion, she was inspired by the minister's lyrical words about love and service. She would close her eyes and imagine a life of purpose, contours more than details, but beautiful nonetheless.

The truth came slowly, as political and social upheaval swept the South. Over a roast and hot rolls at the family dinner table, Forrest White excoriated the poll taxes that kept poor blacks from voting and, later, the governor of Virginia for shutting down the public schools in Norfolk to avoid putting black children in the same classrooms as whites. The move, part of Virginia's policy of "massive resistance," was in direct defiance of the US Supreme Court ruling that had declared school segregation unconstitutional.

Forrest White drove to Richmond to see about the matter as head of an organization of white citizens in Norfolk who wanted the schools reopened. He was turned away by the governor, and on the ride home Forrest White decided his organization should figure out a way to sue on behalf of white students since they couldn't go to school either.

"We're all God's children," Forrest White had told his daughter more than once.

Edith White wore proper white gloves and hats to church, but her four children came to recognize that their Yankee mother was far more outspoken than their father. Her activism in liberal and civil rights organizations got her blackballed from the Junior League and shunned by the ladies at the country club, who called her "Comrade Edie."

It wasn't unusual for the Whites to receive death threats.

When the family's minister was abruptly dismissed, fired after insisting that nonwhites would be welcomed at church services, White struggled to make sense of it. Most everyone she knew went to the Methodist church, but something hateful had happened in a place that spread God's love, and the hypocrisy and injustice gnawed at her.

In the seventh grade, when White was asked to give a speech

before her classmates, it seemed only fitting to talk about the foul history of the Ku Klux Klan. "Nigger lover," someone called out afterward, and White finally understood that there were those in her city, with its peach trees and Southern pleasantries and summers that drifted long into September, who harbored an awful secret.

White went to Vassar to study languages but found herself drawn to German history. She wanted to understand why Christians who valued their civilized culture could support a regime that enforced bigotry and murder.

She graduated in 1975, pursued a doctorate degree in history at the University of Virginia, and moved to Washington to research her dissertation at the National Archives, getting by as a part-time government clerk-typist.

The odds of striking up a romance in the basement of a federal office building seemed altogether slim to White, but at a holiday party for the Department of Energy, she met Bill Blackmore, a left-leaning Southerner who spent much of the evening huddled with White in a quiet corner of the room, quoting from Steinbeck, Hemingway, Heller. His mustache was on the longer side, curling over his top lip, but his eyelashes were short, and that made White happy since her mother had always warned her to stay away from boys with long eyelashes.

They became friends over lunches and the occasional drink. One afternoon, he gave White a parting hug and sighed, "Juicy Fruit." Later, they would laugh about whether his decision to recite a line from the movie *One Flew over the Cuckoo's Nest* had been creative brilliance or social suicide. But that night, twenty-five-year-old White was intrigued. A few months later, she was in love.

After a year of research in Germany and another year teaching and writing in Charlottesville, White moved back to Washington. On a visit home to Norfolk for Thanksgiving in 1982, her father pulled her aside.

"I think Bill has MS."

White paused. Bill had a tremor in his hand and had endured a bout of optic neuritis, but doctors had talked of a temporary condition. Startled, White looked at her father, knowing that he had made it a practice over the years to never offer a diagnosis to anyone who wasn't a patient. Something must be terribly wrong. Her father's face was kind but certain.

White decided to keep the information to herself. *You don't stop loving somebody just because he's sick.*

White had been looking for work in Washington for months when historian David Marwell called in 1983 on the recommendation of one of White's former history professors. She became the sixth historian in the Office of Special Investigations, surrounded by a formidable team of men who had lived and worked in European countries and spoke some combination of Russian, German, Polish, Bulgarian, Ukrainian, Serbo-Croatian, Lithuanian, and Latvian.

White fit in quickly. She was one of the few historians in the country who could translate *Sütterlin,* a German script often used by the older generation in Germany, and much to the surprise of the men of OSI she ordered beer over lunch at the local Thai place.

The other historians specialized in certain countries or Nazi units. White became OSI's generalist. During long days, she pored over thousands of documents from the archives in Europe, Israel, and the United States for names of Nazi perpetrators. She compiled data on each suspect, then worked to match the details with people in the United States.

"High-stakes history," she told Blackmore, who had proposed marriage on an old picnic bench in the backyard of the rented townhouse they shared. White said yes, accepting a piece of hard candy in lieu of an engagement ring since they were saving to buy a house.

"In my next life," she told her future husband, "I am going to be high maintenance."

One summer afternoon in 1990, Peter Black stopped by White's office and peered over a stack of file folders. As chief historian at OSI, Black was overseeing dozens of active investigations and would soon travel with two other historians to Czechoslovakia, where four decades of Communist rule had ended.

For the first time, Czech authorities were opening the archives to Western historians, and Black needed another set of eyes on the research trip. White, more than any other historian at OSI, was familiar with the kinds of records most likely to reveal names of potential defendants.

White paused, flattered by the offer to join Black and the others. She knew that the Nazi regime had stashed thousands of war records in Prague because Soviet and Allied troops did not bomb the city or even approach it until the last days of the war. White's mind raced, thinking about what they might uncover.

Spending even a week away from home, however, seemed almost impossible to manage. Her husband had been diagnosed with multiple sclerosis, just as her father had predicted, and already Bill was having trouble walking. Their two-year-old daughter was not yet in preschool, and White knew from early-morning symptoms that she was pregnant with their second child.

She sized up the massive pile of records on her desk and sighed. Under George H. W. Bush, officials in the Justice Department were studying whether OSI historians could be replaced with contractors offering the lowest bid for their services. No one knew how much time the OSI historians had left, whether they would be forced to leave their work unfinished.

That, White decided, would be a tragedy, to the victims of the war and to the record of history, which clearly had not yet been settled.

She looked at Black. She would go to Prague.

IT WAS NEARING midnight, and Peter Black could scarcely make out the rambling rows of shops and houses hidden in the darkness. The night was quiet—no people, no car engines—and the silence was an eerie sort, a restless city struggling to shake the past, moving toward something that wasn't yet clear.

Black was jet-lagged and hungry. After landing in Frankfurt, Black, Barry White, and two other OSI historians had driven due east across Germany in a temperamental stick shift that had wheezed and grunted for five hundred dusty kilometers. They crossed the border into Czechoslovakia and eased into Prague to search for the rental apartment they would share during their visit.

The humming of the car engine on a quiet residential street drew people from their homes, still in their nightclothes, and Black wondered what they were thinking as they watched the curious German car with four Americans creep down streets and back alleys.

They found the rental apartment in a massive, Soviet-style complex that stretched across blocks on the outskirts of the city. Black expected to find it empty, but the owner of the apartment had waited for them, and she promptly advised her American visitors that she had no great love for gypsies or a Czech breakfast that did not include beer and fried potatoes. She wagged a finger at White, the youngest in the group, clearly distressed that White was not married to one of her traveling companions.

Black fell asleep and woke before dawn. He found the landlady in the kitchen, fussing over a sizzling pan of fried pork cutlets. The four historians would start the visit at the city's military archives, searching for anything related to the Gestapo, concentration camps, or the murderous units of the SS and the eastern European collaborators that they had deployed.

Black had waited years for this day. Unlike Poland's government, the Communist government in Czechoslovakia had always summarily rejected research requests from OSI. For the first time, Black would learn the secrets that the Third Reich had hidden in Czechoslovakia at war's end, tucked inside caches of Nazi rosters and records.

Besides White, he had come with Mike MacQueen, who as a younger man thought he would become an engineer until he grew more interested in nationalist movements, and Pat Treanor, who had conducted research in more than a dozen languages and spent months helping OSI investigate the wartime activities of Austrian president Kurt Waldheim. Both men had lived in Communist countries, where toilet paper was scarce but liquor was plentiful. In Bulgaria, Treanor had come to enjoy *Żubrowka*, a dry, herb-flavored vodka from Poland.

After breakfast, the historians set out on an ancient city bus. Black glanced at White, who was three months pregnant and had barely touched her food. Her husband was already walking with a cane, and Black knew that in a matter of years White would become the family's sole breadwinner.

Black sat back in his seat. In the shadows that come just before morning, he could see the city's castles and cathedrals set along the banks of the Vltava River, remarkably untouched by the air raids during World War II, the 1948 Communist coup, or the Soviet invasion of 1968 that had restored hard-line Communism to Czechoslovakia.

The bus pulled up in front of the military archives, a grand building just outside Prague's business district with a sprawling courtyard behind the entryway. The historians were shown to a file room. Ten hours passed quickly as they looked over hundreds of documents, randomly stuffed inside boxes and folders.

"*Fleisch*," MacQueen remarked late in the day, using the German word for "meat." It was a curse more than a comment. The best attribute of a good researcher, he reminded the weary group, was a fleshy rear end for long stretches of sitting.

They came away with a few scraps of information, including SS investigative reports of concentration camp shootings, with black-and-white sketches of prisoners who had been shot trying to escape over a barbed-wire fence. The emotion that had gone into the drawings was striking, and Treanor would wonder for years afterward whether the mystery artist had felt compassion for the dead.

At dusk, the historians went to look for dinner and stumbled into a tiny restaurant near their apartment.

"Don't order the carp," MacQueen told White, who had never traveled in a Communist country. "It's a bottom feeder, and you don't want to know on what."

But carp was the only thing on the menu, and they returned to the apartment hungry, briefcases slung over their shoulders. The first day of research had been relatively disappointing, and Black wanted to sleep and set out fresh in the morning.

"You Americans work too much," their Russian landlady chortled.

At daybreak the next morning, the four historians split up to look over records at different archives. Treanor and MacQueen would return to the military archives and soon leave for the archives of Bratislava, on the north side of the Danube River. Black and White would travel to the Bohemian city of Litomerice, to a memorial museum in Terezin, northeast of Prague, and then to Brno, the capital of Moravia.

On their last day in Prague, Black arranged for a visit to the archive of the Federal Ministry of the Interior. Outside the apartment block, a government sedan pulled up, and Black and White ducked inside. Black glanced silently at the Czech security agents in the front seat, pistols latched to their hips. The sedan crept out of the city, easing past the boxy, Soviet-era cars that crowded the narrow streets.

At the ministry, the sedan pulled into a cobblestone alleyway hidden behind a wooden gate. The agents motioned toward a metal-cage elevator. It stopped at the entryway of a vast, wood-paneled hall, where a half dozen government officers were waiting, standing stiffly on an Oriental carpet that stretched across the expanse of the room.

Black stepped forward, nodded at the Czech interpreter, and said in English, "Thank you for meeting with us. We are historians from the US Department of Justice, responsible for investigating people who were involved in Nazi crimes and now live in the United States. I am Dr. Black and this is Dr. White."

The officers smirked at the names, and Black had no doubt that they suspected he and White were spies. He nearly chuckled himself, imagining what the frowning officers were thinking. *The CIA has no imagination.*

They were shown to a drafty stone room in the basement that smelled of dust and old cardboard. Black sat at a long table, White at another. Fighting morning sickness, she went to search for a bathroom and found one in a nearby airshaft, with a toilet that flushed with a chain.

They were given a long list of the records managed by the ministry, random documents about German employees in France and people who had worked for the puppet state of Slovakia, for the SS, and for police units in Poland. At the end of each hour, White made her way to the bathroom to vomit.

Several hours passed. Suddenly, White stood up. In a faded yellow folder, she had recognized a name. *Streibel.*

She carried the folder to Black. The documents were thin, faded, and sheared at the edges.

"What do you make of this?" White asked, standing over Black's shoulder.

He studied the first page, scanning dozens of names and *Erkennungsmarken*, German military identification numbers. The second page had dozens more. There was a date at the top, 1945, and the

name that had caught White's attention: SS Battalion Streibel. Karl
Streibel had been the commandant of the Trawniki training camp.

Black read the headings across the top of the page:

Dienstgrad	*Name*	*Geb.am*	*Soldbuch Nr.*
Rank	Name	Born on	Identification number

Black was looking at a roster with the names of men who had served
in the battalion as it retreated across Poland during the summer and
fall of 1944, waging operations against partisan resistance movements and guarding Polish civilians forced to dig anti-tank trenches.
Each man had a rank, an identification number, and an assignment;
some documents listed birth dates, most between 1915 and 1925.
The names were Ukrainian, ethnic German, Lithuanian, Russian,
Polish.

Black studied the pages carefully. He stopped short when he saw
the name of Liudas Kairys, identification number 1628. Black's
mind raced, dates and events flashing in quick succession. Kairys
had received a promotion at Trawniki; on the roster, he was listed as
an *Oberwachmann*, a guard corporal. The date—November 1944—
jumped off the page.

Kairys had served at the Treblinka labor camp until July 1944,
when, as Soviet troops approached, the SS and their Trawniki-
trained guard detachment had shot as many as seven hundred
Jewish prisoners before dismantling the camp.

Clearly, Black thought, Kairys had earned his promotion.

Black turned to another page. There was Vladas Zajanckauskas,
the man from Massachusetts, listed on the document as a supply officer rather than a server in the Trawniki canteen, with the mundane
duties that he had once described to OSI attorneys. Another lie.

Black flipped back to the front of the file, to the page with
Streibel's signature. He drew in his breath. Jakob Reimer, identifica-

tion number 865, was listed with the rank of *SS-Oberzugwachmann*, a top sergeant—the highest rank available to a Trawniki-trained man.

"Look, look," he said to White. "Here's Reimer."

White nodded. "These are all Trawniki men."

Black looked at the dates again. He knew from the personnel file sent by the Soviets that Reimer had been at Trawniki from 1941 to 1944. But the roster that White discovered put Reimer in SS service until 1945, which meant that he had served for nearly the entire duration of the war. No wonder the SS had granted Reimer German citizenship.

Black knew of no other guard who had served at the camp longer than Reimer and who had risen from a recruit to the highest-ranking position for a non-German SS auxiliary. Reimer was not a lowly paymaster. He had been an essential part of Trawniki, there from start to finish, among the most trusted recruits in the operation.

Slowly, Black counted all the names on the roster. He sat back in his chair and looked at White.

There were more than seven hundred men.

CHAPTER ELEVEN

CODE FOR MURDER

Washington, D.C., and Hamburg, Germany
1991–1992

Aaron Black was named after baseball great Hank Aaron, so it wasn't entirely surprising to his parents when his fingers crisscrossed a letter board designed for autistic children and spelled out:

I WANT TO COLLECT CARDS

The letter board was a new tool, a form of facilitated communication that gave Peter and Mary Black another way to communicate with their nine-year-old son, who had spoken only a few words when he was a year old—*bath, bye, dad*—and then stopped talking altogether.

"What's your favorite color?" So many crayons. They would finally know.

GREEN

"What do you want to eat today?"

MCDONALD'S

"Why are you sad?" Aaron's fingers moved right, left, back again.

YOU ARE GOING TO DIE ON THE PLANE

His father was struck by the answer. "No, no. It's not going to happen."

Peter Black was once again preparing to leave for Germany, where in 1976 SS commander Karl Streibel, the fair-skinned, pot-bellied commandant of the Trawniki training camp, had been acquitted after a trial on charges of accessory to murder. Black wanted to review the records in the Hamburg state prosecutor's office, which had supervised the case against Streibel.

After reopening the Reimer investigation and the breakthrough in the archives of Prague, Black was searching for clarity. It was one of the ways he measured success as a historian, whether he could piece together the chronology of horrific events, put history into context.

Now, Black studied his worried son. For years after Aaron was diagnosed with developmental delays and then autism, he couldn't speak to his parents or his younger sister, Laura. But he had found his own way to communicate, taking his mother's or father's hand and pointing it toward the refrigerator when he was hungry or to the door in his bedroom when he wanted to relax there.

Once, when Black was working late, Aaron rummaged in his father's closet, walked downstairs, and presented his mother with a pair of Black's trousers. Aaron had determined that it was time for his father to come home. Mary understood in the way that all parents know their children, through an organic combination of instinct and practice, reinforced by dozens of books about childhood development.

With the letter board, Aaron, fiercely protective, could finally let his parents know that he worried when they traveled on planes.

Black took research trips two or three times a year, flying to Germany, Poland, Israel, Russia, Austria. For the sake of his family, he decided he would no longer leave home for more than a week.

BLACK FLEW TO Hamburg alone, made his way to the prosecutor's office, and introduced himself to the lawyer who had helped oversee the case against Karl Streibel fifteen years earlier.

In May 1945, a British armored cavalry unit had found Odilo Globocnik, the SS and police leader of Lublin, hiding in his home city of Klagenfurt in southern Austria along with several of his cronies. As the British closed in, Globocnik bit down on a cyanide capsule and died instantly. He was buried next to an outer wall of a local churchyard.

Streibel, his man at Trawniki, got away.

History books contained few details about the Trawniki commandant, but Black knew that Streibel had been born at the turn of the century in southern Poland, in idyllic Upper Silesia, with its forests and mountain lakes. The son of a carpenter who had fought in the First World War, Streibel joined the Nazi Party and then the SS in 1933, within days of the appointment of Hitler as Reich Chancellor.

Streibel worked for Globocnik in Lublin as early as 1939, mustering and training ethnic German auxiliaries. In October 1941, Streibel took command of the Trawniki training camp, handpicked for the job by Globocnik.

By some accounts, Streibel had been a regular drunk, prowling the grounds of Trawniki in black leather boots and a long wool coat. In the summer of 1944, as the Soviet offensive swept through eastern Poland to the Vistula River, Streibel abandoned the camp with a battalion of men. They withdrew to the west and later to Dresden, Germany, where they assisted with cleanup of the city after Allied firebombing.

In the final days of April 1945, near the German border with

Western Bohemia, Streibel's men burned their papers and scattered, blending into the chaos of a newly defeated Germany.

Twenty-five years after the war, West German prosecutors brought Streibel to trial. The criminal justice system in West Germany had largely gone soft on Nazi offenders by the 1970s, the public no longer particularly interested in another prosecution from a war that most everyone wanted to forget. At high-profile trials in Ulm, Hamburg, Frankfurt, and Düsseldorf, a series of SS men were convicted, but most received lenient sentences and some were even acquitted.

Streibel was indicted in 1970. He denied knowing the true purpose of the Trawniki camp, and German judges six years later decided that he couldn't be held responsible for the grisly role of his men in the mass murder of Poland's Jews. After his acquittal, Streibel found work as a storekeeper in the library of a Lutheran church in Hamburg.

How could he not have known? To Black, it had been a dubious court ruling. A leader of a training camp with no knowledge of the camp's mission?

In 1943, Globocnik had successfully pushed to promote Streibel, writing that Streibel had commanded the Trawniki camp "with the greatest discretion and understanding for the special leadership needs of this unit. These units have proved themselves in the best way in many anti-partisan missions, but especially in the framework of the Jewish resettlement."

Resettlement of the Jews. It was Nazi code for murder.

Black wanted to know more. He had less than a week in Hamburg, but he would take his time, carefully constructing a chronology of decisions, details, and events. He had learned long ago that even the most innocuous fact could fit with another and eventually deliver a watershed moment of understanding after months or years spent navigating wrong turns and dead ends.

In the prosecutor's office in Hamburg, Black readied himself for a long day ahead. The US Justice Department and the Federal Republic of Germany regularly shared information about ongoing investigations, and Black smiled at the prosecutor who had worked on the case against Streibel. But something was off. He could feel it as soon as he introduced himself. The prosecutor was shaking her head, insisting that Black could not review the records without higher authorization.

Stunned, Black pressed her to reconsider. She was adamant. Black wondered whether the reunification of Germany had somehow changed the parameters of the agreement between the two nations. There was no way to know. He had traveled four thousand miles to Hamburg but would have to settle for a limited review of the records, at least until the matter could be sorted out by his supervisors in Washington.

The prosecutor offered Black the criminal indictment, outlining the allegations against Streibel. Black quickly scanned the document. West German prosecutors had argued that Streibel was responsible for the actions of Trawniki men in the Belzec, Sobibor, and Treblinka killing centers.

Streibel's men, according to the indictment, also traveled to the Polish city of Lublin during the 1942 ghetto-clearing operation, when thousands of Jews were deported to the Belzec killing center or shot on the spot.

> Responsible as a perpetrator in the deaths of between
> 35,000–40,000 people.

The indictment went on. Trawniki men participated in at least twenty-one large-scale shooting and deportation operations throughout the Lublin region.

Responsible for the deaths of at least 50,000 people.

Trawniki men went to Warsaw in 1942 during mass deportations of Jews to the Treblinka killing center.

Responsible for the deaths of 300,000–400,000 people.

Trawniki men returned to help the Germans fight Jewish resisters during the bloody Warsaw ghetto uprising.

Responsible for the deaths of at least 7,000 people through the deportations…

· The words were graphic and chilling, and when Black left Hamburg a few days later, disappointed by the turn of events at the prosecutor's office, he was all but certain that he was leaving behind a critical piece of history.

THERE WAS HARDLY a quiet time in the bustling Office of Special Investigations, where in 1991 eleven trial attorneys and eight historians juggled forty-two court cases and more than four hundred open investigations.

Eli Rosenbaum and Neal Sher were scrambling to oversee investigations and hearings. Barry White was working to run the names of the seven hundred men listed on the rosters from Prague through INS records to see who might be living on US soil. It was a tedious affair because a single name could take on many different transliterated versions—*Nikolaus* on a roster might have been born *Mykolaj*, spelled *Nikolai* in Cyrillic on Russian papers and *Mykola* on a US visa. Scores of names lacked biographical details such as birth dates and hometowns.

But the rosters in Prague were among the most significant finds in OSI's expanding Trawniki investigation, and the effort to match names was a critical next step.

While White and Peter Black worked in Washington, other OSI historians were sending back records from archives spread across the former Soviet Union, new details about the operation at Trawniki from Nazi rosters and the statements of former guards. Ukraine had declared its independence from the Soviet Union, and OSI had begun to exploit the archives there. Collectively, the former USSR housed the world's largest body of captured Nazi documents relating to occupied eastern Europe.

As the records poured in, the historians began calling Black's office "Trawniki Central."

Black was particularly intrigued by the work of historian Mike MacQueen, who was preparing to leave for the archives of Vilnius, the capital of Lithuania. Black knew that men of Baltic nationality had trained at Trawniki.

"If you find any reference to Trawniki material, please review and copy it," Black told him.

A few days later, MacQueen called from Vilnius. "Is Demjanjuk 1393?"

"Yes," Black said quickly. He knew OSI defendant John Demjanjuk's Trawniki identification number by heart. "What do you have?"

MacQueen had found a disciplinary report from the Majdanek concentration camp near Lublin. It was dated January 1943, during what had been a particularly lethal winter for the prisoners confined behind the camp's barbed-wire fences. A typhus epidemic had swept the barracks, and the SS placed the entire facility under quarantine. Prisoners who didn't die from disease were gassed with carbon monoxide or Zyklon B, a cyanide-based pesticide that had been used to delouse ships and clothing until the SS applied it to the murder of human beings.

The documents discovered by MacQueen described two

companies of Trawniki guards stationed in Majdanek that January. Over the phone, he quickly translated:

Subject: Report of the Canine Officer Detachment
   The above-named guards left their barracks and the camp without permission, despite the repeatedly announced camp quarantine order. According to their statements, the above named went into the village to buy salt and onions.

The report contained the names of four Trawniki men, including John Demjanjuk. For breaching curfew and leaving the camp during a typhus outbreak and quarantine, Demjanjuk and each of the three other men had received twenty-five lashes from a whip.

Black thought quickly. OSI already knew that Demjanjuk had trained as a guard at Trawniki, worked at an SS estate in the Lublin District in September 1942, and served at the Sobibor killing center from March 1943 until some unknown date. Gaps in his service record before and after Sobibor had left open the possibility that he could have also been the so-called Ivan the Terrible at the Treblinka killing center.

At Demjanjuk's criminal trial in Jerusalem in 1987, Israeli prosecutors had argued that Trawniki men could have moved between one killing center and another. Black found the argument contrived, an unsupported theory to justify the claim that Demjanjuk had served at Treblinka.

After Demjanjuk was convicted and sentenced to die in 1988, Israeli prosecutors and private investigators had gained access to archives behind the collapsing Iron Curtain and found that the Soviets in the 1960s had brought criminal charges against a series of men who had trained at Trawniki and then worked in Treblinka. As many as forty former guards were interviewed, and in tens of thousands of pages of court records, Demjanjuk's name did not appear a single time.

Demjanjuk may have been at Treblinka, Black thought when he learned of the discovery in Israel, but he certainly could not have been there long enough to earn a reputation as Ivan the Terrible.

Soviet authorities eventually provided more documents, rosters from 1943 showing that Demjanjuk and dozens of other Trawniki guards had been transferred from the Sobibor killing center to a concentration camp in Flossenbürg, Germany.

At OSI, Neal Sher made a similar discovery in a stack of Flossenbürg records. But the earlier gap in Demjanjuk's service record had remained, a span of six months between 1942 and 1943, the last possible link to Treblinka.

MacQueen's discovery in the archives in Vilnius, Black quickly realized, shredded what was left of the Treblinka theory. As a trusted Trawniki man, Demjanjuk had served at Majdanek in the months before his deployment to the Sobibor killing center, then gone on to Flossenbürg afterward. Despite the findings of US and Israeli courts, he could not have been the notorious Ivan the Terrible of Treblinka.

Black was reminded of the titles of two chapters in an Isaac Asimov science fiction trilogy that he had read as a boy: "The Answer That Satisfied." "The Answer That Was True."

Clearly, erroneous information had been used to build a death-penalty case, and the historical and legal record needed to be set straight. There was also the matter of the conviction itself. Demjanjuk, in solitary confinement in Israel, was waiting on a ruling from the Israeli Supreme Court. If the court confirmed Demjanjuk's conviction and sentence, he would hang for crimes that he had not committed.

Yet Demjanjuk, Black knew, was far from innocent. Demjanjuk had begun his SS career at Trawniki, his base unit and training ground, and gone on to serve in a Nazi-run killing center and two lethal concentration camps. Black wanted to see Demjanjuk properly called to account, made to answer for his participation in the persecution and mass murder of Poland's Jews, beginning with his service at Trawniki.

IN 1992, THE prosecutor's office in Hamburg relented, and Black received thick batches of records from the Karl Streibel criminal case. One was the protocol of an interview with Streibel himself, taken in preparation for his trial in West Germany. Streibel had described working in his father's carpentry business and joining the far-right Nazi Party, convinced that it could cure the country's economic problems.

"The Jewish question was not an issue in my family and for myself at first," Streibel told the investigators. "As far as I know, my parents did business with Jewish suppliers. My tavern also had Jewish customers."

"Were you aware of [the party's] attitude towards Jews when you applied for membership in the party?" an investigator asked.

"Yes, but the Jewish problem was unimportant for me and my circle at the time. Important citizens in our town were members of the SS."

Streibel went on to describe his work as the commandant of the Trawniki training camp. "When I reached Trawniki, it held around 300 Ukrainian prisoners. In reality, there were also people of other nationalities, but they were all called Ukrainian.... On orders of the SS head of police in Lublin, the Ukrainians were to be trained as guards. They received weapons as well as uniforms. Ukrainians with knowledge of German were used as noncommissioned officers."

Jakob Reimer among them, Black thought grimly.

Streibel had also described one of the most dreadful events of the Holocaust, a massacre planned by Heinrich Himmler to eliminate the remaining Jewish workers in the Lublin District of occupied Poland. The Nazis had given the plan a cynical name: Aktion Erntefest. Operation Harvest Festival.

On November 3, 1943, SS and police units shot as many as six thousand Jewish prisoners working in a forced-labor camp adjacent to the training camp at Trawniki. Men, women, and children had been made to stand on the edge of a trench before a firing squad, and soon, Black knew, the earth had been filled with bodies.

During Operation Harvest Festival, at least forty-three thousand Jews were murdered at the Trawniki labor camp, the nearby Majdanek concentration camp, and the Poniatowa forced-labor camp, the largest single-day killing spree carried out by the SS during the war.

"I gave the order to cover the moat with the dead bodies with dirt," Streibel told German investigators about the mass shooting at Trawniki. "I ordered the burning of the bodies. A transport of Jews came to Trawniki to do the work. The burning of the bodies lasted approximately two weeks. After finishing the burning, the Jewish people who burned the bodies were shot."

Black read carefully, absorbing the clinical description of murder. He moved on, digging deeper into the Streibel files, and came upon a statement from one of Trawniki's German officers.

The entire battalion, the officer reported, had been deployed to the Jewish ghetto in Lublin in March 1942. Odilo Globocnik had just opened the Belzec killing center, located about 130 kilometers southeast of the city.

It had been a chaotic, terrifying month for the condemned Jews of Lublin, thousands of people forced to assemble at the Great Synagogue in the heart of the ghetto and then sent to the newly operational gas chambers at Belzec, with pits that would serve as mass graves. Belzec had been designed for assembly-line mass murder, Black knew, stunning in its efficiency.

Did the Jews of Lublin know they were about to die? According to the officer's statement, armed Trawniki men had roamed the Lublin ghetto from the very beginning of the liquidation, emptying houses block by block until more than thirty thousand people had disappeared, from dinner tables and backyards and nurseries, generations of families carted off to their deaths.

Black found a statement from a second guard, a professional musician who had volunteered for the SS marching band before he was transferred to Trawniki. Black paused over his words.

"I personally saw dead bodies of people who had been shot, lying in the streets. No one who was present during the operation can deny that.... The general talk during the operation was that Jews who were ill or unable to walk would be shot. Jews were coming out of houses, some were beating the Jews, others were shooting. It was all a disorder."

In the years since the war's end, Black had read rudimentary facts about Trawniki. How Globocnik had set up the camp near the abandoned sugar refinery. How the Germans had recruited an auxiliary force of captured Soviet soldiers, men like Liudas Kairys and Jakob Reimer, as well as Ukrainian and Polish civilians from West Ukraine, Lublin, and the Krakow District. How the camp had become a training facility for guards, and how, on a single day in November 1943, thousands of Jewish prisoners had been murdered at the adjacent labor camp, shot by firing squad.

But against the backdrop of the three notorious Nazi-run killing centers, the better-known forced-labor camps, and the horrific conditions inside the Jewish ghettos of occupied Poland, Trawniki—at least outside Poland—remained a footnote in history, an ancillary operation.

Sitting in his office in Washington, grotesque accounts of murder and destruction piled around him, Black was beginning to see that Trawniki men had been everywhere, operating the gas chambers and guarding the perimeters at the killing centers, screaming and beating and firing until Jewish ghettos were cleared and trucks and train cars packed tight, body against body in the darkness.

There was no way the Germans could have killed so many, so

fast without a reliable and ruthless workforce comprising hundreds, if not thousands, of loyal collaborators, the muscle behind what was surely the most sustained mass-murder operation in the history of the war.

"What was Trawniki?" a prosecutor had once asked a witness in the Liudas Kairys case.

"A camp for—a training camp."

"Training for what?"

"I don't know. To murder Jews."

The Trawniki men had done their jobs so well that the Germans had been able to kill 1.7 million Jews, along with Roma, Poles, and Soviet POWs, in less than twenty months. The doomed Jews of Poland had called their violent captors "the Ukrainians" or "Black-ies," a reference to the black uniforms and caps that many Trawniki men wore.

To Black, they were the foot soldiers of the Final Solution.

And Trawniki, tucked into the countryside of southeastern Poland, had been nothing less than a school for mass murder.

BLACK HAD TAKEN to working on the weekends, when the hallways of OSI were quiet and he could muse out loud about the operation at Trawniki. His son, Aaron, often came along, content to sit on the floor with a cheeseburger and watch Black type notes and questions on index cards, mumbling the details out loud as he recorded them.

Black was beginning to piece together what life had been like in-side the training camp, with five barracks for the recruits, a dining hall, shops for boot making and sewing, a stable for horses, and stor-age rooms for clothing and equipment. He also saw the emerging outline of standard operating procedures for mustering and training personnel.

Karl Streibel had created a comprehensive system of ranks at Trawniki, based on the noncommissioned ranks of the German

police. He had given his men uniforms, military identification numbers, and promotions for loyalty and performance. And as the men
spread out across occupied Poland, Streibel had armed them with
carbines, automatic rifles, and pistols.

Black found the statements and interrogations of former Trawniki
men particularly helpful.

Statement of Abram Thiessen, August 26, 1964, proceedings
against Karl Streibel:

> In Lublin, the Ukrainians had orders to seal off the ghetto and
> remove the Jews from the apartment houses. Though they were
> told that the Jews would be sent to a labor camp, the circum-
> stances of the evacuation convinced them that the Jews would
> be killed.

Statement of Kurt Reinberger, May 21, 1962, proceedings
against Karl Streibel:

> The Ukrainians detailed to Lublin had the task of sealing off
> the ghetto in Lublin.... Heard shooting and saw corpses dur-
> ing the first day.

Statement of Hermann Reese, March 26, 1962, proceedings
against Karl Streibel:

> The Jews were beaten with whips and rifle butts to move them
> along.... It was generally known that those unable to walk were
> to be shot on the spot.

Interrogation of Erich Lachmann, March 3, 1969, proceedings
against Karl Streibel:

We all knew what was going on. I would believe that there was no German and no Ukrainian in Trawniki who did not know what was happening to the Jews.

On index cards, Black wrote out the career data for every Trawniki-trained guard he could identify through the records. He would eventually have more than four thousand index cards, enough to fill a dozen drawers.

Aaron had always kept himself busy at the office, and Black didn't think much about what his son saw or overheard. But at home early one Saturday morning, Aaron pulled out his letter board.

ARE WE DOING TRAWNIKIS TODAY?

CHAPTER TWELVE

SEVEN FLOORS ABOVE MANHATTAN

New York City
1992

Would there be something in Jakob Reimer's eyes, some hint in the way he carried himself that betrayed what he once was, a commander and a collaborator, so loyal to the SS that he had earned the promise of a future in postwar Nazi Germany?

Eli Rosenbaum settled into the conference room at the US Attorney's office and waited. It was a bright spring morning in Manhattan and the city was on edge, gripped by whispers about unrest and violence. A California jury had acquitted four white police officers in the videotaped beating of young black motorist Rodney King, setting off days of rioting in South Central Los Angeles.

But seven floors up, in the teeming offices of the Southern District of New York, Rosenbaum was thinking only of the man whom Peter Black would come to call "Mr. Trawniki."

Reimer had come from nothing, a tiny farm village in the Ukrainian countryside, but he had turned himself into an experienced and skilled leader, once as a lieutenant in the Red Army and again when he collaborated with the Germans, the very enemy he had fought against.

Rosenbaum sighed. How easily Reimer had disappeared after the war. With an angular face and thick, dark hair, he had blended into the immigrant community of New York City in the 1950s. How easily he had lived for the better part of a half century, a salesman and a family man, complicit in the mass murder of Poland's Jews but allowed to prosper in the country that had fought to free them.

Now Reimer had agreed to come in for questioning. And he had decided not to bring an attorney. Would he appear anxious? Distressed? Rosenbaum had his doubts.

Twice before, once under questioning by US Army investigators and a second time before OSI attorneys, Reimer had insisted that he never played a role in the persecution of Poland's Jews. He would tell a good story, how he only handled money at the Trawniki training camp, better to cooperate than to starve in a prisoner-of-war camp for captured Soviet soldiers. *Schrecklich, schrecklich,* dreadful, awful.

Except Rosenbaum knew better. History had finally caught up to Reimer, chronicled in a detailed biographical report that Black had provided before Rosenbaum, Neal Sher, and OSI attorney Michael Bergman left for New York.

Black's account of Reimer's potential role at Trawniki had been nothing less than chilling. About five thousand Trawniki guards, instruments of death in occupied Poland, had served in the killing centers, Jewish ghettos, and forced-labor camps. Reimer had been there from the very beginning, and for his service he had received promotions, vacations, service medals, and German citizenship.

The door to the conference room opened. At seventy-three, Reimer was still lithe and slender, with silver hair and skin that had darkened from the sun. He walked in slowly and offered a friendly nod. Someone was talking loudly in a nearby office, but Rosenbaum barely heard the chatter. He stood up and offered Reimer his hand, an excruciating pleasantry.

"Mr. Reimer. Thank you for coming here this morning. We appreciate your cooperation."

"Yes." Reimer's voice was soft, his accent still heavy.

"You understand that this is a voluntary interview on your part."

"Yes, of course."

"We would like to ask you about your activities during the war and then your immigration to the United States and the process through which you became an American citizen."

Rosenbaum had asked Reimer to bring records and photos relating to his immigration, naturalization, and wartime activities. Reimer pushed a document across the table. Rosenbaum recognized the certificate of US naturalization that Reimer had been given in 1959, seven years after emigrating from Germany on the recommendation of a Red Cross supervisor.

"My name was changed," Reimer said lightly. "It used to be Jakob."

Rosenbaum pointed. "You are holding a small photograph?"

"I would say it was taken when I was a prisoner of war," Reimer replied.

Rosenbaum pretended to study it, but he had seen the photo before. It had been attached to the upper-left corner of the Trawniki personnel file that the Soviets had sent to Peter Black.

"You would say this was taken in 1941?"

Reimer began to tell his story, starting with his capture by the Germans and confinement to a POW camp for Soviet soldiers.

"Let me give you a picture of the prison camp," he said, in a grand show of cooperation. "It was an open field, no buildings, no trees, no shrubbery, nothing, just barbed wires and machine gun towers, and there were hundreds of thousands of soldiers. It was cold, especially the nights. And we had every day a truckload of dead bodies, and they were naked because the ones that were still alive, they were ripping off the clothes."

"When I walked into there, one of my soldiers . . . recognized me. He yelled, 'Hey lieutenant!' And I put a finger on my lips. I said, 'Please, be quiet' because I, quite frankly, was afraid they would shoot me because being a German, being in the war against Germany, I did not know what was going to happen."

Reimer appeared lost in thought. In some ways, Rosenbaum understood the silence, how memories lurked in shadows.

Reimer went on. "My soldiers kept on saying to me, 'You speak German. Why don't you tell them? You maybe can help us, food and whatnot.' So finally, I did. I saw there were some other German soldiers and they did work as translators. So I identified myself and they took me out...all those who spoke German were taken out. And we were brought to a new camp, which was called Trawniki."

"Let's spell that," Rosenbaum said carefully. "T R A W N I K I?"

"Yes. And the first thing they did when we got there, they lined us up and they told us, 'Drop your pants.' I didn't have the slightest idea what that was all about. Later on, we found out what that meant. They were looking if there were Jewish people among us. Now...a German was training us in the German command, the formation, you know, and the turns and whatnot, without weapons, just marching and so forth."

"At Trawniki?"

"Yes. Then they start bringing in soldiers from that same camp that I came from, Russian soldiers. Because they knew I used to be an officer in the Russian army, I then trained those Russians."

"Was it military training?"

"Yes. Just marching, and they called us *Wachmannschaften*."

Just marching, Rosenbaum thought wryly. "I want to explain really why it is that we are here."

"Yes," Reimer said. "Why I am here?"

"You spoke with an attorney from our office...some years ago. Do you recall that?"

"About fifteen, I would say, twelve, fifteen years ago."

"You told him that you had been at Trawniki continuously from 1941 to 1944 and that you had worked exclusively in the orderly room."

"Well—," Reimer started.

"Hear what I have to say," Rosenbaum said more firmly. "Since that time, my office, which only works on these kinds of World War II cases, has done an enormous amount of research. We have been able to gain access to your personnel records...also records about what was going on at Trawniki, what you and other members of the Trawniki unit were doing."

Reimer was quiet.

"I want to explain at the very outset that you are under oath now and under affirmation in your case, and Mr. Sher and Mr. Bergman and I are federal officials. If you testify falsely to us, that is a federal offense, for which, frankly, one can be imprisoned. Nobody here wants to see that happen. What we want is the truth. And you will see from my questioning that we know a lot of it already."

"You're finished with your introduction?"

"Yes, I am."

"In all candor, this was so many years ago that there could be false statements that I make."

"That's fine," Rosenbaum said. "I am not really concerned about what was said in 1980....What I am concerned about is what is going to be said here this morning. All right? If you don't remember something, tell me...but obviously, there are going to be things that no human being could have forgotten and that I will expect you to be able to tell me about. There are events and assignments and duties and actions that you certainly will remember."

Early in his legal career, Rosenbaum had learned to recite facts that had been uncovered in investigations. It was a strategic bluff, a way of showing reluctant suspects that he knew where they had served and what they had done, even if the details were still fuzzy. *Don't bother lying. I already know the truth.*

Rosenbaum asked about Reimer's background. "You consider yourself an ethnic German?"

"Well, the village I lived in, they were Germans from the Hamburg area of Germany," Reimer replied. "What can I say? I am German descent. What can I say?"

"Fine. German descent."

Reimer interrupted. "I consider myself American, quite frankly. I have been living here more than in any other country."

Rosenbaum went on. "You were sent to this Trawniki camp in 1941. But you were not stationed in Trawniki all the time during your assignment to this Trawniki unit. You received assignments in other cities. Isn't that right?"

"No," Reimer said. "I was just—I was in Trawniki."

"But there were also assignments to Czestochowa and to Warsaw. Isn't that right?"

Rosenbaum pulled out Reimer's personnel file from Trawniki, which listed the two deployments. He passed it across the table and waited, wondering whether Reimer was going to try to explain how a so-called paymaster in the office at Trawniki had ended up in two cities at the exact time the SS and police were deporting thousands of Jews to Nazi-run killing centers.

"Why don't we try that again?" Rosenbaum said. "From Trawniki, you were, as we say in English, detailed, temporarily assigned to some other places, correct?"

"Well, it shows that I was sent to Czestochowa." Reimer sounded anxious.

"Right," Rosenbaum said. "And also to Warsaw?"

"And also to Warsaw."

Rosenbaum pictured the devastated Jewish ghetto after the uprising, burnt-out buildings, air choked by ash, bodies on the ground, shot or burned. "Heil Hitler!" SS general Jürgen Stroop, the commander of the Warsaw ghetto operation, had cried when he celebrated the defeat of the Jews by blowing up the city's Great Synagogue, one of the largest in the world.

"I recall one thing," Reimer said, "and this probably will crack you...up. I sold a truck of vodka to a Polish restauranteur....I was supplying the food and the payroll in each one of these cities and specifically, I remember in Warsaw."

He stumbled over the word. *War-shaw.*

"How you pronounce it?" Reimer asked.

"Warsaw," Rosenbaum corrected.

"Warsaw," Reimer repeated diligently. "I sold a whole truck of vodka to them. When I think of it, if the Germans found out, they would have shot me right there. I don't know how I had the nerve to do it."

"This was the vodka that was—?"

"For the men. They were half loaded all the time. So I felt they had too much to drink as it is. I took a whole truckload and sold it to a Polish restaurant."

"One of your jobs was to account for this vodka?"

"That was the only job....Same in Czestochowa. I was never in field duty," Reimer said. "I tried to tell you that at the very beginning. I was never involved in that. I was involved in one assignment. We were brought to a city block—now we know it is a ghetto."

"This is in what city?" Rosenbaum asked carefully, intrigued.

"In Lublin. That's near Trawniki. And they brought us over there on guard duty."

Rosenbaum knew that the men of Trawniki had been deployed to Lublin in 1942 during the mass deportations to the Belzec killing center. Now Reimer had confirmed that he had been there at some point, a third deployment outside Trawniki.

Rosenbaum didn't flinch. After a significant admission by someone he was questioning, Rosenbaum had been known to yawn to feign boredom, as if to telegraph to suspects that the information was unremarkable or already known to him.

Reimer explained. "I was in charge so I had men placed around this block....I would walk into these buildings. There was everything, china and dishes, bedrooms and clothes, no people. There was not a soul in this whole block. That was the only assignment I had."

"What were you doing in Lublin?" Rosenbaum asked. "Why were you sent there?"

"This was a training."

"It was not an operational assignment?"

"No. There was no people in there."

"This was the Jewish ghetto?" Rosenbaum asked again.

"I assume. It must have been. What happened to the people? It must have been the Jewish ghetto."

"There were other training missions outside of camp?"

"No. That was the only one. From then on, I asked for desk duty."

Rosenbaum turned to the single day in November 1943 when the SS and police had shot as many as six thousand Jewish prisoners in the forced-labor camp adjacent to Trawniki.

Rosenbaum had read about the mass shooting carried out under Operation Harvest Festival, how local villagers and Trawniki men had been ordered to stay inside, how radios were turned on to drown out the sounds of machine guns and the desperate cries of victims who had been forced to undress, put their coins in a pile, and stand before a trench that spanned a grassy field. There had been blood everywhere, glowing in the late-afternoon sun. Afterward, Trawniki men had searched the camp for anyone still in hiding.

"Did you see people trying to escape from these killings?" Rosenbaum asked Reimer.

"The only thing I saw is one, a young Jewish man," Reimer replied. "He looked like an athlete who was jumping up and trying to get away. But he didn't make it, of course."

"Did the mothers try to protect their children?"

"They held them in their arms."

"Did you see them crying?"

"Screaming and crying."

"Here is the problem I have," Rosenbaum said a short time later. "I appreciate your coming here today, but you are asking us to believe quite a bit, that for all these years that you served at Trawniki, initially helping to train men, train a force that existed solely to take part in German operations against innocent Jewish civilians, that you never picked up a rifle, you never left your office, you were exempted from all of this, even though you were promoted, promoted, promoted to the highest rank that a former POW could have achieved."

Neal Sher sat forward in his chair. Over the years at OSI, he had met a long list of Nazi defendants who had come to believe their own stories. Time could do that, bend and twist events, make killers into victims. For most, Sher decided, it had been the only way to go on living, to pray to God, to love a wife, to rock a newborn.

"I am going to ask you a few questions because I have been sitting very patiently listening to you," Sher said to Reimer. "You clearly are an articulate man. You are an intelligent man. You have not been truthful with me. You have not been truthful with Mr. Rosenbaum. You have not been truthful with yourself. All these stories about that you have a clean conscience and you have spoken to your lord about this, you are not telling the truth. Now, Trawniki, you got there in 1941, correct? Yes or no?"

"Must have been '41," Reimer replied.

"These Trawniki men with whom you served—you were a Trawniki man," Sher said. "In fact, you got two promotions, correct?"

"Right."

"And the SS used these Trawniki men for what? You said for guard duty, correct? Did you ever hear of [Operation] Reinhard? Do you know what that was?"

"No."

"You can't recall? You seem to be hesitant."

Reimer's voice rose. "I don't like to disappoint you, for crying out loud."

"You are not disappointing me," Sher shot back. "I assure you, Mr. Reimer, you do not disappoint me. You are everything I expected."

He continued. "The first place you know that Trawniki men went to was Lublin, the ghetto of Lublin, yes?"

"Yes."

"We also know that Trawniki men, yourself included, went to Warsaw, the Jewish ghetto. Correct?"

"Yes."

"And to the Jewish ghetto of Czestochowa, correct?"

"Right."

"Now those are just three places we know of. Name some of the camps where the graduates of Trawniki were sent to serve. You know them."

"No, I don't."

"How about Treblinka? Did you ever hear about Treblinka?"

"Sure. I heard of Treblinka."

"How about Sobibor? Did you ever hear of Sobibor?"

"After the war."

Sher paused. "You must really think we are stupid. You must really think we are thick. You served at Trawniki for over three years. The men were being sent continuously to Sobibor and you never heard of it?"

"No."

"Did you ever hear of that extermination camp Belzec?"

"Maybe. Here I am not sure. Maybe."

"You see, we know quite a bit about Trawniki, an awful lot. You were there for as long as anybody was there, by your own admission. The fact of the matter is that Trawniki men went to Belzec, Sobibor, Treblinka.... What happened to the Jews who went to these camps?"

"They exterminated them."

"Trawniki men who went to these camps sometimes came back to Trawniki. Isn't that correct? They never talked about their service at Treblinka and Belzec and Sobibor?"

"I never talked to anybody."

"You talked to the men who came back from these missions. Everybody knew what was going on."

"No." Reimer said. "Suppose, let's say, I would know what was going on. What? Was I going to stop it singlehandedly? What are you accusing me of?"

"Mr. Reimer. I am not accusing you of anything."

"I was not in no position. And one more thing. When you say I trained the men, you are telling me I trained the men how to kill Jewish people? That is wrong."

"Mr. Reimer, the fact of the matter is the entire purpose of Trawniki, the only reason that facility existed, was to train men to murder Jews. That was the only reason it was built."

"Right," Reimer said.

"It had no other purpose?"

"Right."

"It was one of the most diabolical facilities in history?"

"Right," Reimer said.

"I will suggest something else to you," Sher went on. "If you had any explanation as to what you did at that camp, you should have given that explanation after the war when you made application to come to America."

"Right." Reimer said again.

"This is not the time for it. It is a little late."

"Mr. Sher. Are you saying that I am responsible? That I should be put on trial, too, that I committed those same outrageous crimes?"

Rosenbaum watched the exchange silently. When he was twelve, he had come upon a black-and-white teleplay on NBC, a courtroom drama about the Auschwitz trials in Frankfurt in the 1960s. He had lain on his belly on the living room floor, cupped his chin in his hands, and listened to a female survivor describe gruesome medical experiments conducted by a German doctor. Was this woman a real person or an actor? Rosenbaum had never heard of such atrocities.

At home and in his synagogue on Long Island in the 1950s, the Holocaust was often a taboo subject, much like cancer—*shush now.* But just before he would become a Bar Mitzvah, he finally caught on to the intense suffering, and it would see him through to a career at the Office of Special Investigations.

He looked at Reimer. "You told us about this terrible time that they killed all the Jews at the Trawniki labor camp.... There was another time, wasn't there, that you saw Jews being killed? That wasn't the only time, right?"

Rosenbaum was fishing, crafting questions based on instinct.

Reimer grew quiet. "There was another time, but I did not participate."

Rosenbaum had no idea what Reimer would say next. "Mr. Reimer, just, in your own words, tell me about the incident, whatever you can remember."

Reimer's voice was shaking. "Um. We stayed in a barrack someplace outside of Trawniki. Where, I don't know. We all woke up and they were all sent to exterminate a labor camp. I did not get up. I slept. I know you are going to say I think you are crazy to believe me, but I did not participate. I was not involved in the shooting."

"You saw it?"

"The German SS man must have realized that I wasn't there.... He sent a man after me and he came and woke me up."

Reimer went on. "They had a board across a ravine or something, and all the people, they were dead in this grave."

"It was a mass grave and they had all been shot," Rosenbaum repeated. It was a statement, not a question. Reimer needed to believe that Rosenbaum already knew the answer.

"They were all shot," Reimer repeated.

"And your colleagues did the shooting?"

"Right."

"They didn't just cordon off the area. They did the actual shooting."

"They did the shooting," Reimer repeated.

"Weren't there some people who were still alive down there who had to be finished off?"

"There was one—I don't know—was he half dead or whatever. He was pointing with a finger to his head."

"He wanted to be shot?"

"Yes. And I don't know who but he was shot. That is all I saw. That is the only one that I saw that was shot in my presence when one of them already in the grave pointed the finger to his head, begged for mercy, so to speak."

"There's something about the man who pointed to his head that you haven't told me?" Rosenbaum was fishing again.

"Yes."

"You finished him off."

Again, Reimer paused. "I'm afraid so. I don't know if I hit his head. I don't know that."

"But he died?"

"I just say that I had to make one effort at least while the German was looking at me. I shot at the direction.... I couldn't very well just stand there. I had to make an effort or something."

Sher was looking at Reimer. "It's clear now that you participated in this execution of Jews. Correct?"

"It seems that way, that if I shot at that person that pointed at his head."

"Yes, sir," Sher said.

"Then I did."

"And this person that you shot at, he had already been hit but wasn't dead yet. Is that right?"

"That's what I assumed, you know."

"How close were you to him when you shot him?"

"Fifteen feet, maybe."

"After you shot, he was no longer pointing to his head, was he?"

"No."

Clearly, Rosenbaum thought as he listened to the exchange, Reimer had always excelled, as a Red Army lieutenant, as a commander at Trawniki, as an immigrant, as an American. And somewhere deep in the woods outside Trawniki, Reimer had excelled as a participant in a mass-killing operation. It was a devastating thought.

Reimer went on. "My whole life you think about these things. You try to forget them. I come here before you, and voluntarily, and I finally told you."

A thousand barbed responses coursed through Rosenbaum's head when Reimer brought up his own absolution.

"Do you feel better that you told the truth now?" Sher said. "Were you carrying this? Were you ashamed of this?"

"I was," Reimer said softly.

"I am trying to understand people like you."

"I only have one fear, that you would send me back for no reason."

"No reason?" Sher spit the words. "You just admitted you participated in a bloody execution."

"Did you [hear] me?" Reimer said, his voice rising. "They were finished when I got there."

"Not everyone," Sher said slowly. "There was one man that we know of who you finished off, one man. He had a family, Mr. Reimer, in all likelihood. He had people who loved him. He was a human being."

BACK IN WASHINGTON, Rosenbaum found Peter Black and Barry White and recounted the confession, the first of its kind in the history of the Office of Special Investigations. Rosenbaum described the scene at the ravine, a sea of people, dying or dead, and a single, desperate man, inviting a bullet to his head because that was all he could think to do, beg for death to come quickly.

"We are going to file this case," Rosenbaum told the historians. "And we are going to win."

PART THREE

POLAND AND THE UNITED STATES 1941–1951

In 1941, the city of Lublin became the headquarters of Operation Reinhard, the secret Nazi plan to exploit Polish Jews as forced laborers, secure their homes, factories, land, and possessions, and ultimately deport them to three killing centers fitted with gas chambers. The Jews in the Lublin ghetto were among the first to die. Of more than forty thousand Lublin Jews, fewer than two hundred survived the Holocaust. Here, Jewish boys pose in the ghetto. *Credit: AP Images*

The city of Lublin was a vibrant hub for Jewish life in prewar Poland until the Germans ordered tens of thousands of Jews into a freezing, crowded ghetto rife with disease, hunger, and a sign outside forbidding entry to members of the German military. In spring 1942, most of the ghetto's inhabitants were rounded up and sent to the gas chambers at the Belzec killing center. *Credit: United States Holocaust Memorial Museum*

Before the war, Lucyna Stryjewska and her brother, David, lived in an affluent Lublin neighborhood of stately apartment homes. Their father was a court interpreter, their mother a dentist. The family survived together for months until Lucyna's mother was deported to the Majdanek concentration camp and her father was shot in the Lublin ghetto. Lucyna escaped to Warsaw with David and her boyfriend, Feliks Wojcik, whom she married in the Warsaw ghetto. But her brother was caught and sent to a concentration camp in Germany. Lucyna never saw him again. *Courtesy of the Wojcik family*

To carry out Operation Reinhard, the SS needed manpower. In 1941, Odilo Globocnik, the SS leader of the Lublin District, set up a training camp for auxiliary police in the nearby village of Trawniki and began to recruit hundreds of captured Soviet soldiers. These so-called Trawniki men would do the dirtiest jobs under Operation Reinhard: liquidating Jewish ghettos and guarding the killing centers, concentration camps, and Jewish forced-labor camps in occupied Poland. The operation was of great personal interest to SS chief Heinrich Himmler, who visited the camp in 1942. *Credit: Staatsanwalt beim Landgericht Hamburg*

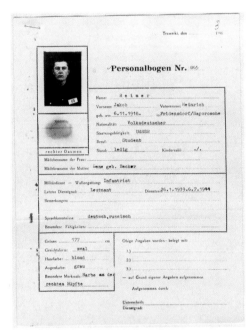

Jakob Reimer, Trawniki recruit 865, was born in 1918 in a Mennonite settlement in the Ukrainian countryside north of the Black Sea. In 1941, when his Red Army platoon was captured by German soldiers in Minsk, Belarus, he was taken to a POW camp. Soon he was recruited by the very men who had captured him and sent to the Trawniki training camp to serve the Third Reich. His personnel sheet, maintained by his supervisors at Trawniki, listed his deployments in the Jewish ghettos of Warsaw and Czestochowa. He also helped liquidate the Lublin ghetto. *Credit: US Department of Justice*

When Reimer arrived at Trawniki, he posed for an official photo and signed a service oath to the SS and police: "I herewith declare that I am obligating myself for service in the guard detachments of the Commissioner of the Reichsführer-SS and Chief of the German Police…." He went on to receive four promotions, vacations, service medals, and the promise of a future in Nazi utopia. *Credit: US Department of Justice*

About seven thousand Jews were killed by the Germans and their auxiliaries during the Warsaw ghetto uprising in 1943. Another seven thousand ghetto inhabitants were sent to the Treblinka killing center and gassed on arrival. The remaining forty-two thousand were deported to the Majdanek concentration camp or to forced-labor camps in Nazi-occupied Poland. The Jewish resistance inspired other uprisings in occupied Poland. *Credit: United States Holocaust Memorial Museum, courtesy of the National Archives and Records Administration, College Park, MD*

Three hundred and fifty Trawniki men, including Jakob Reimer, joined the SS and German police in Warsaw to suppress the ghetto uprising. At night, the men, armed with rifles, bayonets, and ammunition pouches, retreated to a bunker in a schoolhouse a half mile west of the ghetto. In this photo, Trawniki guards look through a doorway over the bodies of ghetto inhabitants killed in the fighting. *Credit: United States Holocaust Memorial Museum, courtesy of the National Archives and Records Administration, College Park, MD*

Relatively few Germans staffed the SS-run killing centers and forced-labor camps in occupied Poland. Most of the work was left to Trawniki men, who had been taught Nazi ideology and the inhumane treatment of Jewish prisoners. At the forced-labor camp in Belzec, in southeastern Poland, Jews were made to build fortifications and anti-tank ditches along the Bug River. A group of Trawniki guards, including one who played the mandolin, pose for a picture. *Credit: United States Holocaust Memorial Museum, courtesy of Instytut Pamieci Narodowej*

Feliks Wojcik and his wife, Lucyna, managed to survive the war together by hiding in Lublin and then on the Aryan side of Warsaw, but their families were lost. They spent four years in Vienna, where Feliks finished medical school, before emigrating to New York. *Courtesy of the Wojcik family*

The fledgling Office of Special Investigations brought one of its most infamous cases to court in 1982 after it was discovered that Valerian Trifa, the sixty-eight-year-old leader of the Romanian Orthodox Church in the United States, had helped provoke days of deadly riots against the Jews of Bucharest during the war. "Trifa's speeches, articles, and newspaper editorials," OSI historian Peter Black concluded, "had pounded home the themes of hatred towards Jews and foreigners." *Credit: Bettmann, Getty Images*

The case against Trawniki man and death-camp guard John Demjanjuk of Cleveland vexed the Office of Special Investigations for years until records behind the Iron Curtain were made available to Western investigators. Demjanjuk was sent back to Germany in

2009 and convicted as an accessory to the murder of more than twenty-eight thousand people at the Sobibor killing center. He died while his appeal was pending. *Credit: Johannes Simon, Getty Images*

Demjanjuk's Trawniki identification card. *Credit: US Department of Justice, Getty Images*

In 1987, émigré groups, joined by conservative journalist Pat Buchanan, publicly denounced the Office of Special Investigations for the pending deportation of a Long Island man who had been the commandant of a Nazi concentration camp in Soviet Estonia. Just before Karl Linnas was set to be deported to the Soviet Union, the groups convinced then US Attorney General Edwin Meese to strike an eleventh-hour agreement to send Linnas to Panama instead. Eli Rosenbaum, a former OSI lawyer who would go on to lead the unit, helped block the deal. Rosenbaum (left), shown here at the Panamanian embassy, was joined by Elizabeth Holtzman, who, as a US congresswoman, helped pass the legislation that created OSI. *Credit: Bettmann, Getty Images*

Buchanan (left) made one final pitch to keep Linnas out of the Soviet Union, squaring off on CNN's live nightly news show, *Crossfire*, with Eli Rosenbaum. Buchanan's push frustrated Rosenbaum. "In Panama," Rosenbaum said, "[Linnas] will spend the rest of his days living very comfortably under palm trees." Linnas was deported to his native Soviet Estonia; he died a few months later of heart, liver, and kidney failure. OSI faced pushback and criticism for years from émigré groups that wanted to see the unit shut down for good. *Credit: CNN*

OSI lawyer Michael Bernstein died in 1988 on his way home from Austria, where he had negotiated a deal with the Austrian government to take back native-born Nazi perpetrators found on US soil. Bernstein, a father of two, was on Pan Am flight 103, which went down in a ball of fire over Lockerbie, Scotland. OSI director Neal Sher publicly blamed the Austrian government for Bernstein's death, pointing out that the thirty-six-year-old lawyer would never have flown to Vienna if the Austrians had been willing to take back Nazi perpetrators. The lack of cooperation by Germany and Austria, over time, became the single greatest frustration faced by OSI. *Courtesy of Eli Rosenbaum, US Department of Justice*

In 1990, after four decades of Communist rule, authorities in Prague granted access to its archives to OSI historians Peter Black (far right), Elizabeth "Barry" White, Patrick Treanor, and Mike Mac-Queen (far left) for the first time since the war's end. There, Black and White discovered rosters from the Trawniki training camp that would help trigger a years-long investigation into the operation of the camp and the men who served there, including Jakob Reimer, Trawniki recruit 865. *Courtesy of Elizabeth B. White*

OSI prosecutor Ned Stutman was charged with overseeing the denaturalization cases against Jakob Reimer and John Demjanjuk. Stutman litigated thirteen cases at OSI and won twelve of them, including the cases against Reimer and Demjanjuk, before dying of cancer in 2005. *Courtesy of the Stutman family*

Jakob Reimer, seventy-nine, testified that he was a victim of the Nazi regime, not a perpetrator, during his denaturalization hearing in federal court in New York in 1998. The Office of Special Investigations argued that he had loyally served the SS, helping to liquidate three Jewish ghettos and participating in at least one mass shooting before returning to the Trawniki training camp. *Credit: Stan Honda/AFP/Getty Images*

Jakob Reimer's account of a mass shooting or shootings in a ravine in occupied Poland changed on the witness stand during his denaturalization hearing in New York. OSI attorney Ned Stutman pressed him for specifics. "You and your other Trawniki men fired the last volley, is that correct?" *Credit: Shirley Shepard*

Two eyewitnesses placed Jakob Reimer at the site of a mass shooting of Jewish prisoners in the Krepiec Forest near Lublin, Poland, in 1942. Today, a small memorial sits behind a chain-link fence. *Courtesy of Jeff Rohrlick*

OSI attorney Jonathan Drimmer (right), shown here with historian Peter Black, stepped in as lead prosecutor for the John Demjanjuk denaturalization hearing in Cleveland in 2001 after Ned Stutman fell ill. Drimmer spent hours learning about the operation at Trawniki from Stutman, Black, and OSI historians Todd Huebner and David Rich. *Courtesy of Eli Rosenbaum, US Department of Justice*

In February 2002, eighty-one-year-old Trawniki man John Demjanjuk was stripped of his US citizenship. A federal judge in Cleveland called the government's evidence "devastating." At the Office of Special Investigations, Eli Rosenbaum (right) and Peter Black react to the news. *Courtesy of Eli Rosenbaum, US Department of Justice*

When the Office of Special Investigations opened in 1979, most everyone believed that the Nazi-hunting unit would remain in operation for only a year or two. In 2004, OSI historian Barry White and director Eli Rosenbaum celebrated the unit's twenty-five-year anniversary. Over more than three decades, OSI investigated and prosecuted hundreds of Nazi perpetrators. *Courtesy of Elizabeth B. White*

Peter Black spent years investigating the operation at the Trawniki training camp and the men who once served there. In 2013, he spoke at an international workshop on Trawniki and visited the village for the first time. He has become known as the world's foremost expert on the camp. *Courtesy of Peter Black*

"In my life," Holocaust survivor Lucyna Wojcik once told a rabbi, "God taketh away and then God giveth." Lucyna's husband, Feliks, a doctor who cared for generations of families, died at age ninety-two. Lucyna died six months later, at age eighty-seven. They had two children and six grandchildren. *Courtesy of the Wojcik family*

CHAPTER THIRTEEN

HEALTH AND WELFARE

Lublin and Trawniki, Poland
1941–1942

The Germans had commandeered a middle-school gym in Lublin, and from inside the yellow building SS and police leader Odilo Globocnik was preparing to travel to Berlin to meet with one of Adolf Hitler's closest confidantes.

Years later, one historian would call Globocnik "the vilest individual in the vilest organization ever known," but in the heady days of October 1941, when the German army had conquered much of eastern Europe and was advancing toward Moscow, he was an intrepid thirty-seven-year-old from Vienna with slicked hair, a long face, and a fanatical devotion to the Nazi Party.

His hatred of the Jews wasn't grounded in religion. To men like Globocnik, Jews were an impure race, a threat to German health and welfare, and to talk about them was more of an epidemiological discussion than one about God or history or faith.

It wasn't in Globocnik's nature to wait for instructions, so he had crafted a plan to present to SS chief Heinrich Himmler in Berlin. So much was at stake, the gateway to the occupied east, beginning with the territory between the Vistula and Bug Rivers. Generations of Poles had traded salt, timber, grain, and stone along the rivers, which flowed over the plains of Poland. The region was a strategic stronghold for the Reich, the center of Europe, with lush farmland that Nazi leaders planned to turn over to ethnic German settlers living in Yugoslavia, Hungary, Romania, and the Soviet Union.

Already, Globocnik, working with the German security police, had ordered the killings of Jewish and Polish intelligentsia, lest they try to organize and resist. He had supervised the roundup of able-bodied Jews and Poles for construction projects along the roads and rivers, looted Jewish homes for jewelry and money, and started to build an extensive network of labor camps, prison camps, and ghettos.

The largest ghetto in Lublin proper was confined to the oldest part of the city. Lined with narrow, brick apartment houses, the ghetto was surrounded by police and bounded on the southernmost corner by an arched stone gate that for centuries had separated the Jewish quarter from Lublin's more affluent Christian neighborhoods. Inside the ghetto, typhus had claimed its first victims.

They were welcome deaths to Globocnik, who kept himself sufficiently removed from the suffering, living across town in a mansion with a nine-pin bowling alley and working in a leafy, hushed neighborhood of large homes and government offices that had once been occupied by the Lublin elite.

Soon he would leave for Berlin to discuss the most important mission yet: *Judenbereinigung.* Clearing out the Jews.

It was the opportunity Globocnik had been waiting for, a critical moment to show Himmler and the civilian occupation authorities in the Lublin District that he was not only an unflinching ideologue but a loyal and enterprising SS leader with a plan to address the enormous task at hand. Globocnik wanted full authority to manage the removal of the Jews throughout the Government General and beyond, including the yet-to-be-conquered Soviet Union.

To Globocnik, the upcoming meeting in Berlin was an opportunity to assume a leading position in shaping the future of the Reich.

He had been born in 1904 in the port city of Trieste, then a part of Austria-Hungary, on a narrow stretch of land along the Adriatic coast. His father was a postal official, his grandfather a professor, his great-grandfather a physician. Globocnik had found work servicing water-power plants in southern Austria, but his passion was for politics, and like other disgruntled young men in the Austrian Republic of the 1920s, he became involved in underground German nationalist organizations and, eventually, a virulent Nazi Party.

He had ferreted out intelligence information for the Reich and channeled Nazi money into Austria even after the Austrian chancellor vowed to subdue the Nazi agitators who had disrupted and divided the country. Hitler himself had ordered underground Nazi factions to tone down the talk and violence, at least until matters between Germany and Austria could be stabilized to Germany's advantage.

But Globocnik had soldiered on, focused and fearless, risking prison time to spread Nazi propaganda. When Austria was incorporated into Nazi Germany in 1938, Globocnik had been named *Gauleiter*, or party leader, in Vienna.

"I will not recoil," Globocnik had declared, "from radical interventions for the solution of Jewish questions."

But subordinates found his management skills weak—one visiting British journalist had called Globocnik a "great enthusiast without much leadership"—and the Nazi ideologue quickly fell from grace, accused of mishandling public and party finances. Demoted to the rank of corporal, he could have been jailed or executed, but in Globocnik, Himmler saw a fierce and passionate comrade.

In 1939, Himmler named Globocnik SS and police leader for the Lublin District, responsible for creating an SS power base in one of Germany's most critical positions in the east. Globocnik settled in Lublin and confiscated an estate home. He found the sight of a nearby, rundown area where some of Lublin's poorer Jews lived altogether unpleasant and in May 1940 quickly ordered the destruction of the houses.

By 1941, Himmler had decided to Germanize the region. Poles would be moved into Jewish homes and Ukrainians into Polish homes to make space for German colonists. That was the natural order, Globocnik believed, decreed by Hitler, the leader of the German race.

But what to do with the Jews? There were as many as 320,000 in the Lublin District, more than forty thousand in Lublin proper. Jews had lived in Lublin since at least the fourteenth century, as much a part of the fabric of the city as the non-Jewish Polish population.

Globocnik had found synagogues, schools, prayer houses, storefronts, Yiddish newspapers, and a five-story Talmudic building, the largest in the world, with thousands of books and a model of the ancient Temple Mount in the old city of Jerusalem.

He assembled a group of intellectuals to plan for long-term German rule. There had been half-hearted talk about shipping Jews to the island of Madagascar. Killing them, Globocnik thought, would be a far more effective way to neutralize the threat.

Globocnik dove into his life in Poland, setting up a casino and social events for his comrades and going out of his way to be kind to young women. But he paid scant attention to his appearance, to his romances, or even to his advancement in the Nazi Party.

The mission itself moved him, exercising absolute power over the lives of Jews, Poles, Ukrainians and planning the future of the Reich's eastern settlements. It was righteous work, building an Aryan world, and Globocnik saw himself as its most devoted champion and architect.

In July 1941, Himmler gave Globocnik the go-ahead to build a massive concentration camp on the outskirts of Lublin. More importantly, Globocnik had authority to plan for the ethnic makeup of the territories.

Globocnik knew that a euthanasia program had killed Germans with disabilities by pumping pure, chemically manufactured carbon monoxide into stationary killing centers. The SS had also used carbon monoxide to murder several thousand people in specially fitted mobile gas vans at a manor house on the outskirts of the Polish village of Chelmno.

Globocnik was interested. At the end of September 1941, he wrote to Himmler, outlining actions against the Jews "of a security policy nature" and arranged to have several officials from the Reich euthanasia program permanently transferred to the Lublin District.

But there was a problem. Globocnik had a staff of fewer than two hundred SS men. He needed an operation, preferably in Lublin and under his direct control, that could take the lead in the destruction of the region's Jews. Quietly, he started to recruit a small army of helpers to flesh out his plan.

In prisoner-of-war camps for captured Soviet soldiers, Globocnik's staff had found hundreds of candidates: German speakers, skilled workers, and men who looked reasonably healthy. They had been sent to the grounds of an abandoned sugar refinery southeast of Lublin in the village of Trawniki, set against rail lines that snaked across Poland in every direction. The first recruits had arrived at Trawniki in late summer.

By the time Globocnik left for his October 13 meeting with Himmler in Berlin, where Globocnik would present a plan to annihilate Poland's Jews, recruits were pouring into Trawniki.

"Gentlemen," Globocnik would say later, "if ever a generation will come after us which is so weak and soft-hearted that it doesn't understand our task, then indeed the whole of National Socialism has been in vain. To the contrary, in my opinion, one should bury bronze plates on which it is recorded that we have had the courage to carry out this great and so necessary work."

IF IT WEREN'T for a sugar plant and a railway station, there may never have been a thriving Polish settlement in Trawniki. Traders and craftsmen migrated to the area at the end of the nineteenth century, turning the sprawling countryside fed by the Wieprz River into a small village, with thatched-roof houses and farms that in the summer months grew bright-yellow canola flowers.

A hundred Jewish families from a nearby congregation had settled on land near the sugar mill, and even after the mill closed a few decades before the war, the modest village of Poles and Jews on the outskirts of the Lublin District maintained a tiny industrial core, linked to the rest of Poland through the rail lines.

An ideal place to train and deploy a makeshift army.

In late summer 1941, Jakob Reimer arrived at Trawniki in a convoy of seventy captured Soviet soldiers, altogether surprised that he was still alive. The Germans had overrun his platoon in Minsk, and Reimer had been taken to Stalag 307 in eastern Poland.

He was an ethnic German, captured as a Red Army officer with the 447th Soviet Infantry Regiment. If the Germans discovered his rank, Reimer knew there would be no mercy. Hitler had instructed the high command of German armed forces to summarily shoot officers and Communist officials at the time of capture, and word of the order had spread among Red Army soldiers.

Reimer had been sure to destroy his papers, but in Stalag 307 it had seemed only a matter of time before the Germans identified him, an artillery lieutenant who had commanded a platoon of Russian men.

But he had been recruited, not killed, a startling twist of fate, and now he stood in a barrack in the training camp Trawniki, posing for a service photo as a newly dubbed German police auxiliary. Black hair, gray eyes, the lines of his mouth drawn into something of a grimace.

Did he ever belong to the Communist Party? Reimer said no. Was he racially pure? Did he have Jewish ancestors? Reimer knew quite well that Germans routinely shot Jewish soldiers of the Red Army. No, he said again. He was given a declaration in German and Russian:

I declare that I am of Aryan descent, that there were no Jews among my forefathers, that I was neither a member of the Communist Party nor the Communist Youth Organization.

Reimer was fingerprinted and offered a hand-me-down Polish army uniform that had been dyed black. He was also given an identification number that would follow him throughout his career as a Trawniki man: 865. The number was etched onto a metal disc he would wear around his neck.

Reimer followed the others to a barn in the shadows of a watchtower, where they would remain in quarantine until it could be determined that no one had lice, typhus, tuberculosis, or influenza. At least he would get to rest.

Soon, under the command of SS captain Karl Streibel, who had been appointed by Odilo Globocnik, the recruits would undergo basic training: military drills and lessons on how to use rifles, machine guns, and grenades. They would be taught German marching songs and German commands—March forward! Fire at will!—and attend lectures about the superiority of the German race.

If they served with honor, they would be paid one half a reichsmark per day as Trawniki *Wachmann*. The rank was guard private, the lowest rank of all, but at least they would have bunks and full bellies. For that, Reimer was grateful.

He had been born twenty-two years earlier in a farm village in the Soviet Ukraine, the sixth of seven children. His father had come from Holland, but his mother's family was ethnic German, among the *Volksdeutsche* who had migrated to the Ukrainian countryside under the rule of Tsarina Catherine the Great in the eighteenth century. Drawn by the prospect of work in agriculture and of exemptions from German military service, thousands had settled in the region.

Reimer's village, along a half-mile stretch of dirt road, was filled with families from northwestern Germany that spoke a dialect known as *Plattdeutsch*. On a plot of land lined with rose bushes and fruit trees, Reimer's father had grown wheat and taken it to the windmills to grind into flour. The family attended a small church in the village, and Reimer went to school with other *Volksdeutsche* children.

In the 1930s, famine swept the countryside, and Soviet authorities confiscated the family farm, every pig and cow. Reimer's father was sent to a labor camp and his older brother to Siberia. The Soviets likely would have sent Reimer away, too, if his mother hadn't fled the village with her youngest children. Reimer had enrolled in a Russian school, a sure way to survive under the rule of Joseph Stalin. He would study to become a librarian.

But he had been drafted into the Soviet army at the start of the war, and because he was well schooled and able to speak German, Russian, and a bit of Polish, he was commissioned an officer and given his own platoon of Soviet soldiers.

In the barn at Trawniki, hundreds of miles from home and wearing the uniform of his enemy, Reimer studied the eclectic group of recruits: fellow ethnic Germans, Lithuanians, Latvians, Ukrainians, the occasional Pole. Most were young, like Reimer, still in their early twenties. They were filthy and starving, but the Germans had offered food and straw for bedding, a much-welcome gesture after imprisonment behind barbed wire.

Reimer would make do, just as he always had.

IN MARCH 1942, seven months after Reimer arrived at Trawniki, the entire battalion prepared to head north for a first major deployment in the nearby Jewish ghetto of Lublin. Reimer, once again in charge of his own platoon, rounded up his men.

The first months at the camp had passed quickly enough. Reimer and his new comrades trained until dinner and cleaned their weapons at night. They learned the German salute and the ideology of Adolf Hitler. Nearly a thousand recruits were training at Trawniki, divided into four companies. The camp would soon grow larger, with a dining hall, shops for boot making and sewing, and a stable for horses that Reimer would often visit.

As the camp expanded, recruits with German-language skills had been elevated to leadership positions and offered higher wages and better living quarters. Some received more base pay than junior Reich German Waffen-SS men.

By the time the recruits at Trawniki got word that they would soon leave for Lublin, Reimer bore the stripes of a platoon leader. Some of his men called him Sashka.

The instructions in Lublin were clear. The Jewish ghetto would be emptied, save for the four thousand Jews who had a *Sicherheitspolizei* stamp on their identity cards because their jobs were considered critical to the Reich. They would be moved to a smaller ghetto on nearby farmland. The rest would be deported east, never to return to Lublin.

German officials had issued an expanded shoot order: *Shoot in place. Kill anyone who tries to escape or refuses to go.*

The Trawniki men arrived after nightfall to a sleeping ghetto and fanned out along the perimeter, with rifles cocked and ready. They lighted the street lamps and summoned families outside.

Some of the Trawniki men panicked. Most were captured Soviet soldiers with weapons training, but the German and Polish rifles were new, the men hadn't all mastered Germans drills, and they had received orders through interpreters. Some of the German personnel were new, too.

Soon, gunshots rang out into the night air. Rifle butts cracked against bone. Whips snapped against flesh. Jews with work permits, told they would get to remain in Lublin, were mistakenly forced to the holding center for deportation.

Years later, witnesses would recount how the men of Trawniki had tossed children out the windows of apartment buildings and shot the elderly and sick on the spot, how afterward bodies lay on cobblestone streets.

The Lublin ghetto was one of the largest in Poland, packed with Jews from the city as well as thousands who had been sent on trains, famished and near frozen, from the surrounding towns of Piaski, Glusk, and Belzyce. Clearing the ghetto would take weeks.

Fifteen hundred people a day were ordered to the Great Synagogue for deportation and then taken two miles away to waiting boxcars. Children in winter coats and old men with straw baskets. Mothers. Fathers. Babies in tight bundles.

Every day, teams of three—a German police official, a Jewish policeman, and a Trawniki guard—went from building to building to round up those inside, leaving behind deserted rooms that still smelled of the families who had lived there, who had gone to bed the night before thinking that perhaps the four walls would keep them safe from the bedlam outside.

Some Germans and Trawniki men went to the Jewish hospital, where two hundred patients were loaded onto trucks, taken outside the city, and shot. Residents of a nursing home and children from a Jewish orphanage were also murdered.

Early one morning, a company of Trawniki men climbed onto SS trucks. The trucks headed north, winding fifteen kilometers along country roads to the entrance of the Krepiec Forest, hushed and still in the springtime. Another truck pulled up, this one filled with several dozen Jewish prisoners from what was left of the ghetto, a terrified mass of men, women, and children.

The prisoners were told to drop their belongings on the ground by the side of the highway. The Trawniki guards drove the prisoners deep into the woods, down a trail with twisted branches and crushed leaves, the air chilled by a dense canopy of trees that blocked out the daylight.

There was a clearing a kilometer away. Some of the Jewish men had been told they would be put to work in the woods, but they found only a large, jagged hole in the ground. Women started to wail as the Trawniki men used their rifle butts to prod the prisoners closer to the pit. Gunfire erupted. In seconds, the bodies were motionless, a mass of tangled limbs.

More transports showed up, each truck filled with fifty people. The shootings lasted well into the night, and when it was over the forest floor was covered with blood.

THE JEWS OF LUBLIN were taken to Belzec in southeastern Poland, where gas chambers were built only a few hundred feet from the train platforms. It was a convenient location for the SS because Belzec was linked by rail to Lublin, Krakow, Lwow, and other cities in southern and southeastern Poland, many with large Jewish populations.

Belzec was built solely for death. For weeks, train cars filled with Jewish families eased into the railway station. When the train doors were opened, prisoners had no time to think or resist. Desperate and disoriented, they were made to turn over their valuables, undress, and run through a narrow passageway known as the "tube" into double-walled gas chambers insulated with dirt.

When it was done, dentists hammered out gold fillings and crowns from the mouths of the dead before the bodies were turned over for burning.

In May 1942, a second killing center opened, this one in a swampy pine forest at the edge of the village of Sobibor, about an hour and a half east of Lublin. Sobibor had three gas chambers, each with a capacity for two hundred people, built with a small opening for hand-pushed wagons that were used to move bodies to mass graves.

A third killing center opened in July in a forest northeast of Warsaw, with two rows of barbed-wire fencing stuffed with pine tree branches between them to hide what was happening inside. On the train platform at Treblinka, the SS put up a wooden clock, fake ticket window, and fake rail-terminal signs to fool prisoners into thinking the facility was a transit camp for deportation east.

It was the assembly-line killing that Globocnik had imagined. Only a few dozen SS personnel managed each killing center. Trawniki men did the rest, unloading the train cars long into the night, and shooting, beating, and screaming as thousands of people stumbled toward their deaths.

Some guards used valuables looted from the prisoners to buy schnapps, chicken, sausage, and sexual services from Polish women. Others deserted the unit.

But Globocnik and Karl Streibel, the Trawniki commander, had built a mostly reliable force of zealous executioners, some far more violent than their German supervisors. It was exactly the manpower the SS needed, brute force on the front lines of the most aggressive mass-murder operation in the war.

In July 1942, Heinrich Himmler toured the Trawniki training camp, shaking hands with the recruits. Their work, he recognized, was invaluable. And as the months went on, the men of Trawniki would be needed more than ever.

CHAPTER FOURTEEN

COURAGE AND DEVOTION

Warsaw and Trawniki, Poland
1943

On April 19, 1943, in the days between winter's end and the promise of summer, Jakob Reimer arrived in Warsaw.

The largest ghetto in German-occupied Poland had once confined more than four hundred thousand people, squeezed into barely three square kilometers of space. By the time Reimer showed up, during the Jewish holiday of Passover, the SS and police had killed or deported to Treblinka most of the ghetto's residents. About sixty thousand Jews were left, and there were whispers about an uprising.

In 1940, when the German Department of Hygiene ordered the establishment of the *Jüdischer Wohnbezirk in Warschau* behind ten-foot walls, Jewish leaders had organized secret libraries, prayer houses, recreational facilities, concerts. Children attended schools disguised as medical centers and soup kitchens. But the ghetto was slowly starved, hundreds of thousands of people surviving on miserable scraps of bread, flour, turnips, and rotten potatoes, rations that totaled a mere 175 calories a day.

Underground workshops manufactured goods that children smuggled outside the walls through tunnels and sewers, but the weak died from hunger or from diseases that spread quickly in rooms crammed with too many bodies. On Grzybowska Street in

the southern end of the ghetto, the Jewish Council had set up or-
phanages and agencies for the destitute, the scavengers, the beggars,
and the gaunt, mute children who squatted in the shadows of alleyways and public squares, puny bundles of rags and filth. Still, the
death toll climbed.

And then, in the summer of 1942, SS and German police forces,
reinforced by a battalion of Trawniki men, had rounded up most
of the ghetto's inhabitants. Some were shot in their homes or on
the streets. Tens of thousands were forced onto suffocating train cars
bound for the gas chambers of Treblinka.

Rumors spread about death camps, a place where Jews were
turned into smoke and ashes. Those who remained in the ghetto
had lost everything, bloodlines that spanned centuries. Soon, amid
a desolate group of orphans and mourners, talk began of armed resistance. Leaflets circulated in the streets.

> Jews! Citizens of the Warsaw ghetto, be alert! Do not believe a
> single word, a single pretext of the SS criminals. Mortal danger
> awaits.... Let us defend our honor with courage and dignity!
> Let liberty live!

When the SS and German police entered the ghetto for an early-
morning round of deportations in January 1943, only a small group
of people appeared at the assembly point with their identity papers. Jewish insurgents ambushed unsuspecting German troops with
Molotov cocktails and handguns smuggled into the ghetto with help
from the Polish Underground. One thousand Jews were shot in the
main square in retaliation for the fighting, but the deportations were
temporarily called off.

WHEN REIMER ARRIVED in Warsaw in April 1943, a full-fledged uprising had begun. After his work in the Lublin ghetto, Reimer had

been deployed to the Polish city of Czestochowa, an industrial and religious center on the Warta River northwest of Krakow.

In 1942, on Yom Kippur, the Jewish holiday of atonement, German police, reinforced by Trawniki men, began ordering the city's forty thousand Jews to assemble on the streets with their hand luggage. The elderly and frail were shot on the spot. The rest, made to remove their shoes to deter the possibility of escape, were forced onto fifty-eight train cars bound for Treblinka.

It was a second successful mission for Reimer, who had positioned guards in the ghetto and coordinated with the Germans and local authorities. He was promoted to *Zugwachmann,* a guard staff sergeant.

Now in Warsaw, Reimer reported to the German security police just inside the ghetto. Three hundred and fifty Trawniki men were already there, ready to support the operation.

Crushing the Jewish resistance was a matter of the utmost importance to the Reich, and Heinrich Himmler had chosen a particularly tenacious police official for the job. SS brigadier general Jürgen Stroop, the opportunistic son of a German police chief, had decided long before the war that Jews were cowards by nature and that Hitler had been placed on earth to purify all of Europe.

The Germans had no idea how many resistance fighters were prepared for battle or what kinds of weapons they had managed to sneak inside the ghetto. Stroop had brought in combat engineers, demolition experts, a squad of flamethrower specialists, the German air force, tanks, armored carriers, machine guns, and explosives.

On Stroop's order, his men pushed through the gates and fanned out in every direction. In an instant, the sound of machine-gun fire filled the air. Stroop expected to round up thousands of people, pack the train cars one after another, but the apartments in the ghetto were empty, prayer books still open, kitchen tables set as if awaiting dinner guests.

Later, the Germans would learn that Jews who still had means and access to the outside world had gathered in kitchens to celebrate Passover with smuggled wine and matzo, unleavened bread that for generations had symbolized the Israelites' hasty exodus from Egypt. When lookouts on rooftops warned of the advancing assault, the inhabitants of the ghetto had fled to a labyrinth of dugouts, bunkers, cellars, and passageways dug deep beneath the earth, some equipped with cots and food supplies meant to last months.

Stroop's men moved north to Moranowski Square, which, in prewar Poland, had been a picturesque gathering spot with trees and trolley cars. The inhabitants of the ghetto, with some support from Polish resistance fighters, attacked with force, lobbing hand grenades and firing from carbine rifles and a smuggled machine gun.

Shooters took aim from sniper holes. Several dozen fighters mounted a German truck and drove off. Jewish women fired pistols with both hands and tossed grenades that they had concealed in their undergarments. Later, on the roof of a building in the square, someone hoisted a Polish flag and a Star of David.

It was the start of a fierce, bloody operation, and at nightfall Reimer and the men of Trawniki, armed with rifles, bayonets, and ammunition pouches, retreated to a bunker in a schoolhouse a half mile west of the ghetto.

On April 23, after four days of fighting, Stroop issued a new order. Jews were hiding in underground bunkers and passageways, a bedeviling development. Some had blown up the valves of the city's sewer system just before the Germans tried to have it dammed up and filled with water to drown those hiding inside.

Stroop decided to burn the ghetto, street by street. "Utter ruthlessness," he declared. He called in a group of sappers, demolition experts trained in heavy explosives. Soon flames charred apartment buildings, warehouses, stores, and workshops. The Trawniki men watched acrid plumes of smoke darken the sky above Warsaw. On streets filled with soot, glass, and the bricks of fallen buildings, Jews jumped out of windows and off roofs to avoid the flames.

German forces threw tear-gas bombs into sewers and poison gas into dugouts and bunkers. Those still in hiding scrambled out into the light, hands on their heads, dirt on their faces. A first glimpse of black leather boots. A final surrender into the eye of a cocked machine gun. Trawniki men stood over the bodies of the dead.

The Warsaw ghetto uprising ended three weeks later, with all but eight buildings leveled, more than seven thousand Jews killed, seven thousand deported to the gas chambers of Treblinka, and forty-two thousand sent to the concentration camp at Majdanek or to the forced-labor camps at Trawniki and Poniatowa.

Stroop praised his patchwork army for "pluck, courage and devotion," including the men of Trawniki, who had suffered a dozen casualties in the gunfire. "We will never forget them," Stroop would say.

A lavish celebration followed at the Great Synagogue of Warsaw, which had been designed by Polish architect Leandro Marconi in the 1870s and was one of the largest in the world.

"Heil Hitler!" Stroop shouted as he pushed a lever and blew the building to pieces.

He would send a detailed accounting of the ghetto operation to Himmler, bound in leather and bearing a triumphant title:

The Jewish residential quarter in Warsaw is no more.

JAKOB REIMER NEEDED a break, and in July 1943, his commanders gave him two weeks off with pay. Some Reich Germans had invited ethnic German Trawniki men like Reimer to their homes during holidays or leave. But Reimer opted to find his sister in the Ukrainian countryside.

He returned to Trawniki later that summer and was transferred into camp administration as a bookkeeper.

Next to the training camp, beyond a wall and a fence, thousands of Jewish prisoners were at work in a forced-labor camp. Some had come from the surrounding countryside, but most were newly arrived from the Warsaw ghetto.

Jewish women sorted, washed, and mended clothing from the dead, delivered in heaping piles from the killing centers and stored in the sugar refinery in the center of Trawniki. Other prisoners made hairbrushes or winter uniforms for the German army in two factories that Odilo Globocnik had relocated from Warsaw to Trawniki.

In the early years of the war, fewer than two thousand Jewish prisoners had been confined to the forced-labor camp. By the fall of 1943, the camp population swelled to as many as six thousand.

In November, a special SS and police unit arrived in Trawniki and instructed Reimer and his comrades to stay inside the barracks. Though Reimer didn't know it, Heinrich Himmler had ordered the death of every Jewish prisoner at the labor camp, including women and children. He had also called for the killing of Jews at the nearby Majdanek concentration camp and the Poniatowa forced-labor camp—some forty-three thousand people in total.

Operation Harvest Festival would be carried out as a single, sudden strike.

Himmler wanted it done quickly. At the Sobibor killing center in 1942, prisoners had staged a daring uprising. Led by the son of a rabbi and a captured Soviet soldier, they killed nearly a dozen German staff and Trawniki guards with makeshift axes and knives, set fire to the camp, and bolted across a minefield fifty feet wide. About three hundred people had escaped to the woods, though many were later captured and shot.

The ghetto uprising in Warsaw, the longest and largest of the war, had inspired prisoner revolts at Treblinka and in the Jewish ghetto in Bialystok, a city in eastern Poland.

Himmler was furious. There could be no more trouble, not with the Red Army bearing down on German-occupied territories in the east.

At dawn at Trawniki, the SS and a particularly violent German reserve police battalion surrounded the perimeter of the forced-labor camp and marched the prisoners to a point just outside that was marked by zigzag trenches cut into the fields, six feet deep and four feet wide. Under orders from the SS and police, they were forced to undress at gunpoint near the edges of the pits.

From inside his barrack, Reimer peered out the window. The SS played music over speakers, but he could hear the machine guns and the groans and cries of the prisoners just before they were gunned down by a firing squad. Desperate mothers clutched their children. Bodies big and small tumbled into the trenches. A struggle. A young Jewish man was trying to get away. Gunfire. The man crumpled to the ground, dead.

The shootings lasted long into the evening, and when it was done Trawniki men searched the grounds of the camp for anyone still in hiding. Soon, a small detachment of Jewish laborers was brought in for clean up. The Jewish men were told to use a piece of railway track to carry bodies out of the trenches and then burn them in batches. The women, many of whom had been found hiding in the camp during the massacre, were permitted to live to sort and mend the clothing of the dead.

It took three weeks to burn six thousand bodies. When the work was done, Trawniki men helped shoot the last of the Jewish laborers.

ON THE SAME day as the massacre at Trawniki, eighteen thousand Jewish prisoners at the nearby Majdanek concentration camp were ordered to roll call, shot behind field number five, and burned in trenches. Most had been among the Jews who had survived the ghetto uprising in Warsaw.

No Trawniki men were at Majdanek at the time, but at the Poniatowa labor camp, just west of Lublin, they performed perimeter duty as fifteen thousand people were forced naked into trenches and shot over the bodies of the freshly killed. As gunfire erupted, some Jewish prisoners had refused to come out of one of the barracks, and the Germans set fire to the building, picking off the prisoners as the flames drove them outside.

By then, the Nazi plan for occupied Poland was complete. More than 1.7 million Jews had been murdered, and currency, gold, silver, watches, jewelry, and property collected from the dead.

To hide traces of the crime, the killing centers were dismantled, buried bodies exhumed and burned, fields plowed over. At Belzec, Trawniki men planted small firs and wild lupines. At Treblinka, a manor house went up, surrounded by trees and fields. Sobibor was the last to close. It was bulldozed in the spring of 1944, and over the bone fragments and ashes of the dead, the Germans planted rows of pine trees.

Six weeks before the November massacre, Himmler had transferred Odilo Globocnik back to his birthplace, Trieste, where, as higher SS and police leader for northeastern Italy and German-occupied Slovenia, he set in motion a new operation to deport Italian Jews to Auschwitz.

In Trawniki, Reimer started making plans for a new life after the war, when he would settle in Nazi Germany. In 1944, he applied for German citizenship and was recommended for immediate naturalization.

"Applicant is 100 percent German descent and is totally immersed in Germanness," the examiner wrote. "He makes a very good impression."

CHAPTER FIFTEEN

AMCHU?

Southeastern Poland
1944–1945

The ride out of Warsaw was killing him, Feliks Wojcik thought, as he struggled for air on a train car meandering to who knows where—a labor camp, a killing center, an execution site. One hundred people were sealed in tight, with no food or water, no place to sit, barely enough room to stand. The darkness was impenetrable, the kind behind closed eyes.

The upper window of the car was covered with barbed wire. Feliks, bleeding on the head, shaking from fever, itching with lice, nevertheless climbed onto the shoulders of others for a glimpse of the passing world. He could see two guards, one at the beginning of the train and one at the end, and miles and miles of wounded countryside, bombed-out train depots, and crumbling stone farmhouses.

The train shuddered to a stop before a stretch of destroyed track. Feliks could see no one in the fields outside, and he wondered whether the whole country was hiding or dead. For two days he stood there, pressed against the bodies of strangers, certain that he would surely stop breathing before he ever again stepped into daylight. But the train rambled on to one last stop. North? South? Feliks wasn't sure.

Barely a week had passed since a German bomb had torn

through the building where Feliks had been hiding in a rented apartment with Lucyna, his wife of two years, on the Aryan side of occupied Warsaw. Lucyna had been able to live in public because she had false papers that identified her as Lucyna Stryjewska, a single Catholic woman with blond hair and blue eyes. Others like her were scattered about Warsaw, Jews who had paid sympathetic priests for the birth certificates of dead parishioners.

While Feliks and Lucyna's younger brother, David, had crouched inside the walls of the apartment building, Lucyna had boarded city buses with Polish women. She had learned Catholic hymns. She had attended Sunday mass, sitting side by side with pious, pleasant congregants who she was certain would have turned her in to the Gestapo for the single sack of sugar that the Germans were offering as a reward for captured Jews.

Some of Lucyna's neighbors had taken to the streets to celebrate when German forces, led by a famous commander named Jürgen Stroop, burned the Jewish ghetto to the ground. "The Jews are frying, and all the cockroaches together with them," one had declared as a flash of fire spread across the night sky.

Lucyna could barely nod, thinking about the people she had left behind when the Polish Underground had helped her escape the ghetto with Feliks and David shortly before the uprising.

On the Aryan side of Warsaw, Lucyna's biggest challenge was finding food. She had three mouths to feed but needed to appear as if she were buying for only one. She shopped at different markets, bringing home potato flour and beans at different times of day with money that Feliks had scraped together by selling a suitcase of old clothing from Lublin. At night, when it was time for dinner, Feliks and David crept from their hiding place behind the toilet, where Feliks had fashioned a double wall with a hole behind it, barely large enough for sitting.

Lucyna had worried most about her brother, who wore the shell-shocked gaze of an orphan. They had lost their father in the last days of the Lublin ghetto, and their mother and Feliks's parents and sister had been deported to the concentration camp Majdanek.

Perhaps they had been put to work, Lucyna and Feliks thought. Perhaps they had been sent farther east, to a new Jewish settlement. Lucyna and Feliks could only hope, pray to God in the middle of the night when the world was still and there was space to imagine the tight, safe embrace of a parent, the soft whispers in Yiddish.

Mishpocheh, mishpocheh. Family.

If only David had been able to live outside the walls, where there was fresh air and light, but he had been circumcised like all the other Jewish boys, and German soldiers had been known to make suspected Jews drop their pants for inspection. Lucyna and Feliks decided it was safest to keep David hidden away.

They had been living on the Aryan side of Warsaw for several months when Lucyna and Feliks heard that the Germans, in exchange for German POWs, were allowing Jews to buy travel documents and leave occupied Poland. It was an unexpected opportunity, a chance to escape to neutral countries, mostly in South America, and Lucyna had made her way to the gathering point at 29 Dluga Street. Several hundred Jews who had abandoned their hiding places were already camped out at the Hotel Polski, buying passports with Polish zlotys or gold.

The transports had no room left for adults, but the Germans were promising to take Jewish children to Switzerland. Lucyna thought of her brother, whose plump face had grown gaunt. She could scarcely imagine sending him alone, a boy of eleven with no family, no money. But at least he would be safe there, no longer hungry, free from the darkness and the walls. It seemed an impossible choice.

"Go," Lucyna's father had said when he pushed Lucyna, David, and Feliks through the barbed wires of the nearly empty Lublin ghetto, a lifetime ago. "Go and see what you can do for yourself."

Of course, David had to go. Lucyna found a suitcase and scrounged together some money to buy her brother new trousers and shoes. At the hotel on the morning that the transport was scheduled to leave for Switzerland, she clutched his small hand.

"I'm going to write to you," David promised. Lucyna watched his brown head, bobbing among the others, disappear inside a truck crowded with children.

It didn't take long for Lucyna and Feliks to get word from the Polish Underground. The children had been taken to a concentration camp in Hanover, Germany. The Germans had set a trap to entice Jews out of hiding in Warsaw, and now the last of Lucyna's family was gone.

OF ALL THE people that Lucyna and Feliks had met on the Aryan side of Warsaw, it was a janitor at their apartment house who grew suspicious. He had come up from behind Lucyna in the market, flanked by two Polish police officers.

"We heard that you are hiding Jews."

Lucyna protested, but the officers demanded to search the apartment. She fought panic, thinking about Feliks, in the dark behind the double wall. He had instructed her to knock loudly on the apartment door if there was ever any trouble, but a conspicuous knock would most certainly make matters worse.

The janitor and the police officers followed Lucyna back to the apartment. "We know that there are Jews here," the janitor insisted.

"There's nobody here."

"Open the door."

Lucyna thought quickly. "I lost my key."

She knocked twice instead, hoping to warn Feliks. One of the police officers called a locksmith, who showed up moments later and pried open the door. The threadbare apartment was utterly still.

"We're coming back at four o'clock," one of the officers promised.

He took Lucyna's identification papers and slammed the door behind him. Lucyna stumbled to the sliding door in the bathroom to call for Feliks. Their entire existence depended on Lucyna's false identity, and now her papers were gone.

I am nothing, Lucyna thought. *I am dead.*

The police officers never returned. On a streetcar a few days later, Lucyna's purse was stolen with what little money she had left. She had been on her way to see a Jewish friend from Lublin, who was also living on the Aryan side of Warsaw with false papers. Lucyna was sobbing by the time she arrived at her friend's apartment.

"My God. What's the matter with you?"

Lucyna turned from her friend to the unfamiliar Polish man in his forties who had asked the question. "You're so young," he said. "You can't be so desperate."

"Right now, I have no means of survival." Lucyna told the story about the janitor, the locksmith, the stolen purse.

"You know what?" the man said. "You look very well. You look like an Aryan. Why don't you want to work a little?"

"Work?" Lucyna replied. "What can I do?"

"I can get a job for you. I can help you out."

Sometime later, Lucyna would learn that Feliks Cywiński was a career officer in the Polish air force who considered helping his neighbors a Socialist imperative and a moral obligation. He had hidden Jewish families in apartments around Warsaw and sold his own house to rent properties for additional space.

He advanced Lucyna money, took her to get new papers and introduced her to other men and women in hiding. They passed the time by making hairnets, cutting elastic threads from abandoned inner tubes and attaching them to bits of white fabric that had been dyed bright colors. The nets were a great commodity among Polish women, Cywiński explained, because so many factories were closed and fashion accessories hard to come by. Lucyna could sell them in street markets.

Feliks didn't much like the idea of Lucyna traveling alone to outdoor markets, but they needed money for food and a new apartment since their old one had been compromised. From his hiding place inside the walls of their flat, Feliks started making hairbands for Lucyna to sell.

Under the cover of night, Polish friends helped Lucyna and Feliks move to a second rented apartment. It was smaller than the first, and the only place for Feliks to hide was in a wood-burning stove in the center of the front room. Using a fork and knife, he ripped out the guts of the stove so that he could step inside and squat over a pipe that stretched across the center.

Feliks had hoped he would never need the hiding place, but one afternoon the landlady stopped by with her cousin, who was drunk and insisting that he stay the night. Feliks huddled in the stove until the next morning, sucking in smoke and fumes, and by the time Lucyna let him out, he was nearly unconscious.

BY THE SUMMER of 1944 the Red Army was creeping closer to Warsaw. Soviet soldiers were just on the other side of the Vistula River, liberating towns and villages. Lucyna and Feliks watched Jewish men swim across the river, clinging to the cable wires that dangled beneath bridges and dodging gunfire from the Germans. Freedom was only seven or eight kilometers away, but it could have been hundreds, thousands.

One day, Feliks Cywiński showed up with a warning. "Things are going to be tough," he told Lucyna. "I want you to prepare food. Money is going to be no good."

The Poles were planning massive attacks against the Germans to liberate Warsaw. Lucyna thanked him, certain that she would have been dead without his help. She took all the money she had earned selling hairbands and bought bread and eleven gold wedding bands, a small, portable treasure that she could trade in a pinch.

When German bombs started falling, Lucyna and Feliks raced to the cellar with their Polish neighbors. Other Jews in hiding crept out from behind the walls, and in that moment—bombs shrieking, buildings burning—Jews and non-Jews huddled side by side, a trembling, unified group of Poles.

The walls shook and groaned, the stairwell collapsed, and in an instant Lucyna was buried beneath bricks and rubble. Feliks couldn't get to her, not with his hands. He looked around the cellar, desperate. With the tips of his fingers, he freed two wooden planks from under the window frames and used them to clear away the debris. He hauled Lucyna out by her leg.

Though he was bleeding from the head and had shrapnel lodged in his abdomen, he hoisted Lucyna onto his back and carried her to a local hospital. At the first-aid station, Feliks flagged down a doctor.

He sucked in his breath when he saw the familiar face from the early days of the war. Feliks nodded discreetly at his friend, one of the Jewish boys from medical school in Lwow who had survived the firing squad alongside Feliks.

"We don't know each other," the young doctor whispered and quickly explained that he had finished medical school with help from the Polish Underground.

He tended to Lucyna, bandaging her face and upper body, and squeezed Feliks's hand. "Best of luck," he said and disappeared down the hall.

The Germans were evacuating Warsaw, and Feliks and Lucyna were directed to a transit camp a few kilometers away. No one questioned their identities, and Feliks began to suspect that all of Warsaw believed there were no Jews left in Poland. In line at the entrance of the camp, a doctor approached Feliks.

"I'm a medical student," Feliks said.

"Why don't you go to the right?"

"Why should we go to the right?" Feliks replied carefully.

"Go to the right. Don't ask any questions. Go to the barrack named C."

Feliks hesitated. From the grim days in the ghettos, Feliks knew that the sick and disabled always died first, garbage to be destroyed. But the other alternative was just as terrifying. Healthy men from Warsaw were being sent to work in Germany, where Feliks would surely be discovered as a Jew. An impossible choice. What would be waiting in barrack C?

The building, it turned out, held hundreds of hacking, bleeding, moaning people, a makeshift infirmary for the sick and injured.

"What's going on here?" Lucyna asked.

No one seemed to know. The barrack was filthy, and Feliks curled up on a straw mat ridden with lice, sweating and shaking from fever. The next morning, they were pushed onto a railcar with no talk of a destination.

As the hours passed on the journey, Feliks had nearly passed out, squeezed next to Lucyna in the darkness of the train. He expected to find Germans at the end of the line, but when the railcar finally stopped and he stumbled outside, gulping deep breaths of chilly air, he found only peasants. The train was stopped at a depot on the outskirts of Krakow, and the local villagers had come to offer their homes to the displaced residents of Warsaw.

In icy rain, the local mayor stepped forward. He loaded Feliks and Lucyna onto a horse-drawn carriage and dropped them in front of a nearby farmhouse. Feliks and Lucyna walked to the door and knocked lightly.

A man peered outside, frowning. "I am not taking freeloaders in my house."

"As soon as we feel better, we'll work for you," Feliks offered. "We'll work for you on your farm."

"I am not going to take nobody," the man said and shut the door.

Feliks had no idea where to go and so he stood there with Lucyna on the farmer's front porch. They had no coats, no boots. He hugged Lucyna tight to try to keep warm. The night passed ever so slowly. Eyes open, eyes closed, counting raindrops.

WHEN THE MAYOR came back the next morning, he motioned to another farmhouse nearby. Feliks was burning up with fever and unsure if he had the strength to walk. He barely noticed the couple that opened the door, fed him chicken soup, and settled him into their bed. Blessed sleep.

Had an hour passed? A day? A light flashed in his eyes. Feliks thought it might be the Gestapo, but the man by his bedside whispered, "I'm from the Underground, the Home Army in this area."

Feliks spoke, but his words sounded garbled. The man mentioned the farmer who had turned Feliks and Lucyna away the night before. "We are sorry that we couldn't come to help."

Feliks drifted off. He sweated and shivered, mumbled incoherent thoughts. Another hour? Another day? He was being dragged through snow and hoisted onto the back of a wagon. Whispers about a Polish doctor. Wait, Feliks wanted to shout. He couldn't be examined. He would be found out a Jew.

The doctor lived a dozen kilometers away, and the farmer that Feliks and Lucyna were staying with helped Feliks to an office on the second floor of a stone house. The examination was thankfully brief, sympathetic talk of hepatitis and jaundice, and Feliks fell into a deep sleep on the ride back to the village.

Finally, several days later, his head cleared. He found Lucyna peeling potatoes and tending to chickens. Feliks decided to wander the modest village, spread across the rolling fields of southern Poland.

It was a poor community with no running water, but there was church every Sunday and a grand feast with ham at Christmas. The farmers seemed generous and kind, but Feliks soon heard stories about local men who butchered Jews found hiding in the woods.

Feliks and Lucyna would go to church and celebrate Christmas.

The farmers made Lucyna a coat from rabbit fur and offered the couple a sack to sleep on, which Feliks positioned between four chairs. He was grateful for the help and one morning went to see the mayor to inquire about teaching local children math and geography. Schools had been closed since the start of the war, and Feliks would have to teach in secret.

The mayor sent Feliks to a nearby village to collect Polish primers, crayons, pencils, erasers, arithmetic books. Feliks stationed one of the schoolboys on the roof of the school to keep watch for German soldiers, who would surely burn the building to the ground if they discovered a Polish school.

The days passed quickly. In the final months of 1944, the Red Army and Polish forces were moving quickly across Poland. Just after Christmas, Feliks heard movement in the woods, a rumbling at first, then blasts of artillery, coming closer to the village. The magnificent sounds of war. He crawled through the forest on all fours and spotted Soviet tanks a hundred feet away, preparing to liberate the region.

The next morning, Soviet soldiers marched into the village.

"Who are you?" a Soviet commander asked Feliks.

"I am the teacher here," he answered in Russian. And then he lowered his voice so the villagers couldn't hear and said for the first time in months, "I am also a Jew."

The commander frowned. "You're lying. There are no Jews here. You must be a spy. All the Jews were killed."

"That's not true," Feliks protested. "I escaped with my wife. I am telling you, I'm Jewish."

The commander summoned a young Russian soldier. "Take a load of this. This guy is telling me he's a Jew. You're Jewish. You find out."

The soldier turned to Feliks and explained that he had worked as a plumber in Leningrad before the war. "Are you a Jew?" he asked, frowning.

Feliks nodded.

The soldier started speaking Yiddish. Feliks struggled to make sense of the words. His family had always spoken Polish at home in Lublin.

"If you're Jewish, speak Yiddish," the soldier demanded.

"Believe me, I am a Jew, but I don't speak Yiddish."

"Then you must be a spy."

When Feliks was a boy, his father had hired a rabbi to teach Feliks how to recite Jewish prayers. They sat around the kitchen table, and when the rabbi nodded off, Feliks quickly flipped to the last page of his prayer book to prove that he had finished his readings.

From someplace in the depths of his soul, bone tired after five years on the run, Feliks remembered.

"*Sh'ma Yisrael, Adonai Eloheinu, Adonai Echad.*"

The most important prayer in Judaism, recited morning and night. Hear, O Israel, Adonai is our God, Adonai is One.

Feliks started to cry as he said it, and then the Soviet soldier kissed his cheek and pulled him into a long embrace.

"You," the young soldier whispered, "really are a Jew."

THE PEASANTS MADE Lucyna boots out of rabbit fur for the long journey back to Lublin, about eighty kilometers through the dense winter snow. The mayor begged them to stay, to make a new life in the village. Feliks secretly suspected that the mayor knew that he and Lucyna were Jews, and Feliks was grateful that he had kept their secret. But it was time for Lucyna and Feliks to go home.

Lublin had been liberated early, in July 1944, and with it the Majdanek concentration camp, where Feliks's family and Lucyna's mother had been sent. More than forty thousand Jews had lived in Lublin before the war. Surely some had survived. On foot, Feliks and Lucyna trekked through village after village, shivering in the cold for

ten days. On the outskirts of Lublin, an old man in a red hat stared
as they passed by.

"*Amchu?*" Feliks called gently in Hebrew. You are one of us?

The old man hesitated.

"Don't be afraid," Feliks said.

"I have no one left," the man answered and then offered Feliks
and Lucyna a scrap of bread.

Other Jews were coming out of hiding, heads down, frightened.
Lucyna and Feliks could spot them instantly. "Like dog to dog,"
Lucyna would say later.

What does home look like in an upside-down world, on streets
filled with ghosts and memories, in forests filled with corpses? To
Lucyna and Feliks, Lublin looked like death, every stone covered in
blood, every neighbor a stranger.

There was a Jewish registry in the town square, established by a
committee of Polish Jews to connect survivors from across Europe.
Feliks and Lucyna searched the list for the names of family members, more than one hundred between them. But they found no
parents, no cousins, no younger brother who should have been safe
in Switzerland. They returned every day, praying for a familiar
name, walking away with red, wet faces.

Without graves to tend to, Lucyna and Feliks had no way to connect to the family they had lost.

Feliks soon learned that two uncles had survived. One was living
in Yugoslavia, but the other had returned to Lublin. He gave Feliks
some gold coins to sell on the black market to pay for food and a
place to stay.

Feliks and Lucyna wanted to leave Lublin, but they needed more
money. Though the furs, radios, silver, and jewelry that Feliks's family had stashed with neighbors at the start of the war were gone, he
was the sole owner of his family's apartment house. He contacted a
lawyer, and because the building was not subject to state control and

Feliks could prove ownership rights, he was able to sell the property to a local butcher for the equivalent of $1,000.

Feliks bought Lucyna a dress, a hat, a gold watch, and, finally, a proper wedding ring. He bought himself some clothes. He had $400 left.

"We cannot bring back what we lost," he told his nineteen-year-old wife, who couldn't bear to go near her own family's home. "We can only live with the memories."

Feliks had never thought much about fate, but now he found himself in postwar Lublin, no smarter than the millions who had perished but somehow still alive, in a new suit and bow tie, Lucyna safe by his side. Had it been fate or sheer luck, like a good hand at cards, chance over choice?

On a cold night in October 1946, with help from an agency in Palestine, Feliks and Lucyna crossed the border into Czechoslovakia, two of only two hundred Jews from Lublin who had lived to see the end of the war.

CHAPTER SIXTEEN

GOOD FORTUNE

New York City
1950–1951

Lucyna Wojcik's first impression of the Western world was forged off the coast of Nova Scotia on a blustery early morning in November 1950. From the deck of the *USNS General R. M. Blatchford*, she looked across the Halifax harbor and spotted a boy no older than seven, bundled against the cold, swinging fat batches of newspapers high into the air and over the side of the ship.

Most of the twelve hundred war refugees on board couldn't speak or read English, but they were hungry for news. They took the papers and knotted money to the end of the rope. One good toss and the rope landed back on the dock's wooden planks with a thud.

How hard these people work, Lucyna thought as the sun rose over the icy waters of the north Atlantic.

She remembered what her parents had said when she had been a girl at home in Lublin, back when Lublin was still home. *In America, people find money on the streets.*

This new world wasn't what Lucyna had expected.

It had been a stormy crossing from Bremerhaven, Germany, to northeastern Canada, and Lucyna and Feliks had huddled below deck on the crowded US Navy ship for nearly two weeks. They had come with only ten dollars, a satchel of Feliks's medical books, and two microscopes that he couldn't bear to leave behind in Europe.

The war had uprooted millions of people, who crowded roadways, waterways, and displaced-persons camps, searching for family, searching for work, hoping to find someplace to settle when all of Europe was in a chaotic state of transition. After leaving Lublin, Feliks and Lucyna had settled in Vienna so that Feliks could finish medical school.

His tuition had been free, part of a reparations pact that the Austrians had struck with the Allies. Feliks and Lucyna took classes with four hundred other young Jewish refugees who had found their way to the Austrian capital from Nazi-run camps and hiding places across eastern Europe. Most were orphans, and they had instinctively banded together in an old schoolhouse that served as a dormitory, pooling postwar food rations to make communal pots of soup.

Lucyna was grateful that she was no longer in Poland, where she had lost her family, her identity, her God. Late into the night, the Jewish students in Vienna gathered to talk about their studies in engineering, medicine, or architecture and the professors who were loath to pass and promote foreigners, particularly Jews. Some professors, Lucyna discovered, had been members of the Nazi Party.

Mostly, Lucyna, Feliks, and their new friends talked about where they would go once they had earned their diplomas. Where was home when no one was waiting to welcome them, when every street, every neighborhood, every town, every country, seemed more foreign than the next?

The decision almost always came down to a tenuous family connection, a second cousin in France, a great uncle in Italy, an aunt by way of marriage in Palestine. And when there was no connection at all, a continent wiped clean of even the most distant relative, Vienna was no better or no worse than anyplace else. It was a city, not a home, but maybe that would change after memories gained distance, after some series of summers and winters and birthdays.

Unlike many of the others, Lucyna wanted to leave Europe altogether. She had attended two years of medical school, but the sight of blood so soon after the ghettos had been too much to bear, and she stopped going to class.

"I just want peace," she told Feliks one night. "I have to rest."

Feliks wanted to finish his medical degree in Vienna. "I promised my mother that if I survived, I would go back to school."

He suggested Israel after graduation. Lucyna shook her head, unable to imagine herself living in another tumultuous part of the world. She had a distant cousin in New York, an older man with a family of his own. Lucyna had never met him, but he had sent winter coats and American money through Switzerland. In the United States, they could start over.

"Let's try," Feliks said.

In 1950, after four years in Vienna, they left for Germany's North Sea coast, where Allied forces had established a displaced-persons camp in the port city of Bremerhaven. They stayed for six weeks before boarding the military transport ship with their new immigration visas, squeezing into narrow passageways alongside hundreds of other refugees wearing overcoats and nametags. Lucyna had spotted the Jewish refugees easily enough. They hauled suitcases filled with china, one set for meat and one set for dairy, to be sure that they could keep kosher in America.

The voyage across the Atlantic passed slowly, the ship rocked by North Sea winds. In the galley at dinner one night, Lucyna and Feliks ate roasted turkey to celebrate a holiday that the ship's captain called Thanksgiving. It would become Lucyna's favorite day of the year.

When the ship docked days later in Nova Scotia, the first stop on the way to America, Lucyna paced the deck, looking out across

Canada as the chill from the water numbed her fingers and toes. Soon, she would arrive in the United States, in a city she didn't know to see a cousin she had never met. Lucyna felt adrift, caught between worlds, the wailing of seagulls growing louder overhead.

In America, people find money on the streets.

Lucyna sighed, took one last look at the paperboy, and went back inside to find Feliks.

THE SHIP PASSED a towering copper statue that appeared bluish-green in the morning light. Lucyna gaped at the robed woman on a pedestal high above the sea, holding a torch straight into the sky. And then, in the distance, the sprawling harbor of New York City, bigger and busier than any place Lucyna had ever seen.

Ships bobbed in swirling clouds of steam. Loading cranes swiveled right and then left, hauling the day's cargo. The air was raw, a smelly mix of fish and gasoline. The dock itself was a sea of red, and as the ship drew closer Lucyna could make out hundreds of Americans waving bright-red flowers that someone called carnations. She blinked, overwhelmed by the sight of it all, but then there was the bedlam of the vast processing center. Immigration agents corralled a mass of frightened people into lines for health screenings.

Once outside, Lucyna and Feliks were whisked to a Jewish assistance center near the harbor, past a dizzying blur of buildings that seemed to block out the sun. Her cousin appeared, a stranger really. But he was polite and kind, and he showed them to a hotel in a village called Greenwich. It was in lower Manhattan, but Lucyna couldn't tell up from down, only that the hotel was on Lafayette Street near pretty brick walk-ups and cobblestone streets lined with crisscrossing streetcar tracks.

Lucyna and Feliks spent their first night in New York City in a pitch-black hotel room, listening to a never-ending symphony of strange sounds—car horns and sirens and slamming doors.

The next morning, Feliks combed his closely cropped hair. Even
in the ghettos he had been a meticulous dresser, clean and neat, and
Lucyna admired her young husband as he set about seeing some
Jewish doctors for help finding a job. Lucyna made her way back to
the Jewish assistance center for breakfast.

Several Jewish families asked Lucyna to keep their children while
they went in search of work, and she quickly accepted. Until Feliks
found a job, twenty-five dollars a week seemed like a small fortune,
enough money for a cup of coffee and the occasional trip to a theater on 42nd Street, where Feliks and Lucyna could practice their
English watching *Sunset Boulevard.*

The hotel where they were staying charged a quarter for twenty
minutes of radio time. Lucyna saved most of her earnings, and
after several weeks she squirreled away enough to buy a twenty-five-
dollar radio. Alone at night, Feliks and Lucyna listened to American
news stations for hours, picking up English, and then wandered
outside to explore the streets and alleyways of their bustling neighborhood, filled with young artists and jazz musicians.

Six weeks passed while Feliks searched for a job. Lucyna's cousin
lived in a sprawling apartment overlooking Central Park, and more
than once he had tried to slip Feliks and Lucyna some money. But
Feliks wanted to find his own way, and he had politely declined the
offers.

Feliks and Lucyna went to see a Jewish committee that was helping survivors find jobs and housing. They were shown a map of
the United States. Where would they like to live? Without thinking,
Lucyna put her finger on a place called Rochester, in upstate New
York.

"That sounds nice," she said, "wherever it is."

The Jewish committee arranged an internship for Feliks at the
hospital at the University of Rochester, and soon they were renting
a room in the home of a Jewish family who had emigrated from

Germany just before the war. Lucyna found a job at a store called
Woolworth, selling sweet fried cakes that someone called doughnuts.

She brought home six dollars after each shift. They had no money
for meat, and Feliks often complained that he looked like a rucksack
without a new suit and shoes. But Lucyna couldn't believe their
good fortune, the doctors, nurses, and Jewish organizations that
wanted to see them settled in New York.

The United States was a magical, generous place. And when
Lucyna and Feliks had a baby boy two years later, she decided that
America was also, finally, home.

THE COMMANDERS OF Trawniki issued one final order in the spring of
1945 as Soviet forces pushed west into the Czech lands, headed for
Prague: burn your papers and run.

Jakob Reimer, always one to follow directions, ditched his
Trawniki uniform, slipped into civilian clothes, and made his way
south and west toward Munich. His life depended on his ability to
keep his identity a secret, to blend as a civilian into the mass of displaced persons milling through central Europe at war's end.

If he was found out, the Soviets would call him a traitor; the
Americans, a Nazi collaborator. He struck up a relationship with a
twenty-two-year-old Polish woman for cover. To survive, he would
have to put his past behind him.

The retreat from Trawniki had begun in July 1944, four months
after Reimer was granted citizenship in Nazi Germany. As the Soviets advanced toward Lublin, Trawniki commander Karl Streibel
ordered his troops to withdraw west. Hundreds of Trawniki men deserted the battalion, diminishing the ranks, but Reimer and seven
hundred others had faithfully stayed on, guarding bridges, buildings,
and Polish forced laborers.

The men had pressed further west, to Dresden, Germany, and
then south into the Czech lands, before the unit dissolved and the

men scattered in every direction. After Nazi Germany surrendered, Reimer found his way to Munich. Bombs had leveled much of the city, but construction crews would soon rebuild block after block to preserve the prewar street grid.

US forces controlled Munich, which meant that Reimer would have to find a way to appeal to the Americans. In Trawniki, his ability to speak German had earned him a job as a platoon leader. In Munich, Reimer decided to once again leverage his language skills. He got a job with the US Army's 26th Station Hospital, chauffeuring GIs to Hollywood movies. At night, he frequented dance halls.

Still, it would be best if he could start again. Safest. By 1951, ships with thousands of refugees were leaving Germany, bound for the shores of America. In passing the Displaced Persons Act of 1948, the Congress of the United States had offered to provide refuge to hundreds of thousands of Europeans, particularly those who said they were fleeing Communism.

Reimer filled out an immigration application, careful to note that he had worked only as an interpreter for the German army during the war. He presented the application to American authorities, along with a letter of recommendation from a Red Cross supervisor whom Reimer had worked with in Munich:

A conscientious worker whose concern for his job takes priority over personal interest. Honest and dependable. Neat in appearance and has a pleasing outgoing personality. Would make a good American citizen.

Reimer likely would have received quick approval, but US authorities flagged the case after learning that he had applied for citizenship in Nazi Germany in 1944. The US Army Counterintelligence Corps launched an investigation. What was Trawniki? Reimer had noted his service at the camp on his German citizenship application.

He told the Americans that he had been only a guard-soldier and interpreter, and later a paymaster in the Trawniki administration. It had been mundane work for the Germans, he said, bureaucratic in nature.

Luckily for Reimer, the US State Department had little information about the significance of the training camp that Odilo Globocnik had created to prepare thousands of recruits for some of the bloodiest jobs in occupied Poland.

In June 1952, eighteen months after Lucyna and Feliks Wojcik set sail for America, the *USS General M. L. Hersey* left Bremerhaven, Germany, and crossed the choppy waters of the Atlantic. It eased into the harbor in New York City, where David Garroway was anchoring the *Today Show* and Mickey Mantle and Yogi Berra were on a winning streak that would take the Yankees to their fourth consecutive World Series.

Hundreds of European refugees spilled out onto the streets of the city. One of them was Trawniki recruit 865.

PART FOUR

UNITED STATES
1996–2013

CHAPTER SEVENTEEN

LONG AFTER DARK

Washington, D.C., and New York City
1996–1997

How much easier it might have been, the people of OSI often mused, if the Soviet Union had remained an ally in the years after the war, eager to share evidence about the lethal operation at the Trawniki training camp and the men who had so faithfully served the Third Reich. Instead, the Soviets had kept their own investigations secret, and there had been hundreds, conducted from the late 1940s to the 1960s, long before the Office of Special Investigations began its work.

For years after the fall of the Iron Curtain, Peter Black had dispatched his team of OSI historians to the archives of former Soviet states. Amid thousands of pages of notes and rosters, the historians found criminal files for former Trawniki men who had returned to their homes at the end of the war. Most had been found guilty by the Soviet courts for deserting the motherland and fighting for the enemy. They had spent years in prison.

The documents provided firsthand accounts of the Trawniki operation, a window into the minds and methods of the men who had served there, and Black had devoured every word. By Black's count, Trawniki commander Karl Streibel had recruited and trained more than five thousand men, the force that Odilo Globocnik had imagined in those early, dizzying months of the war.

Black had studied the movements of Trawniki units and collected biographical information on the recruits. On particularly intense days, when the office seemed to fade away, lost to the words on the documents sprawled across his desk, Black could see the military drills, imagine the weight of the mission, sense the fear in the barracks where Jews were held as laborers until Heinrich Himmler decided that every remaining prisoner in the Lublin District had to die.

How many Trawniki men were living in America? Black had no way to know for sure, but by the mid-1990s, investigations of the men who served there had become a top priority.

On the rosters in Prague, Barry White had found the name Bronislaw Hajda, Trawniki recruit 3069. An initial check with the Immigration Service had turned up nothing, but on a second try White identified a retired machinist living in the suburbs of Chicago. Hajda had trained at Trawniki, served with Liudas Kairys as a guard at the Treblinka labor camp, and in July 1944 participated in shooting as many as seven hundred prisoners in a nearby forest, just prior to abandoning the camp.

White had also identified Trawniki man Wasyl Lytwyn, a shipping clerk in Chicago, who had fought to suppress the Jewish uprising in the Warsaw ghetto.

Vladas Zajanckauskas, the Massachusetts man who claimed he had only served in the canteen at Trawniki, was under investigation too, since the rosters in Prague reinforced the suspicion that such lowly duties did not fit with his high rank. A second roster from the Federal Security Service archive in Moscow had come in, identifying Zajanckauskas as a senior instructor at Trawniki who had participated in the destruction of the Warsaw ghetto.

Using military identification numbers found in the avalanche of documents, OSI for the first time could track the career paths of Trawniki men from when they were put into the system at the training camp to their deployments in Jewish ghettos, forced-labor camps, and killing centers. Some men, like Jakob Reimer, had stayed on until the very end, following Streibel as he fled the Soviet invasion of south-eastern Poland with a battalion of seven hundred men.

It was tedious work, with historians scattered among the archives across Eastern Europe and Black scrambling in Washington to synthesize the findings. White, as head of research and development, was trying to match names from the European records to those on American records from INS, army background investigations, POW camps, and military hospitals.

One day in October 1996, Black closed the door to his office and settled in for a long afternoon of reading. A thick batch of documents had come in from the provincial Federal Security Service archives of Krasnodar in the North Caucasus, a region in European Russia between the Black Sea and the Caspian Sea.

Black was tired, which wasn't unusual. At home he was busy helping to care for his son, Aaron, who had slipped away on several occasions. On a weekend visit to OSI, Aaron had worked his way down a back staircase into a parking garage and ended up caught behind some fencing. He had once wandered into a birthday party in a neighbor's yard, picked up a Pepsi, and sat down between two strangers. To keep Aaron safe at night, Black and his wife, Mary, slept lightly, listening for footsteps on creaking floors.

In his office, Black started sorting through the new documents, discovered by OSI historian David Cameron. He settled on an eyewitness statement by an ex-Trawniki man that had been taken by the Soviets in 1964. The document, stamped by the directorate of the Federal Security Service in Moscow, included a name that Black quickly recognized: *Rajmer.*

It was a phonetic transliteration of *Reimer* from Russian Cyrillic, used by the translator that OSI had commissioned. Black read on.

One day in the spring of 1942, about twenty to thirty of us SS men were placed into motor vehicles and driven from Lublin along a highway about fifteen kilometers from the city. This group included RAJMAR, AKKERMAN, and BEK. They were our commanders. A guard unit…then began to bring groups of thirty or more Jews—including men, women, children, and old people—in covered trucks up to the place on the highway where we had got out of our vehicles.

The first group of perhaps thirty doomed people delivered there was surrounded from all sides and led deep into the forest. During the march, they began to throw their things away and were very upset. The children and women were crying.

Deep in the forest, about one kilometer from the road, we saw a large pit that had been dug out and around which some [Security Service] officers with submachine guns were standing. There were about four or five of them. All the doomed people had to sit down about ten meters from the pit. We *Wachmanner* were posted in surrounding positions.

Then AKKERMAN, RAJMAR, and BEK used their rifle butts to prod the victims and force the fear-crazed people to stand up in groups of five to seven people. They marched them to the pit and then, along with the Germans, shot those people.

After having finished off all the adults and children, we returned to the road, and the escort unit gave us the next group of twenty-five to thirty people who had been delivered there by vehicle. We escorted them to the pit in the forest, where they were shot in similar circumstances by the fascist officers, with the direct participation of BEK, RAJMAR, and AKKERMAN. A total of about 250 to 300 people were shot during that day.

It was a detailed description that placed Reimer at a pit shooting in a forest near Lublin in the spring of 1942, when the first massive ghetto deportation had taken place.

Black picked up another eyewitness statement, also taken by the Soviets in 1964. A second Trawniki man had placed Jakob Reimer at the site of the shooting, though this statement inexplicably used both *Rajmer* and *Rajmont*.

When the doomed people realized they were in a forest with us SS members, some of them started to cry and throw their things, and eventually, all of the adults and children were doing this. They apparently understood they were going to their deaths. The doomed people we had delivered were ordered to sit down on the ground about fifteen to twenty meters from the pit. The crying and moaning continued among them.

We *Wachmanner* were posted at points five, fifteen, and twenty meters around the execution site. Then, on orders from the fascists, AKKERMAN, RAJMONT, and one of the other *Gruppenwachmanner* used their rifle butts to hit the terrified men, women and children and old people—many of whom were crying hysterically—to make them stand up, pushed them to the pit in groups of five to seven people, and then they and the fascist officers shot the Jews.

Was this the same shooting that Reimer had described to Eli Rosenbaum and Neal Sher in New York in 1992? Black had no way to know for sure, but whether there had been one mass shooting or many, the statements were graphic confirmation that Reimer had participated in an execution of Jews as an armed Trawniki platoon leader. Black paused, taking in the eyewitness accounts, murderers describing murder in the most ordinary way.

He thought about Ned Stutman, OSI's newest lawyer. Black had been raised without religion, but he knew that fifty-one-year-old Stutman was deeply connected to his Jewish identity and to family that had escaped the Ukraine region in the years before the war.

Stutman had grown up in a kosher home. His father had been president of the neighborhood synagogue.

Yet in interviews with accused Nazi perpetrators, Stutman was congenial and unusually sensitive, keenly aware that he was talking to a damaged human being who was, above all else, innocent until proven guilty. How would such a compassionate man react to the particularly devastating images described in the eyewitness statements?

IN MATTERS OF love and law, Ned Stutman had never seen a need for equivocation, which is why, in the winter of 1967, twenty-five years before he would become a prosecutor at the Office of Special Investigations, he had straightened his shoulders, studied the young woman in front of him, and said simply, "I love you, I know it. Can I marry you?"

She declined the offer, finding a marriage proposal on a first date altogether peculiar. When he called the next day to say that he had smuggled a transistor radio out of her brother's bedroom and would return it only if she agreed to a second date, she nearly said no again. They married six months later, swaying to Mozart's Piano Concerto No. 21 as the sun streamed through the glass ceiling of their wedding hall.

At twenty-one, Ned Stutman was devout, both as a Jew and as a son of Philadelphia, where cheesesteaks and Eagles games were considered something of a religious experience. Law school seemed the most logical choice for a career path, given his ability to fill a room, dominating conversations about Vietnam and civil rights and presidential politics.

White hot light, his wife Suzanne decided, impossible to turn away.

Stutman enrolled in law school at Temple University and took a job teaching history at a Catholic school in Camden to pay the bills.

"Mr. Stutman," one of the nuns had said, sizing up his olive skin, long eyelashes, and thick beard. "We've never had an Italian here before."

He grinned. "Sister, I hate to tell you this, but I'm Jewish."

She paused. "Well, we've never had one of those either."

He launched his law career prosecuting criminals for the district attorney's office in Philadelphia and eventually became a public defender, taking on a widely watched case of a black man accused of killing a white police officer.

"Aren't you conflicted about defending this man?" Suzanne asked early one morning as the case dragged into 1975. "It's a terrible thing to kill a cop."

"Everybody deserves a just trial," Stutman answered.

By way of good-bye, he lowered his face to hers so that their fluttering eyelashes touched. A "butterfly kiss," he had come to call it.

Suzanne sized up her husband, striking in his Brooks Brothers suit. He was a fastidious dresser, likely because he had spent much of college with holes in his gym socks. Suzanne knew that her Birkenstock sandals and tousled hippie hair made an odd contrast to his polished wingtips and silk ties the color of salmon.

Stutman turned to public-interest law, helping people with disabilities find transportation and housing, and in the early 1980s he moved with Suzanne and their children to a red-brick row house in a leafy neighborhood of Northwest Washington. He practiced disability law and then went to work for the Justice Department's Civil Rights Division.

Stutman had transferred to OSI in 1992, soon after Jakob Reimer met with Eli Rosenbaum and Neal Sher at the US Attorney's Office in Manhattan. Reimer had left that day a free man and Rosenbaum had left with a headache, stunned by Reimer's murder confession.

OSI would seek to strip Reimer of his US citizenship and then deport him, perhaps to Germany, Poland, or Ukraine. Stutman would lead the prosecution.

By October 1996, after several years of tedious pretrial work, the office was in full trial mode. Stutman huddled with Peter Black for hours, poring over the history of the Trawniki training camp and

Reimer's confession about the shooting at the pit near Lublin. The conversations were grueling, and at home after work, Stutman often poured himself a glass of vodka on ice and sat alone on the porch, trying to distance himself from images of war. His children waited in the kitchen, knowing that when their father was ready, his head clear, he would bound into the house and bellow in a deep, silly voice, "The Holocaust eez ma life!"

Friday nights were reserved for Shabbat dinner, served in a dining room that smelled of baked chicken and salty kugel. While his children wiggled in torn leather chairs, Stutman would sing in Hebrew, resting his hands on their shoulders.

"*Yevarechecha adonai ve-yishmerecha.*" May God bless you and keep you.

But some nights, long after dark, he'd crawl into bed and cry. Suzanne knew that her husband believed in divine justice as much as he did God and family.

"You're trying to make things right," she'd whisper, kissing his wet eyelashes until he fell asleep.

WITHOUT A DOUBT, the eyewitness statements would help forge a legal case against Jakob Reimer. But Stutman almost wished he had never seen them, the words that twisted themselves into images and lodged deep in his gut, a chronic condition.

Stutman thought about the man he would soon take to federal court. Some months after the interview with Rosenbaum and Sher, Reimer had appeared in his bedroom slippers on the front porch of his house in Lake Carmel and complained to a reporter from *New York Magazine* who was planning a story about the case.

"They have the wrong man," Reimer told journalist Jeffrey Goldberg. "I did not do anything to the Jewish people."

Reimer had hired a prominent defense lawyer and changed his account of the massacre at the pit, arguing that he couldn't have killed the man who had pointed to his head because the man was already dead by the time Reimer fired his shot.

"That's not what you told the OSI," Goldberg said to Reimer during the interview. Reimer did not respond.

To successfully prosecute Reimer, Stutman knew, OSI would have to take on Reimer's disparate accounts and convince a judge to move against an affable, churchgoing man who had stepped off a US Navy ship in the port of New York in 1951 and eased into a new life in America. He had found a job sweeping floors and then tending bar at Schrafft's restaurant in Times Square, serving vodka martinis for eighty-five cents and scotch sours for a dollar. He married, had two sons, and opened a Wise potato chip franchise.

Unlike some other OSI defendants, Reimer had never guarded Jewish prisoners at a Nazi-run killing center. But Reimer's service to the Reich, Stutman believed, was just as egregious. Reimer had been deployed to three Jewish ghettos to participate in mass deportation operations, and at least once had led a platoon of Trawniki men to the perimeter of a ravine, where Jewish men, women, and children were slaughtered.

The Holocaust, Barry White often said, was the product of a vast criminal conspiracy that involved the work of thousands of collaborators. Jakob Reimer, Trawniki man, had loyally played his role. Prosecuting him would not only bring a trusted Nazi perpetrator to justice but finally expose the extent of the horrific training operation at Trawniki, stitched together by Black and the OSI historians.

Stutman scanned the eyewitness statements again. Doomed people. Large pit. Submachine gun. He looked around his office, crowded with maps of Eastern Europe and photographs from concentration camps. A quote from the Torah scrolled across his computer screen.

It was one of the central tenets of the Old Testament: *Justice, Justice You Shall Pursue.*

OSI, Stutman decided, would take on Jakob Reimer and his Nazi past, bring the whole damn thing out into the open.

SOME PROSECUTORS AT the Office of Special Investigations preferred to handle interviews alone, but Ned Stutman believed that historians could use historical facts to detect the tiniest of lies, to tease out the truth through context and detail. The Reimer case was no exception, and Stutman asked Peter Black to join him during Reimer's deposition before the case headed to court.

On a crisp February morning in 1997, five and a half years after Eli Rosenbaum and Neal Sher had first questioned Reimer, Black and Stutman settled into a conference room at the US Attorney's Office in Manhattan.

Reimer was smaller than Black had expected, with a narrow face and a mane of silver hair. He offered a slight smile, a graciousness that instantly struck Black as practiced and intentional. This time, Reimer had not come alone.

Black turned to Reimer's lawyer and nodded, studying the man whom Black had seen in newspapers and television news segments. Ramsey Clark, the son of a US Supreme Court justice, had been a driving force in the civil rights movement before serving as attorney general under President Lyndon B. Johnson. Clark had gone on to champion progressive views and vigorously denounce US intervention in the Middle East. He was familiar with OSI, Black knew, since Clark had represented concentration camp supervisor Karl Linnas years earlier.

"There comes a time after the most horrible acts when the possibility of reconciliation outweighs any possible need for retribution," Clark once told a reporter at the *New York Times*.

Black suspected that the sixty-nine-year-old defense attorney would make a formidable adversary in the courtroom.

"Good morning, Mr. Reimer," Stutman said politely. "I am going to be asking you some questions today, and if at any time there is a question I ask that you don't understand, please ask me to rephrase it or restate it and I will be glad to do that. Is there any health matter that you have that I should be aware of, any condition, physical condition?"

"No, not really," Reimer replied. "I would say for age, probably normal."

"I read a magazine article in which you are quoted as saying you are interested in nutrition and the bible. Is that right?"

"Absolutely." Reimer's voice was earnest. "I live by the bible. I came from a very, very conservative family."

Stutman decided to dig in quickly. He turned to Reimer's shifting story about the mass shooting at the ravine.

"Do you recall that you were interviewed by a reporter?" Stutman asked.

Reimer nodded. "Terrible. They called me a Nazi. I was a prisoner of the Nazis. I fought the war against the Nazis. Half of my country was killed by the Nazis."

Stutman interrupted. "I understand, Mr. Reimer. I will give you an opportunity to tell that story. I want to talk—"

"Sorry."

"You don't have to apologize."

"It gets to you, you know?"

Stutman didn't answer. He pressed on. "In that article, you were quoted as saying you are the most hated man in America. Did you feel that way?"

"Yes."

"Did you tell the reporter that you shot into the ravine?"

"I don't remember, but it is in the papers, then I must have said it."

Clark interrupted. "You don't have to assume that they reported it accurately, Mr. Reimer."

Stutman went on. "Now, the *New York Magazine* article...reports that the reporter asked you, 'So, you shot the man?' And you responded, 'Yes, but he was already dead.'"

"Boy, my mind is always different," Reimer said. "I am sorry. I don't remember if I said it."

"At the time you fired your shot, you thought they were all dead?"

"Right."

"How do you know that they were all dead?"

"Well, when I got closer to the edge, they were all motionless. Nobody was moving or anything."

"You said that you observed a man who was pointing with a finger to his head. Did you see a man who was pointing with a finger to his head?"

"Mr. Stutman, I probably said that and it's probably true but...I wasn't the only one who fired at this point....I fired in the direction of the ravine. I did not fire at anybody. To me, that was a no-no."

Reimer went on, insisting that an SS officer had forced him to fire his gun during the shooting operation to prove loyalty to the German cause. "To me, Mr. Stutman, they were all dead. They were all motionless. Suppose I had not fired a shot? They would have called an ambulance or something? No. I only fired over the ravine. I didn't even aim at the man."

If Stutman had his doubts about Reimer's story, Black decided, the lawyer didn't let on. Stutman asked his question again. "Isn't it true that you fired at the man who was pointing to his head?"

"Like I say," Reimer said, "you think of that one incident and it builds on you and builds on you, but was it true? I don't know. Please. God hates liars. Ninth commandment. Believe me, I could not kill anybody or lie."

"Which is the truth? Was he alive or was he dead? Was he moving?"

"I don't know."

"There was no one moving in the pit?"

"No."

"You didn't go down and take everybody's pulse in the pit, did you?" Stutman asked.

"This is too serious to joke," Reimer shot back.

"I am not joking," Stutman quickly replied, his voice level.

Watching the exchange, Black suddenly understood how Reimer had so easily covered up his past. He was one of the more congenial defendants that Black had ever seen, appearing likable and cooperative even in the face of a murder inquiry. And Reimer was smart, carefully sidestepping questions about his role in the pit shooting. He shot but he did not kill. He had been forced by the SS. A crafty way to pivot.

Reimer was describing the men at Trawniki. "They were getting into things that I hadn't dreamed about, that I didn't know what was going to happen."

"What did you learn that they were getting into?" Stutman asked.

"They were shooting civilians, okay? And, it is one thing to be in the war to defend yourself, you go against an enemy in the war, but shooting unarmed civilians, absolutely wrong. And I didn't stand for that."

"You saw this at the ravine incident?"

"Yes. I had to do something and I did," Reimer said. More than once over the years, Reimer had insisted that he spent much of his time at Trawniki as a paymaster, far from the violence. "I should be thanked for getting out of it, but now I am being prosecuted."

Black glanced at Stutman, who did not appear angry or frustrated. Stutman was perfectly poised, a finder of fact rather than an arbiter of justice.

"We were prisoners of the Nazis." Reimer was indignant. "Russia was totally cut off from the world. We didn't get any information. We had no knowledge what the Nazis were all about. It just as well we could have been in China."

Stutman switched subjects to the liquidation of the Lublin ghetto in March 1942. In the interview with Rosenbaum and Sher, Reimer had acknowledged spending a single night in Lublin. A training exercise, he had called it, not an operational mission. His men had simply guarded empty houses in an empty ghetto.

"Did you have occasion to go into any building?" Stutman asked.

"I did," Reimer answered.

"Can you describe the circumstances?"

"Well, the sun went down and it was getting dark and there were no lights going on in these buildings, so I was curious. I just probably walked in one and I saw there were no people. The apartments were completely furnished and everything and the kitchen utensils, everything was here, but no people. It was completely empty."

"What did you see?"

"There was the beds, there was everything there. There were linens. There was everything. Towels in the kitchen. It was...set up for somebody to live in."

Black took in the details. For the second time, Reimer had confirmed that he had been in Lublin during the massive ghetto-clearing operation in March and April 1942. It had been no single-day training event, as Reimer had tried to claim, but a mission that spanned weeks during one of the darkest, bloodiest periods in Lublin.

"You say that you had no expectation about guarding people when you went to Lublin," Stutman said. "You acquired weapons in Lublin?"

"Yes," Reimer replied.

Stutman paused briefly. "So what did you expect the weapons would be used for?"

CHAPTER EIGHTEEN

WINTER IN PENZA

Penza, Russia
1998

The most critical eyewitness in the case against Jakob Reimer lived four hundred miles southeast of Moscow in a factory town along the southern route of the Trans-Siberian Railway. The fastest way to get there was by train, and on a January evening in Moscow in 1998, OSI historian David Rich settled into a second-class cabin with Ned Stutman and padlocked the door.

The Russian train was a behemoth of steel and glass, one of the last carriages manufactured by the East Germans before the collapse of Communism eight years earlier. Over twelve hours, the train would travel through the frozen steppe to the Russian city of Penza, a frontier-fortress outpost built in the 1600s to protect Russia from the Crimean Tatars.

The train cabin smelled of stale sweat and smoke, but Rich was thankful for the narrow foldout beds and the cheese and wine that Stutman had thought to pick up in Moscow before the overnight journey. The night air was frigid. Rich glanced at his traveling companion, bundled up in a fur hat. Rich was warm enough in his long underwear, but he made a mental note of the babushka who was selling hot tea in the back of the train car.

Soon, they would meet Nikolai Leont'ev, one of the two former

Trawniki guards who had described Reimer's participation in a
shooting at a pit in a forest near Lublin during the liquidation of the
Jewish ghetto. Stutman suspected that Reimer's lawyer would argue
in court that the 1964 eyewitness accounts had been strong-armed
by the Soviets. Stutman wanted to interview Leont'ev himself.

Eli Rosenbaum had quickly approved the request. He had become director of OSI four years earlier, after Neal Sher left the unit
for a job with the American Israeli Public Affairs Committee. Authorities in Moscow could have taken months to coordinate the visit,
but approval came swiftly, and Stutman and Rich had flown to Russia four days into the new year.

Rich studied the chain he had used to secure the cabin door,
a precaution that seemed only logical during the tumultuous, post-
Communist presidency of Boris Yeltsin. Drug traffickers and mob
bosses had commandeered much of Russia, violent criminals known
as Vory v Zakone who had murdered bankers and businessmen and
pushed the country's homicide rate to one of the highest in the world.

Tourists had also been targeted, particularly on the Trans-
Siberian Railway and other remote routes. Rich had read news
stories of train gangs that had pistol-whipped, raped, robbed, and
murdered travelers. Though Western passengers had been generally
left unharmed, Rich decided to leave nothing to chance.

He had once chased Soviet submarines through the depths of the
Mediterranean, but the thought of street thugs slipping onto the
train in the middle of the night with axes and iron rods was down-
right terrifying. He would sleep with one eye open. He doubted
Stutman would sleep at all.

The lawyer was bent over his legal pad reviewing the questions
he would ask Leont'ev, the cheese and wine untouched. Night fell
around them, dark and lonely. The train lurched, and Rich could
feel the seat twitching beneath him. *Don't mess this up*, he told himself.
It was his first major trip and his first major case with OSI.

A navy man, Rich had been a helicopter pilot in the Pacific during the Cold War. He spoke Russian and Ukrainian and had spent time in the post-Soviet archives doing sensitive work for the federal government. When Peter Black had offered him the job at OSI only months earlier, Rich had never heard of Jakob Reimer or the obscure Nazi-run camp where he had once trained.

How did the SS convince a mass of largely uneducated Soviet prisoners of war who came from different places and didn't speak German to function as a cohesive SS unit, day after day, month after month? They had labored through two Polish summers and two brutally cold winters, until every ghetto in German-occupied Poland was emptied, money and valuables sorted and sent back to the Reich, 1.7 million Jews dead.

Over long conversations with Black, Rich finally understood. The answer was both stunning and simple. The Trawniki complex had functioned as a militarized police organization, with squads, platoons, companies, promotions, service medals, training, and clearly defined images of the enemy.

Trawniki men who were injured in the line of duty had been hospitalized in SS facilities, Black explained. Those who died were buried in military cemeteries. It had been purposeful work with a mission that few men had questioned, their war years spent away from combat. They had received spending money and vodka, enjoyed full bellies, and engaged in dalliances with Polish women. And Reimer had been at the center of it all, an educated ethnic German, perfectly positioned to earn the trust of his SS superiors.

As the train to Penza rumbled through the Russian countryside, Rich turned to Stutman. "Do you want to chat?"

"No, no," Stutman said, without looking up. He was reading the eyewitness statement again, a blood-curdling account that Rich knew had been delivered with absolute dispassion. "I'm just going to work."

Rich stared at the thin line of fluorescent light that stretched beneath the cabin door. Was there anyone else in the car with them? Perhaps the whole train was empty. He looked out the window at the passing countryside and for a split second thought he saw a den of wolves, yellow eyes glowing in the darkness.

Don't mess this up, he told himself a second time. He thought about Black, who had left OSI after nearly twenty years to become the senior historian at the United States Holocaust Memorial Museum, a few blocks away from the OSI offices in downtown Washington. Black would continue to help the unit with its Trawniki cases, and for that Rich was grateful.

Black had gathered more information on the camp and its recruits than any other scholar in the world and had spent two and a half years helping to craft an expert report about Reimer and Trawniki that expert witness Charlie Sydnor would present in federal court. Rich had taken part too, and now he was officially the OSI historian on the case.

Just before he drifted off to sleep, he decided he could have been a character from *Doctor Zhivago*. How absurd this all was, the way life jerks and turns, padlocks on trains, wolves in the shadows, the mysterious man waiting at the end of the line.

THE TRAIN ROLLED into Penza at dawn. David Rich squinted into the bright early-morning sunshine at the lone figure who stood on the platform.

"Come with me," the city's chief prosecutor said in Russian and led the two Americans to a Volga limousine dusted by a fresh layer of snow.

Stutman offered a quick nod. He was in no mood for small talk. He had barely uttered a word on the train, and Rich noticed that the light over Stutman's top bunk had stayed on all night. Stutman slipped quietly into the back of the limousine alongside their Russian interpreter, who would help with the Leont'ev interview. Rich sat in front with the prosecutor.

Penza was an industrial city, and one of Russia's poorest, with factories that produced steel and lumber along the banks of the Sura River. In the fifteenth century, a Russian architect on orders from the tsar had built a fortress in Penza, with a wooden kremlin and a compact village with housing for nobility, tradesmen, and merchants, mostly of Ukrainian descent. By 1801, about thirteen thousand people lived in clusters of stone houses, and over time the western Russian city grew into an industrial hub, with a railway junction that linked Moscow to Chelyabinsk.

The limousine sped through the morning haze and stopped moments later in front of a classic Soviet-style apartment complex, squat and imposing. Much to Rich's surprise, the elevator in the building was working. This way, the prosecutor gestured, and they walked silently to the apartment where Nikolai Leont'ev had lived for years, fixing watches and clocks to earn a meager living.

Leont'ev opened the door and stared at his American visitors, extending a terse greeting. He led them into a kitchen that held a single table and four plastic chairs. There was no offer of tea.

The former Trawniki guard was eighty years old, but he looked much younger. Such a gentle descent into old age, Rich thought, for a man who had once served the Nazi killing machine.

Leont'ev had spent nine years in a Soviet gulag after the war. He was eventually released when Joseph Stalin died and the Russian government opted to amnesty thousands of convicted traitors. In 1964, as a Soviet witness in cases against other Trawniki men, Leont'ev had provided the account about Reimer and the shooting at the pit near Lublin.

Stutman settled into a chair. Rich noticed that he made no move to shake Leont'ev's hand. Instead, Stutman made introductions and advised Leont'ev that he was obliged to tell the truth.

"I'm with the United States Department of Justice," Stutman began, speaking slowly to give the interpreter time to convert the words to Russian. "My office works on matters related to people who entered the United States after the war and became citizens—"

Leont'ev interrupted. "We didn't have anyone. As far as I know, all these people were not Americans."

"I know," Stutman answered. "The people we investigate are people who became Americans after the war."

Leont'ev shook his head. "I have no way of knowing."

The man was on edge, clearly. In front of an American prosecutor, he would offer nothing freely.

"I have come many miles to speak with you just to get truthful information about what you saw during the wartime period and some people that you may have known during that period," Stutman said evenly.

He turned to the Trawniki camp. "Did you have officers over you at Trawniki?"

"Of course."

"And were these officers Germans from Germany or were they Russians of German nationality?"

"How would I have known?" Leont'ev shot back. "How would I know?"

"When you were at Trawniki, were there other Russians there?" Stutman repeated.

"I don't know. There were thousands. How many? I don't know but there were thousands of them."

"And when you got there, didn't the Germans train you to become *Wachmanner*?"

"What do you mean the Germans gave us training?"

"Did they teach you German commands?"

"I don't know. I don't know. I really don't remember."

Stutman looked dubious. "You don't remember? Did they teach you how to do guard duty?"

"I've already said I really don't remember a thing. How many years ago was it? I just don't recollect."

"When you were in Trawniki, do you remember the names of any of the people who trained you?"

"No."

"Among the ethnic Germans, do you remember anyone by the name of Reimer?"

Leont'ev paused. "Darned if it isn't familiar.... I think I remember somebody...with that [name], but I can't say anything bad about him. He was a good guy."

"A good *Wachmann*?" Stutman said. Rich doubted that Leont'ev could detect the hint of sarcasm in the question. "What do you remember him from?"

"He was a nice fellow. He was a good guy. He wasn't the type to hand out punishment. He never said an unkind word. Just a very nice person."

"Was he one of those who trained you?"

"He did train us."

"And when you went to Lublin, did your trainers go with you?"

"I don't remember. As far as I know, they were already there when we got there."

"Do you remember how long you were in Lublin?"

"Probably two or three months."

"What was your unit doing?"

"The Jews had been rounded up and put into camps. They were now empty and we were guarding these empty buildings."

The account, Rich knew, solidified OSI's suspicion that Reimer had spent many weeks in Lublin.

"Do you remember something else happening while you were in Lublin?" Stutman asked. "A shooting in a forest?"

Leont'ev paused. "Damned if I... if that happened, I can't say. I don't remember."

Stutman pushed the 1964 eyewitness statement across the table. "Let me help refresh your memory on this. Mr. Leont'ev, we have a statement that was given to us by the Russian government. I want to show it to you. It has signatures at the bottom of each page."

"What is this, by the way?"

"This is a statement that you gave to the Russian authorities?"

Again, Leont'ev paused. He looked at his visitors. "Would anyone like a smoke?"

"They're not good for you, Mr. Leont'ev," Stutman quickly replied.

Stutman pointed to the statement. "I would like you to look, Mr. Leont'ev, and tell me—"

Leont'ev shook his head. "Can anyone remember what happened thirty-four years ago?"

Stutman decided to read an excerpt of the statement. "I want you to listen, Mr. Leont'ev," Stutman said, "and tell me is it true or is there anything in this statement that's not true or correct. Because if anything isn't true, I want you to tell me."

He read aloud. "In about March 1942, Mikhail Korzhikov, Ivan Khabarov, and I, Leont'ev, were in a detachment numbering perhaps ninety people who deployed from Trawniki to the city of Lublin. We were escorted there by...Reimer, Ackermann, Traut, and others."

"Who's Traut?" Leont'ev interrupted.

"I'm asking you," Stutman said.

"I don't remember Traut. Traut I don't know."

Stutman went on. "After we arrived in Lublin, we were quartered in three barracks near a church in the town itself. In Lublin, we guarded some houses of the former Jewish ghetto that contained property."

"That's true," Leont'ev said.

Stutman continued, moving on to the shooting in the forest.

AKKERMAN, RAJMAR, and BEK used their rifle butts to prod the victims and force the fear-crazed people to stand up in groups of five to seven people.... After having finished off all the adults and children, we returned to the road and the escort unit gave us the next group.

"Okay. I'm going to stop now," Stutman said. "Mr. Leont'ev, is there a part of that story that is not true?"

"It's correct. It's true. That did happen. I remember. It did happen."

"And at the shooting, Reimer, Ackermann, and Beck, they were there?"

"Yes. I think they were. I think they were."

"This kind of event probably stays with you in your memory," Stutman said.

"But I want to say that these three did not do the actual shooting. It was ethnic Germans who did the actual shooting."

"In your statement, it says that [supervisors] Ackermann, Reimer, and Beck used their rifle butts to prod the victims and force the fear-crazed people to stand up in groups of five to seven. Then they marched them to the pit, and, along with the Germans, they shot those people."

"As far as I can recall, as far as I know, the Germans did the shooting."

"What did the [supervisors] do?"

"They were the convoy. They brought them to the pit."

"I see. And the [supervisors] were Reimer, Ackermann, Beck?"

"Yes. They were in charge. They were the commanders of the convoying."

"And they were the ones who were giving you orders?"

"Yes, it was they, of course, who ordered us. They gave us our orders."

"And after the first group was shot, the Jews that followed must have known what their fate was. Did any of them try to run away?"

"They were executed. There was nowhere to go. They had no possibility of escape."

Listening to the exchange, David Rich wondered whether Stutman was absorbing the details as a prosecutor or as a Jew, whether there was any way to be one and not the other. Stutman did not appear angry. Instead, he paused.

"Are you warm?" he asked Leont'ev. "Do you want to take a break? Have some tea? You didn't eat. Are you okay? If you get tired…"

"No," Leont'ev replied. "I'm fine."

Stutman went on. "How come you never got promoted?"

For the first time, Leont'ev laughed. "Why would they promote me?"

"Was Reimer with you the whole time you were in Lublin?"

"He was.… You know this was something that should have been addressed immediately after the war. At such a late date, who needs to know any of this? Who is interested?"

"The United States didn't want people to immigrate who had assisted the Nazi persecutors in any way," Stutman replied.

"It's been how many years?" Leont'ev asked. "How many years since the end of the war?"

"Well, it's been a long time, Mr. Leont'ev," Stutman answered. He took a deep breath. "But there are still people who remember."

THE TRAIN BACK to Moscow did not leave until six p.m. To kill time after the interview the prosecutor from Penza suggested a tour of the city. As the limousine scaled a winding road high above town, he grinned and pointed to an island in the middle of the Sura River.

"That," he said, "was once a strategic target for the Americans."

Rich nodded and smiled, knowing that Stutman would say very little. He was lost in thought, rehashing Leont'ev's grudging confirmation that Reimer had led a platoon of Trawniki men to the pit shooting and that he had spent weeks in Lublin during the ghetto liquidation. Both admissions were critical to OSI's case.

The next day, Rich and Stutman sipped vodka in a warm dining room looking toward Red Square. The Kremlin glowed green and yellow against the night sky. It was a majestic sight, and in the silence Rich stared at the twinkling lights and thought about the work that was waiting back in Washington.

THE JUDGE ASSIGNED to hear the Reimer case in US District Court for the Southern District of New York was Lawrence McKenna, nominated to the bench by President George H. W. Bush.

After OSI filed the denaturalization case against Reimer in 1992, Neal Sher had gone to New York to meet in chambers with the judge and defense attorney Ramsey Clark for an initial status conference. Sher had returned to OSI, looking grim.

In case after case, the unit had faced intense scrutiny from judges about the use of documents supplied by the Soviet Union. Turning to his legal team, Sher recounted a question from McKenna, who had grown up in New York City during the height of the Cold War and to Sher had appeared skeptical about the upcoming case against Reimer.

"I don't suppose," Sher recalled the judge asking, "that I can convince you to leave this poor old man alone?"

CHAPTER NINETEEN

THE WORK OF MURDER

New York City
1998

The federal courtroom was packed. Ned Stutman expected that. The New York dailies were on the story, and the *New York Jewish Week* had headlined an exposé: "The Last Nazi Trial of the Century." From the prosecutor's table in the front of the room, Stutman could see journalists squeezed next to Holocaust survivors, some wearing armbands bearing the Star of David.

Jakob Reimer sat at the defense table in sneakers. He was wearing a cardigan sweater even in the August heat, a savvy move, Stutman decided, given the allegations against him. The seventy-nine-year-old defendant looked frail and friendly, an average guy in comfortable American footwear.

Later, an OSI attorney would study a sketch of Reimer in the crowded courtroom and remark, "Who do you think is the Nazi and who do you think is the Holocaust victim?" Based on appearances, it was impossible to know.

Stutman had come to court with eighty-five German documents and 132 written statements from victims, witnesses, and Nazi perpetrators, assembled by Peter Black, Barry White, David Rich, and the other OSI historians. Four survivors were waiting to take the stand, including men who had witnessed the ghetto liquidations in

two of the cities where Reimer once served. The records and witnesses would help detail Reimer's sweeping stretch of deployments
during the two most lethal years of German rule in Poland.

But Stutman was worried. The case was already off to an unfor-
tunate start.

The Office of Special Investigations had asked for a summary
judgment, a ruling against Reimer without the need for a hearing.
The evidence was among the strongest in the history of the Nazi-
hunting unit—a confession, two eyewitness accounts of murder, and
rosters and records that placed Reimer in the three ghettos where
tens of thousands of Jews were whipped, beaten, shot, or forced onto
trains bound for killing centers. But Judge McKenna had denied the
request.

Stutman wasn't the kind of lawyer to leave anything to chance.
He had asked Eli Rosenbaum to skip the hearing and stay behind
in Washington, knowing that the director of OSI would likely draw
attention from Reimer's veteran defense attorney.

"You'll be a lightning rod for Ramsey Clark," Stutman had warned.

Stutman hated distractions. He wanted the judge focused
squarely on the facts, the legal arguments for stripping Reimer of
his citizenship fifty years after he had settled in the United States.
Stutman intended to prove that Reimer had participated in mass
murder not as a grunt or as a passive bystander but as an active,
armed Nazi collaborator. So loyal to the cause that he had earned
promotions and vacations. So loyal that he would receive citizenship
in Nazi Germany when the dirty work was done.

In the quiet courtroom, Stutman pushed back his chair and stood
up. In Washington, he had earned the title of "funniest lawyer" in
a local comedy contest. "Humor," Stutman liked to tell the young
members of his legal team, "is how we get by."

But in court, in stiff dress shoes and ties, Stutman didn't joke. Some
prosecutors liked to fill up the room, bold and loud, performing for

a judge or jury. Stutman spoke softly, carefully. Mass murder didn't need dramatizing.

He glanced briefly at historian David Rich and the three lawyers sitting next to him at the prosecutor's table, then turned to face the judge.

"In Operation Reinhard, which lasted from March 1942 until December 1943, the Nazis killed an estimated 1.7 million Jews," Stutman began. "The Nazis could not have done so without Trawniki training camp, the men who trained there, and men like Jack Reimer to train and lead them. The government will show the Trawniki training camp was, in every respect imaginable, a training ground for persecution and murder, and the defendant was one of its first teachers."

Across the room, Reimer bowed his head, shielding his face with his hand. Stutman knew that Reimer appeared vulnerable, an underdog with a single lawyer. It was sound legal strategy, a subtle way of pointing out that Stutman was part of big government, sitting at the prosecutor's table with the other lawyers, Rich, and a massive stack of documents.

"We have few opportunities," Stutman went on, "as a nation or as individual citizens to express our absolute abhorrence of persecution on the basis of race, religion, or national origin. The Congress of the United States seized one such opportunity when it passed the Displaced Persons Act and declared that individuals who assisted in persecution or misrepresented wartime activity would not be eligible for a visa to come to this country. Congress declared in no uncertain terms that this country would not and will not be a haven for those who assisted in persecution.

"There were only a limited number of visas back then, your Honor, and Mr. Reimer took the visa of a real victim. Jack Reimer assisted in persecution....Moreover, he trained others to assist in persecution as well. Then he misrepresented his whereabouts and activities during the war. On all of these bases, we ask the court to denaturalize Jack Reimer."

The judge turned to Ramsey Clark, who was nearly a decade younger than Reimer and a good head taller, with a narrow face and a G-man's haircut, brown hair swept back off his forehead.

Stutman had read up on Clark's involvement in the defense of Karl Linnas, the Estonian concentration camp commandant who had been deported to the Soviet Union over the protests of Pat Buchanan and others. While awaiting trial, Linnas died of natural causes in a prison hospital in Leningrad. Clark had flown to the Soviet Union to see Linnas a day before his death.

Clark had defended other high-profile and controversial clients, including the Palestine Liberation Organization, sued after terrorists hijacked a cruise ship off the coast of Egypt. Gunmen had shot and killed Leon Klinghoffer, a disabled Jewish man from New York who had been celebrating his thirty-sixth wedding anniversary. Klinghoffer was thrown into the sea in his wheelchair.

Clark stood up and looked at the judge.

"So the question is: why are we here?" the defense attorney said. "I think the evidence will show that Mr. Reimer learned his religion well, although he was cut off from it, that he lived that religion and does to this day. . . . He is a kindly man. You couldn't say he has had a happy life. Early on he told me—I didn't understand it at first—but early on he said that this is his test and he will face it alone.

"I said, 'Your family'—that is, his children, his wife, his preacher, pastor they called him, these people. He said, 'No. This is my test. . . . I have been through this.' He said, 'I went through it alone.' He said, 'They weren't with me.' He said, 'I am not subjecting them to this.' And here he is. I read in the paper this morning that this was the day that Columbus sailed from Palos for the Western hemisphere for the first time, and I hope that in this trial, we will find America again."

DENATURALIZATION CASES WERE decided by judges, not juries, and on the second day of the Jakob Reimer hearing, expert witness Charlie Sydnor turned to face Judge McKenna from the witness stand.

From a historian's perspective, Reimer could have been a Nazi collaborator straight from central casting, an educated ethnic German who had likely understood the German culture far more than he did Russian. Still, Sydnor thought the judge looked doubtful, even bored, sitting with his head in his hands at his desk in the center of the courtroom.

For many months, Sydnor had worked late into the night with David Rich and Peter Black, who, Sydnor often said, understood OSI defendants all the way down to their fingernails. Stutman was like that too, meticulous and obsessive, an irritant to the mildly exhausted paralegals in the unit who were forced to chase down the most obscure details about the Nazi regime. Had an SS guard at Auschwitz worn size eleven boots? Stutman needed to know.

Sydnor appreciated the thoroughness. After the impromptu meeting in the men's room in Charleston with Peter Black and David Marwell in 1980, Sydnor had worked regularly as an expert witness for OSI, testifying in court about concentration camp guards and other Nazi collaborators. Over time, Sydnor discovered that some lawyers considered the historians little more than eccentric scholars, curiosities to be tolerated but never fully empowered.

Ten pounds of shit in a five-pound bag, Sydnor once called a particularly dismissive attorney.

But Stutman was different. He believed that history was the best evidence of all, with the power to make or break a case rooted in faraway events that were decades old and growing more distant with each passing year.

In the courtroom in New York, Stutman was asking about

Trawniki. "Dr. Sydnor, are you able to say whether...Trawniki men knew or came to know what was happening to the Jews?"

"It's very clear that the men initially recruited were not told where they were going," Sydnor explained. "When the first large-scale, lethal actions were undertaken—and the first one was in Lublin in March of 1942—the official explanation that the participants were given was that the people in Lublin were going to be cleared from the ghetto and shipped out, and they were going to be sent to Palestine or they were going to be relocated in work camps further east. The official explanation given even within the SS was, and the clerical euphemism used was, 'resettlement to the east.'"

Sydnor went on. "Pretty soon everybody figured out that something a lot worse than transportation to Palestine or relocation to a labor camp in the east was what was happening to these people, and, of course, the death camps were up and running. Trawniki men who were rotating back and forth from these guard formations in the death camps to the Trawniki camp itself brought back stories with them of what was going on."

Sydnor paused. "At a certain point, every Polish child was aware of what was happening to the Jews who were crammed into those trains."

Stutman asked Sydnor to describe the training protocol at Trawniki and then turned to shooting operations. "Can you describe any...mass shootings that involved Trawniki men?"

From survivor accounts from postwar legal proceedings in West Germany, Sydnor knew that Trawniki men had participated in a massacre of Jews in the woods during the Lublin ghetto deportation in the spring of 1942. He believed that the two Soviet eyewitnesses who had placed Reimer at a pit shooting had likely described that massacre, and that Reimer himself, during his 1992 interview with Eli Rosenbaum and Neal Sher, had likely detailed the same operation.

But Sydnor couldn't know for sure. Because the conduct of the killers at pit shootings throughout eastern Europe was generally consistent, he decided to describe a shooting in August 1942 when as many as two thousand Jews in a village in the Lublin District were taken to a sports complex and then into the woods, where they were shot in groups.

"This shooting created something of an administrative stir... because it was very, by German standards, very messy," Sydnor said. "...The pit had been dug in a location where groundwater seeped into the bottom. The victims were forced to get into the pit and lie down and they were shot. The next group of victims were then forced to lie down on top of the first group and they were shot....A lot of victims in the pit were only being wounded so that at one point, the Trawniki men who were doing the shooting and some of the Germans actually got down into the pit as the groundwater mixed with the blood of the victims and fired with pistols at short range to finish off those who were only wounded."

"These operations sound like they were hard work," Stutman said softly.

"Very hard work. Mass murder is hard work, Mr. Stutman."

ON THE THIRD day of the hearing, Ramsey Clark pressed Sydnor about the pit shooting that he had described in court. "You have absolutely no reason to believe [Reimer] was there, do you?" Clark asked.

"I have seen no evidence that he was there, no, sir," Sydnor replied.

"Why would you go through all that horror in this man's case?"

"Information was given by Mr. Reimer about a shooting....It is, I think, important in trying to understand the context of the time and the circumstances of German rule in the Lublin District....Historians simply look for what information or evidence may be available to provide context with other events."

"Do you think in a murder trial it would be fair to present evidence [from] other murder trials. What Jack the Ripper did?" Clark asked.

"I don't know about a murder trial," Sydnor said evenly. "But I don't think there was any intent or effort to either sensationalize or dramatize anything. Certainly, the nature and character of German rule and the behavior of the Trawniki-trained guards...were of such a nature that any courtroom theatrics fifty years after the fact, Mr. Clark, would be pretty superfluous."

"But if it was your future that was under consideration, you might not think that testimony was superfluous to your case. You would agree with that?"

Stutman cut in. "Object to counsel arguing with the witness."

"To the last question, sustained," the judge said.

"You have no knowledge that he was there, do you?" Clark asked again. "He may have been, but you have no knowledge of it?"

"He may have been. All I have are the statements, the recollections of [the two eyewitnesses], each of whom testified that they participated in a killing operation involving a pit in the woods...in the spring of 1942. And each of those gentlemen identified a number of people who were present at that event. Both of them identified Mr. Reimer."

AFTER COURT, SYDNOR and Stutman met for dinner at Windows on the World on the top of the World Trade Center. The main dining room, which faced north and east, commanded a sprawling view of the Manhattan skyline. Stutman was quiet, staring into his wine glass.

"What were they thinking?" he murmured.

Sydnor looked up. He didn't understand the question. "What?"

"What were they thinking?" Stutman asked again.

He seemed to be referring to Reimer and the Trawniki men who had fired into the ravine filled with Jewish people.

"Well, I—"

Stutman interrupted. "What do you think was in their minds, in their last thoughts, before they were murdered?"

Stutman was asking about the victims, not the killers, and Sydnor found the question unexpected and profoundly unsettling. He tried to think of some way to respond, some factoid from history that would explain the roots of inhumanity. He came up empty.

Stutman went on. "Do you think that a father standing there, holding his infant, in his last thoughts, could he have imagined that one day there would be somebody who would try to effect justice or retribution?"

Sydnor imagined the ravine filled with parents, children, grandparents, stripped of their dignity and about to die in a hole in the ground. Sydnor wanted to comfort his colleague, to come up with a way to make sense of it all, but he couldn't find the words.

Instead, he stammered, "I can't imagine, Ned."

CHAPTER TWENTY

TAKEN UP

New York City
1998

The dreams were back, familiar in the early-morning stillness. *Run.* She is a prisoner in a Nazi concentration camp. *Hide.* There is safety in shadows. For a split second, she can see herself from far away, surrounded by the SS with all the others, but then the light fades, the air returns, and the grisly image finally slips away.

Sitting next to Ned Stutman on the sixth day of the Jakob Reimer hearing, Ellen Chubin wasn't the least bit surprised that the nightmares of her childhood had returned, feeding off the testimony in the courtroom. As a girl in Philadelphia she had learned about the Holocaust in part from the experiences of her grandmother's cousins, a Jewish brother and sister who had fled to Palestine just before the German invasion of Poland. Images of a lost generation crept into Chubin's dreams and lingered there for years.

As the junior member of Stutman's legal team, Chubin had been assigned to prepare two government witnesses, one from the Jewish ghetto in occupied Czestochowa and another from Trawniki. At seventeen, Sophie Degan had been taken to the training camp to sort the belongings of the dead.

"I haven't talked about these events ever," she told Chubin, who listened but didn't push, just as Stutman had advised her.

Degan and three other survivors had agreed to share their stories in court. None had known Reimer personally during the war, but for historical context and detail they would describe the work of the Trawniki guards in the cities where Reimer had been deployed.

In the courtroom, Chubin stole a glance at Reimer, who had stared straight ahead for much of the morning as the first survivor took the witness stand.

Sixty-eight-year-old Samuel Hilton, an accountant from Arizona, had been a boy of thirteen when the SS ordered every remaining Jew in the Warsaw ghetto to report for deportation. Hilton had crouched in a crowded cellar with his father, but his stepmother and two-year-old sister had stayed behind since a crying toddler would have alerted the Germans. Hilton and his father managed to evade deportation for several months, hiding in bunkers around the ghetto until they were discovered by the SS.

"We were sure we were going to be shot," Hilton said. He described standing in a square with his father and the others. "That's when the indignity started. Well, the SS troops with sticks and bayonets ripped the dresses off the women . . . beat them, looking for gold, looking for money.

"They said, 'If we find any gold or money on you, we will shoot you on the spot.' And my father had three very beautiful gold bracelets, heavy gold, and I said to him, 'Dada, please drop it. Drop it.' So he actually dropped it in the cobblestone."

Hilton continued. "They made us sit, and I looked up in the sky. It was a beautiful, blue May day. I looked at my father and I said, 'What did I do? What did I do to deserve to be killed? I haven't hurt anyone. I haven't done anything to no one. Why should I be killed?' . . . My father stroked my head and he said, 'What did your little sister, two years old, do to be killed?' I was a schoolboy and I didn't know. It was mind-boggling to me."

The courtroom was utterly still as Hilton described how the group was taken to a schoolhouse. "That's where the Ukrainian SS came into play," he said. "They were swarming that place...from one end to the other."

Hilton described beatings with sticks, random and indiscriminate shootings. "I looked out from the window. There were a lot of bodies in the courtyard laying in a pool a blood, a lot of bodies. Then they took women—there was a special room in there. You could hear it, the screaming. That was the rape room, where they used to rape the women."

At the prosecutor's table, Chubin glanced at OSI attorney Lisa Newell, who appeared poised and steady as she questioned Hilton.

"You stated a moment ago that the Ukrainians came in," Newell said. "How were you able to recognize these men as Ukrainians?"

"How do I know?" Hilton replied. "They wore the black coats.... This was all Ukrainian. They didn't speak German."

Hilton described being sent with his father to the Majdanek concentration camp, where relatively strong, healthy men were separated from those who would be quickly killed. Hilton knew he was too young to go with the men, and so he had looked at the SS man in charge and started shouting.

"I just yelled out, 'I am sixteen years old, Herr Colonel.' He was a sergeant, and I called him a colonel. He looked down at me and he smiled and said, 'You are a kid'...and let me go with the men instead of going to the death."

Hilton said his father died a few weeks later at a labor camp near Majdanek.

"Mr. Hilton, did you ever obtain any further information about the fate of your stepmother and sister?"

"I looked all over. I am the only one who got out alive."

"I have no further questions, Your Honor," Newell said.

"No questions, Your Honor," Reimer's attorney, Ramsey Clark, said.

Chubin cleared her throat, gave her head of thick brown curls a gentle shake, and stood up. She wanted to impress Ned Stutman, who reminded her of her father and had once even promised to find a suitable Jewish suitor for Chubin to date and marry. More than anything, however, she wanted to give the survivors a chance to be heard.

She turned to the judge. "The government calls as its next witness Carl Langner."

The retired engineer from Rockland County, New York, walked to the witness stand in a blue jacket and red tie. Looking at Langner, Chubin tried to imagine the boy in Czestochowa who had lost his father to deportations in 1940. Langner, his brother, and his mother had been left to fend for themselves in the Jewish ghetto, on a street that had been called the Avenue of the Holy Madonna until the Germans renamed it Adolf Hitler-Allee.

"When exactly did the liquidation of the Czestochowa ghetto begin?" Chubin asked.

"The beginning, just following the Day of Atonement, Yom Kippur," Langner said, staring straight ahead through a pair of square eyeglasses. For a man who had once lost everything, Langner had a voice that was clear and strong.

"What did you see?" Chubin asked.

"I saw yelling and screaming and people running trying to escape through the roofs, jumping from the windows, screams, gunshots."

"Where were the gunshots coming from?"

"From the Germans and Ukrainians that tried to kick out the people from their apartment. They did it in such a way that they didn't have time even to do anything. It was so bad that they had to jump from windows. This period was most horrible, most horrible of all horrors. It was just, I cannot describe. I choke with emotion. How can I express what happened here? You cannot quantify horror."

Once, Langner said, he and his brother tried to reach a workshop outside the ghetto, but were turned back by a Trawniki guard. "The Ukrainian...he was singing, whistling. We thought that he is not dangerous. He saw us. He just turned around without a word, cocked his rifle and tried to shoot us."

"Who was guarding you?" Chubin asked.

"We were always guarded mostly by Ukrainian guards....They were cruel beyond imagination."

SOPHIE DEGAN, CHUBIN thought, looked younger than her seventy-one years as she settled onto the witness stand and brushed back her cropped, blond hair. Chubin smiled, hoping to reassure her.

In November 1943, Degan had been sent to Trawniki with a small group of women to sort belongings left by the thousands of Jewish prisoners who were murdered during Operation Harvest Festival.

"How were you transported...to Trawniki?" Chubin asked.

"On tracks because I remember looking and seeing the world," Degan said. "There were guards, Ukrainian guards sitting with us, and at some point asking us to give all the valuables that we had because we won't be needing them anymore where we are going."

"When they brought you inside the camp, did you see any prisoners?"

"No, nobody. That's what it was, terribly quiet, nothing."

"Did you see any signs that there had recently been prisoners in that camp?"

"Yes, because the barrack there they brought us in, it was like people's household. They had their household things there, their dresses there, utensils, and everything was pulled out from the platforms that they were sleeping on, like bunk beds."

"Bunk beds?"

"Bunk beds, sort of, and you could see that the place was searched through because the bed things were on the floor. Everything was just upside down. So there were signs that somebody was living there, but nobody was there."

"Did you find any survivors of the group who had been at the camp before you arrived?"

"Later on, as we were clearing all the barracks.... We found at one time a little boy, Marek. He may be two years old. And for a while, they let us keep it, but then they took it away."

Jakob Reimer had argued that he was, in most every sense, a prisoner of the SS. Chubin wanted to establish the difference between the Jewish prisoners and the men of Trawniki.

"When you were at Trawniki...were you issued a uniform?" Chubin asked.

"No."

"Did you receive any pay for your work?"

"No."

"Did you receive any vacation time?"

"No."

"Based upon your experience at Trawniki and your contact with the Ukrainians who were there, was there a difference in the status of the Ukrainians versus the status of the Jews?"

"Well, they had guns and they were guardians over us. We were prisoners of theirs."

"Besides yourself, did any family members survive the war?"

"Just one single cousin."

Chubin nodded at Degan. "Thank you very much."

"No questions, Your Honor," Clark said again.

AFTER COURT, NED STUTMAN left to give an update to Eli Rosenbaum back in Washington. Chubin found Degan standing by herself, a lonely figure in the cold, marble hallway. The older woman looked up briefly and Chubin sucked in her breath. After the grueling testimony in court, Sophie Degan appeared utterly serene.

"Thank you," Degan said slowly, "for letting me tell my story."

Chubin had fought to keep her composure all day, but her eyes grew moist as she smiled at Degan, a poetry lover who had come to embrace the words of Henry David Thoreau.

> Every blade in the field, every leaf in the forest, lays down its
> life in its season as beautifully as it was taken up.

As it happened, the tears came later, when Chubin sat alone in her room at a Marriott near the courthouse. As night fell over Manhattan, she felt spent and numb.

What she really needed was sleep, distance from ghettos and guards, but the dreams were back and they were relentless. She was a prisoner in a Nazi camp, crouching in blazing white light, shrinking down to the nothing.

CHAPTER TWENTY-ONE

COMPASSION

New York City
1998

O n the eleventh day in federal court, Jakob Reimer took the stand to face his accusers. Ned Stutman could not detect the slightest hint of surliness in Reimer's demeanor, no flaring temper or the lusty indignation of the wrongly accused. Reimer wore a knit tie and striped shirt, a most ordinary American, and as he settled in his chair on the witness stand, he glanced sheepishly at the judge.

Stutman nodded briefly, intent on staying focused. His wife, Suzanne, had come from Washington and was sitting in the back of the courtroom with their youngest son. Sweet, familiar faces, a lifeline to a place far removed from occupied Poland and the men who had so loyally served the Reich.

For more than two days on the witness stand, Reimer had spun a hard-knock story before the judge. Under questioning by defense attorney Ramsey Clark, Reimer had been a starving prisoner of war, an unwitting Nazi recruit, a benign office manager far removed from the murder of Poland's Jews. Stutman was anxious to address Reimer himself, and he glanced down at his worn legal pad, filled with hundreds of questions culled from strategy sessions with David Rich and Peter Black.

There was no doubt that Reimer made a sympathetic defendant.

Once, he had interrupted his own attorney to praise Simon Friedman, OSI's oldest witness, who had described being shot and left for dead by Trawniki men during a mass execution at the Treblinka killing center.

"I have to give Mr. Friedman a lot of credit at his age," Reimer said moments after he took the witness stand, startling the lawyers in the room.

"I beg your pardon?" Clark replied.

"I have to give Mr. Friedman a lot of credit at his age," Reimer went on, "and I can only say that starting in 1941, I worked in the office and this was all under the strictest secrecy. We didn't know anything about it."

Reimer paused and then added, "I am sorry, Mr. Clark, if you want to ask me more questions."

"We are supposed to do this by questions and answers, as you know," his lawyer scolded.

"Sorry," Reimer said again. "I had to get this off my chest."

From the prosecutor's table, Stutman had listened as Reimer described being taken to Trawniki, filthy and malnourished, and given food and a uniform. He insisted that he had only been deployed to Lublin for a single day, to guard a block of empty houses, and that on the morning of the ravine shooting, he had no idea what would eventually happen in the woods.

"In the army, you know it, never, ever they tell you," Reimer said, stumbling over the words. "When you face the battle, that hill we have to take, then you get the order. You don't know when you are in the army. You are taken there, then you are given the order, what the purpose is."

"Do they tell you what you are going to do?" Clark asked.

"Absolutely not."

Reimer testified that on the night before the ravine shooting, he had been taken with his platoon to a shack somewhere outside

Trawniki. He was woken up before dawn by an SS man and told to gather the guards.

"Did you have to find them in the dark?" Clark asked.

"You have no light. You feel around at first. I felt around, if every bunk was empty. I knew I was late now and I rushed, and as I rushed, I stumbled and fell and I was knocked out, and I was laying there on the spot."

It was a wildly disparate story from the one that Reimer had told Eli Rosenbaum and Neal Sher in New York in 1992. During that first interview, Reimer said he had been late to the operation because he overslept, an implausible explanation given what Stutman knew about the exacting nature of SS operations. Now Reimer was insisting that he had blacked out from a fall.

From the witness stand, Reimer went on, "I fell on my head."

"What happened next?" Clark asked.

"I was laying on my face and somebody came and grabbed my right and left shoulder and started to lift me up and I came to. I got up. I was half in a daze, and then he led me where the group was. I didn't know where the group was. I had no idea where they had gone."

"When you came up to the others…what did you see?"

"I saw a little ditch or a little pit that was a small area where I saw some dead bodies."

"Try and describe the pit," Clark coaxed. "Could you tell how many bodies were in there?"

"No. I am only guessing. I had no idea how many there were. There weren't many, though."

"There weren't a thousand?"

"No."

"Were there a hundred?"

"There were not even a dozen. It was a small group."

"How big was the pit? Can you estimate?"

Reimer paused. "Let me describe it this way. The nine men that were standing around this pit was bigger than the pit itself. That is how I surmised that it was a small pit."

Once again, Reimer had changed his story, drastically scaling back the scope of the shooting operation. In 1992, he had described a large pit covered with wooden planks so that SS and Trawniki men could walk from one end to the other. Now, the size of the pit had changed, and so had the death count, from as many as sixty people to fewer than a dozen.

"Were the bodies clothed?" Clark was asking.

"Yes."

"Did they have uniforms on?"

"No...I thought they were civilians."

"Did you ever find out who these people were?"

In 1992, Reimer had told Rosenbaum and Sher that the victims had come from a Jewish labor camp.

"We had no idea who they were. The Jewish persecution was under the strictest secrecy.... When you are raised behind the Iron Curtain, we didn't know anything about Nazis or what they were all about. We had not the faintest idea. When you live under a totalitarian government, you don't dare ask questions or you wind up someplace. No. No. We had no idea what the Nazis were all about, what their aim was."

"Do you have any knowledge as to whether these were common criminals or whether they were people who were threatening security or anything like that?"

"That is what we assumed. I thought they had been found guilty. We didn't have the foggiest."

"I know it is hard to remember...," Clark said, "but do you remember anybody in the pit moving?"

"Well, I have been thinking about that a lot," Reimer replied. "I don't know why it comes into my head that somebody moved or pointed to his head. I don't know. It is possible."

"When you got over here, did you ever tell your children about it or any—"

Reimer interrupted. "Mr. Clark, I couldn't possibly even talk to anybody or explain. They wouldn't understand. This was with me for over fifty years and every time you look on the TV and you saw Holocaust and this comes in your head what I had seen, so this builds up and builds up and finally, and then in 1992, I said they shot a labor camp."

"Who did you say this to in 1992?"

"To Mr. Rosenbaum and Mr. Sher."

"Was that the first time you talked about it in all these years?"

"Yes. And I told them that we went to exterminate the labor camp....We were nine men with rifles....I should have said, 'Shoot.'"

"Did you shoot?"

"I had to fire a shot."

"Tell me what you did."

"I just shot over it. I was not about to kill somebody. Even if they were already dead, I would not shoot into anybody. It is very simple. In my life, all my life, you shall not kill, and I did not."

"Did you see anyone push people into the pit?"

"No. They were dead when I got there."

"Did you hit anybody?"

"No way."

"Did you believe," Clark asked, "you personally had done any-thing?"

"I personally didn't shoot anybody. I personally did not, nothing more than what the Germans ordered me to do, but I didn't shoot at anybody, dead or alive."

Later, Clark asked, "Have you ever had any hatred or ill will to-ward Jewish people?"

"Oh no," Reimer replied.

"Have you ever persecuted any Jewish people?"

"No, I haven't."

"Have you ever hated any group of people, African Americans or gypsies or Jews or anybody?"

"No way, no. You are supposed to love all the people."

"Did you ever hurt any person from the time you became a German prisoner until the end of the war?"

"No," Reimer replied flatly. "Never."

IT HAD BEEN an astounding few days in court watching the exchanges between Reimer and his lawyer, and finally Ned Stutman stood up and walked to the front of the room. He could feel the stares of the survivors who had come to watch Reimer, to search his face for answers, as if truth lurked behind frown lines.

"You should get an electric chair!" a woman had called out the day before when Reimer stepped down from the stand, carrying a batch of legal folders. Reimer did not reply.

After ten days in court, the air in the room felt flat and stale. Stutman drew in his breath and focused on the tremendous task at hand. Cross-examining a defendant was never simple, but Reimer was nearing eighty, with stooped shoulders and a cough that had developed after hours on the witness stand.

"Is it fair to say that you believed that during your entire time at Trawniki, you were a prisoner of war and were treated like a prisoner of war, with no rights whatsoever, who could be executed?" Stutman asked. "You believed that when you were at Trawniki, you believe it now, and you believed it in the fifty intervening years, is that correct?"

"That's correct," Reimer replied.

"Whatever your assignments at Trawniki, you believe you were always in the status of a prisoner with no rights, who could be executed at will and was ordered to do various things?"

"Yes."

"And you believe that when you were doing the guard duty in Lublin that you have described, it was only because you were a prisoner and were ordered by the SS to do that?"

"Right."

"And your testimony in this court has been that sometime in late 1941, you went into the office in Trawniki permanently, never to have an outside tactical assignment again. Is that correct?"

"Absolutely."

"Since you have told Judge McKenna and all the rest of us that you were a prisoner under the threat of execution, ordered by the Germans, even the lowliest German could order you to do whatever they wanted, is there any reason to believe that you told any immigration official anything different?"

"No," Reimer said, appearing confused. "I don't see."

Stutman produced the US Army Counterintelligence Corps report drawn up before Reimer immigrated to the United States, describing Reimer's whereabouts during the war.

"It says, 'Between 1942 and 1944, interpreter at the Gruczyn sawmill in Poland.' Were you ever an interpreter at a sawmill in Poland?"

"I don't think so," Reimer said slowly. "I don't recall it."

"Right below that statement is another. It says, '1944 to 1945, interpreter at the fortification projects at the Vistula River.' Do you recall what this is referring to?"

"No."

Stutman was seeking to highlight one of the most significant inconsistencies in Reimer's story. If Reimer had been a so-called Nazi prisoner, why would he lie about his activities and whereabouts on his immigration documents?

"You have testified in this court that you were in Warsaw in 1943, correct?"

"Right."

"So you couldn't have been in Gruczyn and Warsaw at the same time, correct?"

"No. That's why I said I agree. It's incorrect."

"Do you have any way at all that you can explain how this statement got on your signed statement...in November 1951?"

"No," Reimer answered. "They were general statements."

"This seems to me to be a...specific statement, not a general statement," Stutman pressed. "I am asking you again, can you explain in any way how this statement appears on your signed statement?"

"Those are not my words. Those are not my statements. They only got in there by suggestion. I don't know who."

From the back of the courtroom, someone shouted, "Why you sign?"

"Let me just stop for a moment, please," Judge McKenna interjected. "I understand that those things cause very painful memories for people.... However, this is a court of the United States. We cannot have people shouting things out."

Stutman went on. "While you were telling various American officials during the period of your immigration that you were a prisoner of the Germans, treated like a prisoner with no rights, who could be executed at will, did you ever tell anyone that you were permitted to travel home from Trawniki on two occasions unattended?"

"No. That didn't come up."

"You state that you were a prisoner during the entire time at Trawniki with no rights, but, in fact, you were paid, weren't you?"

"Yes."

"And you state that you were a prisoner at Trawniki with no rights, who could be executed at will, who carried weapons from time to time. Am I correct?"

"That's correct."

Satisfied, Stutman turned to the ravine shooting. Again, he would focus on Reimer's shifting accounts, starting with the size and nature of the operation. "Now in your testimony in this court...you stated it was a small pit. Do you remember how you described the size in 1992?"

Reimer was quick with a reply. "When I was asked in '92, over the years, this had grown in my head. I even said we went to exterminate a labor camp in '41. Number one, there was no labor camps in '41. Number two, exterminate means gas or like the extermination camps. You didn't go with nine rifles to exterminate a labor camp. It was absolutely all made up in my mind....I actually have been suffering by these things that I had seen, you know, so that's why I exaggerated everything, and it took me a while to put it all together."

"I want to ask you a simpler question," Stutman said. "Do you remember how you described the size in 1992?"

"Yes."

"Can you state how you described it?...You said it was a big hole?"

"Big ravine."

"And looked like it was dug by a bulldozer?"

"Right, and they didn't even exist, bulldozers at that time."

"Yes, that's quite right. But you said it was a big hole?"

"It was all made up in my mind. It had grown over the years."

"Now you testified in this court that there were not even a dozen people in the pit when you arrived there."

"Right."

"Do you remember the number that you gave to me in your deposition?"

"Less than ten probably. Maybe a few."

"You said there were twelve in your deposition."

"Well, how would I know? Did I go down and count them?" Reimer answered, sounding irritated. "It's impossible."

"Do you remember the number that you gave in 1992?"

"I said forty to sixty."

"Now, in your testimony in this court, you stated that you didn't know why you were there or the identity of the people."

"No, I didn't. We didn't know."

"If I may," Stutman said, "I would like to play for you a segment of this tape from '92 so you can hear what you said."

"Well, no, I know it's all wrong what I said in '92, so I want you just to realize that."

Stutman ignored the comment. At the prosecutor's table, Ellen Chubin stood up and turned on a large recorder. The voices of Eli Rosenbaum and Reimer filled the courtroom.

"Mr. Reimer, in your own words, tell me about the incident, whatever you can remember."

"We stayed in a barrack someplace outside of Trawniki, where, I don't know. I think it was a platoon of us. They all woke up. We all woke up and they were all sent to exterminate a labor camp."

"How many Jews were killed in this action?"

"Forty, fifty, sixty; I don't know."

"Did the Jews have to dig their own ditches, their own graves?"

"It was a big hole. It could not have been dug by hand."

"Now Mr. Reimer," Stutman said, "who stated that the men were going to exterminate a labor camp?"

"Well, you heard me say that."

"The word 'exterminate a labor camp' originates with you. Mr. Rosenbaum asked you, 'Tell me in your own words what happened' and the words were, 'We were all sent to exterminate a labor camp.'...How did you learn about exterminate a labor camp at that time?"

"Nobody told me. It grew in me over fifty years. And I made it a labor camp....I had heard this over the years and until '92 when I was asked about it, then I pull it all together."

"I see," Stutman said. "Did you ask anybody where these people had come from?"

"We didn't know who they were. Were they underground or criminals—"

"You keep saying that. I am asking a different question. After this was over or at any time, did you ask anybody about who these people were, why they were lying in a pit?"

"The only one who would know was the SS men," Reimer insisted. "I couldn't very well go and start an argument with the SS men. I would be the next one shot."

"You never asked? You never were curious to find out who these people were and why they were shot?"

"No. I never found out."

Stutman pressed. "You had no curiosity because you knew who the victims were, didn't you?"

"The victims?"

"You used the term 'exterminate a labor camp'—"

"This was—"

"Let me finish," Stutman said. "Who were in the labor camps, Mr. Reimer?"

It was a rhetorical question and Stutman went on. "Now, in your testimony in this court, you stated that you missed the first volley because when leaving the shack behind your men, you stumbled and fell on your head and was knocked out."

"That's correct."

"Now, of course, we have just established that in 1992, you gave a different version or different reason for missing the first volley, am I right?"

"I said I overslept....That's, of course, totally ridiculous."

Stutman motioned to Chubin, who turned on the recorder again to play another excerpt from Rosenbaum's interview with Reimer.

"There's something about the man who pointed to his head that you haven't told me?"

"Yes."

"You finished him off."

"I'm afraid so. I don't know if I hit his head. I don't know that."

"But he died?"

"I just say that I had to make one effort at least while the German was looking at me. . . . I shot at the direction."

The courtroom was still. "You and your other Trawniki men fired the last volley, is that correct?" Stutman asked.

"Yes."

"That's when the man who was pointing to his head was actually finished off?"

"Not by me."

"I didn't say by you. I said, 'And that's when the man who was pointing to his head was actually finished off?'"

"Yes, right. That's my impression. I think that's the way it was."

Later, on the witness stand, Reimer started coughing.

"Are you okay?" Stutman asked. "Would you like to call it a day, Mr. Reimer?"

"Well, no," Reimer replied. "I wish you would finish the subject already."

DURING A BREAK, Suzanne Stutman pulled her husband into an empty corner in the back of the courtroom and touched his hand. After twenty-five years of marriage, she knew exactly what he was feeling and wasn't the least bit surprised when he whispered, "Am I doing the right thing? Am I okay?"

"*Rakhmones,*" he said, using the Yiddish word for compassion.

Reimer was a Nazi collaborator and quite possibly a murderer, but he was also a husband, father, and grandfather. His life, in many ways, had also been tragic.

"You know he's an old man," Suzanne said gently. "But the work that you're doing is so important."

THE NEXT MORNING, Ramsey Clark had one final chance to make his case. "Were you ever a Nazi?" he asked Reimer.

"Absolutely not. I just can't stand that when they call me that because as soon as I had a chance, I got out of there."

"Have you ever opposed the United States at any time in any way?"

"No way."

"In your heart or by your deeds, by your acts?"

"No. I have always been proud and honored to be a citizen of this country."

"Have you been chased and harassed by the press and media?"

"Constantly."

"In the several weeks you have been in the courthouse here, have people said mean and terrible things to you?"

"Yes, but they don't really know that I was not involved. I don't hold it against them. I understand their anger, but—"

"Has the press literally chased you down the street with cameras?"

"Yes. Yes, Mr. Clark."

"Now, Mr. Reimer, my question to you is how do you answer those people and what do you want to say to them?"

"I have been saying this to Mr. Stutman. I got out of it before it even started. So actually, I did something about it. I should be praised to get out of it before it even started."

"What would you say to them about how you feel about them?"

Reimer paused and then wrapped up the end of the twelve-day hearing. "I pray for everybody that prosecutes me."

CHAPTER TWENTY-TWO

SECOND CHANCES

Washington, D.C., and Cleveland, Ohio
2001

Three years had passed without a ruling in the Jakob Reimer case, a preposterously quiet stretch of weeks and months that would have brought on moments of deep despair if there were no other cases to consume Eli Rosenbaum and the staff of the Office of Special Investigations. From the rosters in Prague and Moscow, the historians had discovered more Trawniki men living in Connecticut, Utah, Philadelphia, the suburbs of New York.

Growing old in America, Rosenbaum often brooded, *alongside Holocaust survivors and war veterans.*

Though OSI had opened more than fourteen hundred investigations of Nazi perpetrators by 2001, time had always been the enemy of the unit, the slow churn of the judicial system as great an obstacle as the savviest defense attorney. But the delay in the Reimer case was unprecedented, and every day without a ruling fed a mounting fear at OSI that the judge was simply biding his time to allow Reimer a graceful exit, an untroubled death in his home in New York.

It was a terrible thought, Rosenbaum decided, a backhanded slap to all those who had survived the war. What if the O. J. Simpson jury had been out for a year? Surely the American public would have demanded answers. Rosenbaum couldn't shake the thought, but of course he had been the one to look Reimer in the eyes when Reimer confessed to the shooting at the ravine. After reading the eyewitness statements—"fear-crazed" people forced into the pit with rifle butts—Rosenbaum had imagined Reimer's pleasant face filled with rage in the shadows of Poland's Krepiec Forest.

Rosenbaum would never become a rich man on a government salary, but justice was a righteous payout. He needed that in the Reimer case, if only for the dying man in the pit who had pointed to his head during the massacre, inviting one last shot to end the misery.

"It seems that there is always some crime, some image, perhaps from our latest case," Rosenbaum had told a Jewish congregation in Richmond, Virginia, just before the start of the Reimer hearing, "that won't let go of us."

At least OSI was moving forward, about to take to trial a new case against its most notorious defendant, John Demjanjuk. It would be a high-profile, controversial affair after all that had gone wrong over twenty years of litigation.

In 1993, after newly discovered Soviet records made clear that Demjanjuk could not have been Ivan the Terrible of Treblinka, the Israeli Supreme Court had overturned his conviction and death sentence. Though the court found that Demjanjuk had been a guard at the Sobibor killing center, prosecutors declined to take further action. Demjanjuk was freed after five years on death row.

That same year, the Sixth Circuit Court of Appeals in Cincinnati had lambasted OSI for its handling of the case, pointing out that the original attorneys had had evidence that cast doubt on whether Demjanjuk was Ivan the Terrible but failed to share documents with the defense team. "Prosecutorial misconduct," a three-judge panel had bluntly declared.

The court ordered Attorney General Janet Reno not to block Demjanjuk's return to the United States. Demjanjuk flew back to

Ohio and in 1998 successfully petitioned a federal judge in Cleveland to restore his US citizenship.

Rosenbaum had not been part of the first, tangled denaturalization case against Demjanjuk, which had been launched long before Western historians had proper access to archives behind the Iron Curtain. Armed with hundreds of newly discovered documents, Rosenbaum knew without a doubt that Demjanjuk had trained at Trawniki and gone on to guard the doomed Jewish prisoners at the Sobibor killing center and at the Majdanek and Flossenbürg concentration camps.

Launching a new case against Demjanjuk would surely bring renewed attention to OSI and require a long legal slog through the federal courts. And it was entirely possible that Demjanjuk would die on US soil before he was ever stripped of his citizenship for a second time. But OSI, Rosenbaum knew, had all the evidence it needed to take the case back to court, and he had gone to the Justice Department's criminal division for permission to move forward.

Rosenbaum had been sitting at his desk one fall afternoon in 1998 a few weeks after the Jakob Reimer trial in New York, when a longtime deputy assistant attorney general called with an urgent request.

"We have to present to Janet Reno," he told Rosenbaum. "An hour from now."

Rosenbaum looked at his watch. It was an unscheduled meeting, called to reassure the attorney general that there would be no unwelcome surprises if OSI pursued Demjanjuk a second time. Rosenbaum mumbled something close to yes and hung up.

He phoned Patty Stemler, a senior lawyer at the Justice Department and head of the criminal division's appellate section. She often worked directly with the attorney general, whom Rosenbaum had scarcely met. Rosenbaum explained quickly.

"Who should make the presentation?" he asked, hoping Stemler would volunteer.

"I think it should be you."

Oh my, Rosenbaum thought, knowing that Reno demanded absolute precision, regularly challenging her staff to be sure that every case was built on solid legal ground. Rosenbaum couldn't say he blamed Reno for wanting to sign off on the Demjanjuk case. After the media criticism and the thrashing from the Sixth Circuit Court of Appeals, Rosenbaum for the first time in his legal career had taken to hedging when strangers asked what he did for a living. "I'm a federal prosecutor," he'd usually say, and leave it at that.

Rosenbaum thanked Stemler and hung up. An hour later, he slipped inside the executive suite at the Justice Department. He was seated at a conference table across from the attorney general, who was flanked by senior officials from the criminal division.

Reno appeared calm behind thick, oversized eyeglasses, but Rosenbaum was keenly aware that the country's first female attorney general had been threatened with contempt by Republican members of Congress for refusing to turn over two internal Justice Department memos during the impeachment hearings of her boss, President Bill Clinton. Reno, fiercely independent, had made a point to never let politics sway decision making at the Justice Department.

Reno's team had already read OSI's summary of the Demjanjuk case. Is the evidence solid? Rosenbaum said that it was. OSI had Demjanjuk's Trawniki identification card, his personnel file, and dozens of other records, including rosters that detailed his deployments to Sobibor and Majdanek.

Rosenbaum recounted the facts and arguments, how Demjanjuk had lied about his Nazi service and then sailed into New York City aboard the *USS General W. G. Haan* in 1952. Six years later, Demjanjuk became a naturalized citizen of the United States. He had enjoyed a decent life, with union pay and family.

Reno listened quietly and finally nodded. "You can file the case."

OSI was being given one last chance to set the record straight. Rosenbaum had thanked Reno and her staff and hurried back to the office. He found Ned Stutman and OSI attorney Jonathan Drimmer, who would work with Stutman on the case. Rosenbaum pulled in Barry White, who had become OSI's chief historian, and Todd Huebner, the historian who would take the lead on the case.

"Janet Reno says we can file," Rosenbaum said.

Just after the 1998 Jakob Reimer hearing, syndicated columnist George F. Will had penned a piece published in the *Washington Post*. Rosenbaum had read it often, practically memorizing key passages. As OSI scrambled to prepare for the second Demjanjuk trial in the early months of 2001, Rosenbaum thought of Will's words once again.

"The unspeakable was done by the unremarkable," Will had written, "and it speaks well of American justice that it will not close the books on bestiality until the last participant has felt a *frisson* of fear and is routed from the land of the free."

GIVEN THE SIGNIFICANCE of the case against John Demjanjuk, the first day of the hearing in Cleveland in May 2001 was bound to be tense. The prosecution had once again made international news, OSI's reputation was on the line, and the fate of a man accused of helping the SS slaughter thousands of Jews would be put before a federal judge in the United States for a second time.

Still, OSI attorney Jonathan Drimmer chuckled under his breath as he walked into the courtroom and saw several thick World War II books prominently propped up on the defense table for good showing. He glanced at Demjanjuk's lawyer, Michael Tigar, whose silver and turquoise belt buckle glinted in the morning sun. The veteran criminal defense attorney, once compared by his peers to Clarence Darrow and Thurgood Marshall, had earned a reputation for enjoying a flair for the dramatic in the courtroom.

Later, to needle the defense team, Drimmer would make a good show of laying down *The Complete Idiot's Guide to World War II* on his own table in the courtroom. It wasn't exactly a legal strategy that he had picked up at law school at UCLA or during a stint at the NAACP Legal Defense Fund, but it was too delicious a move for second thoughts.

Drimmer had been twenty-nine when he joined OSI, just before the Jakob Reimer case went to court. He had spent hours with Ned Stutman, Peter Black, and historian Todd Huebner, learning about the operation at Trawniki. Stutman, Drimmer realized early on, had learned to press defendants for details about their whereabouts during the war, knowing that the historians could rebut lies with facts and context.

"These guys know their stories," Stutman often said about OSI suspects, "but they don't know history."

Drimmer was moved by his new colleagues. He had found Black profoundly patient, an educator as much as a historian. For all his time at OSI, digging into some of the darkest moments in history, Black still managed to laugh every time Stutman, sometimes intentionally, sometimes not, mispronounced a Polish name.

"Kozowka?" Black would say, chuckling, his glasses bouncing off the tip of his nose. "Ko-zow-ski."

At home, Drimmer knew, Black and his wife, Mary, were caring for Aaron, who on one afternoon had slipped away from his school, walked into an unlocked house a few blocks away, pulled food from the refrigerator, and started to eat. The homeowner called the police, and one of the officers had pepper sprayed Aaron and tackled him to the ground. Black and Mary rushed to retrieve their son, whose eyes were red and wrists were bruised from handcuffs.

Drimmer had come to know Stutman too, particularly on a trip to Ukraine, where they toured an ancient synagogue that the Nazis had used as a stable for horses during the war. Later, the building was turned into a public theater.

"All these amazing restored churches," Stutman had remarked, gazing at the Star of David that still hung above the building's stained-glass windows, "and with these old synagogues, they don't give a shit."

The moment had helped Drimmer understand Trawniki, how the Germans had leveraged generations of antisemitism in eastern Europe to turn men like Reimer and Demjanjuk into loyal collaborators.

To prosecute Demjanjuk, OSI would present seven German documents showing that he had been sent from the Trawniki training camp to Sobibor, Majdanek, and the Flossenbürg concentration camp. The records included a photo, a signature, a date and place of birth, and a physical description of Demjanjuk, who bore scars on his left arm and his back and had a tattoo listing his blood type, a product of SS service.

OSI also had Demjanjuk's original Trawniki identification card, which had been returned by the Israelis. Eli Rosenbaum had picked it up in Tel Aviv and placed it in a waterproof container inside his briefcase. On the long flight home, he opted not to use the restroom because he didn't want to leave his briefcase unattended above the seat. So much had already gone awry in the case over so many years. Rosenbaum decided to leave no room for another mishap.

Though no survivors would be put on the witness stand in court, Stutman and Drimmer wanted to share small, humane details about suffering and loss, not for dramatic effect but because the awful story of John Demjanjuk could not be told by dates, documents, and deployments alone. Only six Sobibor survivors were still living in the United States, and Drimmer had gone to see each one, traveling to Ohio, Connecticut, California, New York, and New Jersey.

On the first day of the Demjanjuk hearing, the air inside the

Cleveland courtroom felt chilly. Drimmer sat next to Stutman, behind stacks of records gathered by the historians.

When Rosenbaum reopened the case against Demjanjuk, the editorial board at the *Washington Post* had called the move "correct, even
courageous." But Drimmer couldn't know for sure how the judge
might ultimately rule.

Drimmer looked for eighty-one-year-old Demjanjuk, a large man
with a spit of white hair who had been rumored to need extra-large
handcuffs while on trial in Israel. But only his son and son-in-law sat
at the defense table alongside Tigar. Drimmer assumed that Demjanjuk was waiting at home in the suburbs of Cleveland.

Drimmer was eager to hear from Demjanjuk's lawyer, who had defended Oklahoma City bomber Terry Nichols after he was charged
with helping to blow up the Alfred P. Murrah Federal Building, killing
more than 160 people and injuring 680 others. In court, Michael
Tigar would argue that OSI had it wrong again, a second case of mis-
taken identity, and that Demjanjuk had never been at Trawniki.

Just before eleven a.m., federal judge Paul Matia surveyed the
packed courtroom. He was familiar with the case, Drimmer knew,
since Matia had been the one to restore Demjanjuk's citizenship
three years earlier after he had returned from Israel.

"Good morning, Your Honor," Stutman said, rising. "We have
come here with one purpose, to revoke the defendant's citizenship.
Our burden in doing so is heavy, as it should be. Your Honor, this is
a case of maximum contradiction regarding history. Either the government's history is right or the defendant's is. We believe that the
seven naming documents and wartime documents like them are the
very foundation of history itself, and they clearly and unequivocally
show that [the] defendant was a Nazi guard during World War II
and that his version of events is simply not true."

Tigar quickly shot back. "The government once again has got it
wrong."

IT WAS AN exhausting first day in Cleveland, and when Stutman asked Drimmer to come to his hotel room after court, Drimmer braced for another long night of strategizing. Drimmer smiled when he spotted a photograph of Stutman's wife, Suzanne, propped on the nightstand by the bed.

Drimmer half expected the older lawyer to offer some uncanny quip about the day in court, a joke to lighten the mood. For years, Stutman had performed a stand-up comedy act in the nightclubs of Washington, spinning tales about family and fatherhood. "I take humor very seriously," he often said.

But now Stutman's face was ashen.

"I need to fly home."

Drimmer shook his head, unsure if he was hearing clearly.

"The test results came in," Stutman went on, "and it's bad."

Drimmer struggled to manage his thoughts. As the OSI legal team prepared for the hearing, Stutman had complained that he couldn't run as far on his daily workouts, that his legs felt like cement. His focus was off, foggy somehow. "I'm really having to dig in," he had told Drimmer.

"It happens to everybody who works in this office," Drimmer had answered, grinning at his exhausted colleague, who, at fifty-five, had started working nights and weekends to make final preparations for trial.

In meetings, Stutman had begun eating jelly doughnuts. "I'm having problems keeping weight on," he explained, and again Drimmer brushed aside the comment, figuring that stress had caused the weight loss.

Looking at Stutman in the hotel room, Drimmer could finally see it, the way Stutman's suit sagged on his hips, the gauntness around his eyes and cheekbones. Later, Drimmer would learn that a doctor had called only moments before the start of the Demjanjuk hearing with news that Stutman had a rare form of non-Hodgkin's lymphoma. There was no known cure.

Stutman had hung up the phone and gone on to deliver his opening statement in court. He had talked for hours without letting on that he had just been told he likely had six months to live.

"I conducted that inquiry seated. I apologize," Stutman said to the judge at one point after posing a long series of questions to an expert in forensic document examination. "Would Your Honor prefer me to stand at the podium?"

"It doesn't make any difference," the judge had replied. "We are going to be here for quite a while."

Looking at Stutman, Drimmer felt helpless. "I'm really sorry. I can't imagine what you're going through."

Stutman paused, as if he was about to say something more. Instead, he just nodded. "You should keep going. You've got this case. You should keep going."

Stutman was the team's lead attorney, but Drimmer knew the material, the witnesses, the history.

"I'll do my best," he promised.

The following morning, Stutman flew home to prepare for an experimental course of cancer treatment at a medical center in Houston. Drimmer asked for a meeting with the judge and Tigar, whose face softened when Drimmer explained.

Tigar asked whether Drimmer wanted to postpone the hearing. Drimmer thought of his friend and colleague, who had always said that life doesn't move in a straight line.

"No," Drimmer said. "We're ready to go."

CHAPTER TWENTY-THREE

CREDIBLE EVIDENCE

Washington, D.C.
2002

Five months after Osama bin Laden's terror network struck New York, Pennsylvania, and Washington, Eli Rosenbaum sat alone in his corner office three blocks from the White House. The space was packed tight with history books, legal folders, and notepads that Rosenbaum kept around to scribble random thoughts about upcoming speeches and cases.

Taxis sped down 13th Street, which connected Washington's business district to the sprawling federal office buildings along Constitution and Pennsylvania Avenues. Commuters hurried to work, bundled up from the February wind. Official Washington and much of the Justice Department was focused on bin Laden, the extraordinary destruction on American soil, and what had come to be called the "War on Terror."

It had occurred to Rosenbaum when the Twin Towers fell in a plume of smoke and flames that he had spent his entire adult life immersed in the worst behaviors of mankind, violence that had caused so much misery, so much loss. Michael Bernstein, gone in a flash of fire over the skies of Scotland.

Rosenbaum kept a framed photo on his desk, a picture of a billboard that John Lennon and Yoko Ono put up in cities around the world in December 1969 as the Vietnam War raged. "War is Over! If you want it. Happy Christmas from John & Yoko."

For all the scrambling around him, Rosenbaum's office was quiet. He sat perfectly still in the silence, eyes fixed on his computer screen.

Eight months after the hearing in Cleveland, Trawniki man John Demjanjuk had been stripped of his US citizenship for the second time. Federal judge Paul Matia had called the government's evidence "devastating."

> Although the defendant claims he was not at the camps indicated by the documentary evidence, he has not given the court any credible evidence of where he was during most of World War II. The government had the burden of proving its contention to the court by clear, convincing and unequivocal evidence. It did so.

Rosenbaum thought about the killing center Sobibor, a place that he knew had been something close to hell, encased by barbed wire and rigged with land minds. Only about 50 of more than 165,000 prisoners had survived to describe it, and their stories—trainloads of men, women, and children driven into gas chambers within moments of their arrival and suffocated with carbon monoxide—had defied imagination.

A celebration of the Demjanjuk decision would be wholly inappropriate.

Instead, Rosenbaum reached for the phone. He called a Sobibor survivor in New Jersey, whose parents had been stripped naked and forced into the gas chambers by Trawniki guards with whips and rifle butts. "We won," Rosenbaum said gently, thanking the man for being willing to testify.

Rosenbaum told historians Todd Huebner and Barry White, who

had worked on a 176-page report about Demjanjuk and the men of Trawniki that expert witness Charlie Sydnor had provided to the court.

> Trawniki became the training ground, command center, and supply depot for this force, whose members participated directly in the implementation of virtually every aspect of Operation Reinhard. One of these auxiliaries was a young Ukrainian.... Demjanjuk entered German service at Trawniki in mid-1942, beginning a career that would take him to the depths of the Nazi abyss.

Rosenbaum called Peter Black and Ned Stutman, grateful to have something good to share with a man who was promising to return as a lucky redbird after he died so that his grandson could one day sit by a bird feeder and say, "Hi Poppop."

There was silence on the line after Rosenbaum delivered the news of the judge's decision, and he knew that Stutman was crying.

It was a significant victory, even after the embarrassment of the first failed case, and at a press conference later that morning, Rosenbaum peered into a bank of television cameras. He thanked Stutman, the historians, and Jonathan Drimmer, who had stepped into the role of lead trial attorney when Stutman fell ill.

Already, Demjanjuk's lawyer was vowing to appeal, and Drimmer was preparing arguments for the Sixth Circuit Court of Appeals, the same court that had criticized OSI for withholding evidence in the first case.

With any luck, Demjanjuk would be ordered deported and sent to Ukraine or Germany. But there was no telling how long the case might linger before that happened. Demjanjuk, Rosenbaum knew, might live a good long while on US soil.

And yet, the man was no longer an American citizen, his role in the mass murder of Jews finally, officially, correctly confirmed by a federal court.

"Our efforts," Rosenbaum said at the press conference, "were inspired by the courage of the survivors who, in recounting for us their nightmarish experiences of more than a half a century ago, were willing to reopen psychic wounds that of course have never fully healed in order to help us ensure that justice is done on behalf of those who perished.... They should never have been forced to share their adopted homeland with John Demjanjuk."

PETER BLACK WOULD never know exactly what happened over four days in September 2002, seven months after Demjanjuk was stripped of his citizenship. Eli Rosenbaum had complained to a friend about the interminable delay in the Jakob Reimer case, and the friend had placed a discreet phone call to a reporter at the *Wall Street Journal*.

And then, suddenly, four years after the hearing in federal court and fifty years after Reimer had settled in New York, Black received news of a decision.

Federal judge Lawrence McKenna had ruled for the government, stripping Reimer of his citizenship. It seemed a reluctant decision, a half-hearted parsing of facts and arguments rather than an angry denouncement of Reimer's role in the destruction of Polish Jews.

The judge had placed "little weight" on Reimer's initial confession about the ravine shooting, but Reimer had been armed during a mass shooting and had repeated in court his admission that he fired his gun while at least one victim was still alive. As a member of Trawniki, he had "logistically supported" SS personnel during the busiest, most violent months of the Holocaust.

Reimer had thirty days to turn in his passport.

At OSI, Rosenbaum got Ned Stutman and historian David Rich on the line, then called Charlie Sydnor. "Judge McKenna has ruled in favor of the government," Rosenbaum declared.

In New York, US Attorney James Comey, who would go on to become the seventh director of the Federal Bureau of Investigation, told the *New York Times*, "Reimer's presence in the United States is an affront to all those killed in the Holocaust."

After nearly six decades, Black reasoned, a full accounting of the operation at Trawniki was now part of the official public record, memorialized by a federal court. Above all else, Black was relieved.

Unlike nearly every other Trawniki man found on American soil, Reimer had never served in a labor camp or killing center. But his participation in at least one mass shooting and in the liquidation of Jewish ghettos had been enough, and the win would surely allow OSI to more easily prosecute others.

In Sutton, Massachusetts, Trawniki man Vladas Zajanckauskas, who had penned a journal he called "My Bits of Life in this Beautiful World," was insisting that he had played no part in the murder of Polish Jews.

In Queens, New York, Trawniki man Jakiw Palij was fighting to stay in the United States even though OSI had found that he guarded Jewish prisoners in the months before they were shot at Trawniki during Operation Harvest Festival.

Finally, Black decided with a discreet measure of satisfaction, the record of history was complete, with a detailed and somber roadmap of the past that might one day deter others from acting on such inhumane instincts. Jakob Reimer, for all his proclamations, had been brought to justice, and though time was surely the enemy of OSI, it had not won out.

Not yet anyway.

Reimer would appeal the ruling. But as Black read the judge's decision, even rhetoric from Reimer's defense lawyer wasn't particularly troublesome.

"To me, among those who've survived," Ramsey Clark had declared of his client, "he's one of the greater victims of World War II."

CHAPTER TWENTY-FOUR

TRAWNIKI

Trawniki, Poland
2013

The barracks that once housed five thousand men had long been abandoned, the site of the forced-labor camp for Jews replaced by a grassy field. Still, the Polish village of Trawniki seemed familiar, and despite the unusual warmth of the October sun, sixty-two-year-old Peter Black shivered.

He had set out in the morning, walking among the birch trees that grew in the backyard of his hotel. Both perpetrators and victims had described birch trees at shooting sites, and Black paused, taking in the landscape.

He walked along the old railroad tracks that had delivered Trawniki men to ghettos and killing centers across occupied Poland. He walked past buildings adjacent to the former training camp, near the spot where the SS and police had shot to death as many as six thousand Jewish prisoners during Operation Harvest Festival in 1943.

Everywhere Black went, it seemed as if he were standing on the bodies of the dead.

He had traveled to Trawniki to address an international group of historians and prosecutors who had come together, nearly seventy years after the war's end, to talk about the operation at the training camp.

"To manage the murder of two million Jews believed to be re-
siding in the Government General, the Nazis in Lublin needed a
reliable, available and ruthlessly led police auxiliary force," Black
told the group. "Trawniki Training Camp provided this resource.
The Trawniki men not only served as the foot soldiers of the final solution in the Government General but also represented a workable
model for the enforcers of the future in the grim world the Nazis intended to construct."

The Office of Special Investigations had identified nearly forty-
five hundred of the roughly fifty-one hundred men who had trained
at Trawniki. As he walked through the village for the first time since
he had started his research years earlier, Black thought of Jakob
Reimer.

As promised, Reimer had appealed the court's denaturalization
ruling, but in January 2004 the Second Circuit Court of Appeals in
New York upheld the decision to revoke his citizenship. Judge Sonia Sotomayor, who would later accept a seat on the US Supreme
Court, had penned the ruling:

Perhaps most damning to Reimer's argument... is that on at
least one occasion he stood, armed, at the edge of a pit into
which people—some alive and others dead—had been thrown.
When one of the men who lay in the pit moved slightly, Reimer
was ordered to fire. He did.

Reimer had agreed to leave for Germany, but German officials
turned him away. Eli Rosenbaum had been so frustrated by Germany's refusal to take back Nazi criminals ordered deported by US
immigration judges that he later went to Germany and, in a speech
to scholars and prosecutors, pleaded for help.

"The nonacceptance of what to us is a clear moral obligation is
a great disappointment," Rosenbaum declared. "If Germany does

not act to admit these men...they will likely get to spend the rest of their lives in my country, which is the adopted homeland of so many thousands of Holocaust survivors and is a country whose families sacrificed 200,000 of their sons in order to bring to an end the nightmare of Nazi inhumanity in Europe."

Jakob Reimer would die in Pennsylvania in August 2005 before the Office of Special Investigations and the US State Department could find a country willing to take him.

To Black, a more profound tragedy would come one month later, when Ned Stutman died just after his sixtieth birthday. Black missed his old friend, who had come back to work for a stretch when the cancer was in remission. Stutman had been thinner, but his graying hair had started to grow back. "Like the cherry blossoms on the Tidal Basin in Washington," he had said, grinning.

Jews, Stutman explained to friends and colleagues, didn't believe in asking God for miracles. But he figured that God could certainly decide on his own accord to permanently rid Stutman's body of cancer. Wishful thinking or not, Stutman had thrown a party to celebrate his improving health, passing out bagels and baseball caps to thank friends who had sent hats when chemotherapy had cost Stutman his hair.

But there would be no miracle. He would write that his immune system had likely been weakened by his work—"a steady diet of Holocaust horror and sorrow and the emotion that came from recreating it."

From a bed in Georgetown University Hospital, Stutman had given his son-in-law a proposed headline for an obituary: "Justice Department Lawyer, Humorist."

Just before his lungs filled up with water and he started to hallucinate, Stutman kissed his wife and children good-bye. It was a *mitah yafah*, Suzanne Stutman said afterward. A good death.

And when a cardinal built a nest right outside their daughter's house in Philadelphia a few months later, no one was much surprised.

Stutman had litigated thirteen cases at OSI and won twelve of them. Black wished that Stutman had lived long enough to see John Demjanjuk sent back to Germany in 2009, where he was convicted as an accessory to the murder of more than twenty-eight thousand people while he had been a guard at Sobibor between late March and early August 1943. Demjanjuk died while the case was on appeal.

Alone in Trawniki, Black stood on the grounds of the sugar factory, with its towering smokestack and old bricks that had turned a dull shade of white. He could see no visible signs of a training camp for murder, only a small memorial down the street with a few trees and a slab of marble.

Black lingered for a long while, thinking of Reimer, Demjanjuk, so many others. The Trawniki rosters discovered in Prague, and the research that came afterward, helped OSI successfully prosecute thirteen Trawniki men in the United States. Standing in front of the place where they had been armed and trained to kill, Black had a single thought.

The dead never knew their names.

EPILOGUE

FEELS LIKE VINDICATION

In a sprawling brick house cluttered with soccer balls and sparkly pink tutus, Lucyna Wojcik had set about raising her children. There was no extended family to speak of, no grandparents or aunts or cousins, but on birthdays and Friday night Shabbat dinners, she and Feliks would come together with other Jewish survivors, not quite family but kin, people who came from the same place, who needed what they did.

It was what Lucyna wanted for her son and daughter, a world filled with light and sweetness, kisses at bedtime, Chanukah presents wrapped in shiny gold foil, Halloween costumes carefully sewn together with bits of satin and yarn. She had gone about it in the most practical way.

Though Feliks had earned only fifteen dollars a week as a medical resident in the hospital in Rochester, New York, they took long, happy walks in the park, where they put their infant son on a blanket in the grass and munched on day-old bread that Lucyna had learned to soak in milk and bake with sugar. Before bedtime, Feliks played "The Blue Danube" on an old violin since music reminded him of his mother. Lucyna canned apples and tomatoes. When there was extra money Feliks bought his first car, a 1947 Plymouth.

The dark years, as Lucyna called them, faded ever so slightly. *This is our happiness,* she thought.

A baby girl came four years later. Where once there was nothing, Lucyna said at the Thanksgiving dinner table that year and every year after that, now there is a family of four. They moved to the Midwest suburbs in the early 1960s so Feliks could open a medical practice, and there they found a community of Polish survivors who hadn't quite mastered the nuances of the English language but kept American flags firmly positioned on their front lawns.

There were no grandparents for Bar and Bat Mitzvah ceremonies, but friends and neighbors filled the seats of local synagogues for one child after the next. "You don't have family, you make your own family," Feliks liked to say, and instructed the children to call him uncle or papa.

Between the two of them, Feliks was decidedly more fixed in the past. He talked about the guards in Lublin. "The Ukrainians," he said more than once, his voice rising, "were worse than the Nazis. They enjoyed it."

He talked about how his faith in God had died in the ghettos.

"What I would give to have a picture of my sister," he once told Lucyna.

In the early 1980s, Feliks had read newspaper stories about a man named John Demjanjuk. Somehow he had come to the United States, on a ship bound for New York. How could such men be living free? There was no good answer, of course, and soon Feliks stopped asking the question.

To spare her children, Lucyna talked about the past only on rare occasions and in a manner more matter of fact than angry. Once, on a beach vacation in 1974, she sat with her daughter and described the last days of the Lublin ghetto.

"My mother told me, 'You must leave,'" Lucyna said. "I didn't have the chance to say good-bye."

In her own children, Lucyna saw compensation for what she had
lost in Poland. During the Jewish holiday of Rosh Hashanah, the
rabbi at the family's synagogue had once said, "God giveth and God
taketh away."

After the service ended, Lucyna pulled him into a corner. She was
dressed in a suit and pearls, gold earrings neatly clipped to her ears.
"Rabbi, I have to tell you, I disagree with you. You're wrong."

"How am I wrong?" the rabbi asked.

"You said, 'God giveth and God taketh away.' But in my life, God
taketh away and then God giveth." She pointed to her family. "Look
what I produced."

After Feliks's medical practice took off, there had been extra
money for the opera and a timeshare in Acapulco, where Feliks
brought along a Super 8 movie camera and followed his children
as they splashed in the water. On weekends at home, he put on an
apron and hat and grilled steaks in a yard filled with red and white
flowers. Lucyna spent time in the kitchen, grinding meat for kre-
plach, the small dumplings that she had eaten as a girl in Poland.

When Feliks and Lucyna's children became parents, a family of
four became a family of twelve, filling an entire row in the synagogue. Alone at home, Lucyna found herself thinking more about
the war and her lost brother. What had become of him? She knew
only that in Warsaw, his assumed name had been found on a list of
survivors registered in January 1946 in a displaced-persons camp in
the town of Neuburg, Germany, near Frankfurt.

"There was no proof that he ever died," Lucyna told Feliks. "I
need to know."

Feliks pressed her to launch a search, to talk to the Red Cross or to
return to Poland and search for his name in the telephone books. That,
Lucyna said, wouldn't do. "My foot will never step on the Polish soil
under any circumstances, except if I know my brother is there."

Together, they wrote to officials in Israel, Sweden, England,

Australia, and Germany. Lucyna posted a notice on a website set up by Holocaust survivors and their families. She waited for months, but no response ever came.

When a local Holocaust educational group asked if she would be willing to describe her life in Poland during the war, Lucyna agreed to go on camera. When her children were young, she wouldn't have considered it. But as she grew older, she felt an obligation to her family, to history, and to her parents and brother.

Lucyna put on a pink wool suit, gold earrings, and lipstick. She looked somewhere off-camera and paused. "I come from a town called Lublin," she began.

In 2013, after fifty years as a practicing physician, ninety-two-year-old Feliks died in his armchair. Long after Lucyna's legs had weakened, he had managed to twirl her around the dance floor at polka parties, looking, in his crisp white bow tie, every bit the boy Lucyna remembered from Poland.

"I will not live past our wedding anniversary without him," Lucyna told her son.

True to her word, Lucyna fell into a coma and died six months later, at the age of eighty-seven, on the seventy-first anniversary of her marriage to Feliks in the Warsaw ghetto.

NO OTHER COUNTRY has more rigorously pursued Nazi war criminals in the past three decades than the United States. Since 1990, the Office of Special Investigations has denaturalized and deported more than seventy people who once assisted in Nazi persecution. That's more than the total prosecution victories of all other countries in the world combined, including Germany, during the same period.

More than a hundred successful cases were brought by OSI after its founding in 1979. Most OSI defendants did not come from Germany and were instead collaborators who helped throughout the Holocaust.

"To be successful at preventing future genocides," Barry White wrote in 2016, "we must...do the hard work of examining the factors and dynamics that can motivate potentially any ordinary human in potentially any country to collaborate in mass murder."

Peter Black, who retired from the United States Holocaust Memorial Museum in 2016, is now considered the world's foremost expert on the Trawniki training camp and the men who served there. "If legal consequences for mass murder and mass atrocity become habitual to political and judicial behavior in the twenty-first century," he often said at conferences after his retirement, "perhaps we can prevent mass murder in the future."

Though OSI won cases against dozens of Nazi war criminals, eight defendants under deportation orders died on US soil because their native countries and Germany refused to take them back. Reimer, the ninth, died a few months after OSI launched a deportation case against him. Germany had already declined to take him.

Over time, the lack of cooperation from other countries became the single greatest frustration faced by OSI. Eli Rosenbaum brought up deportation policies twice on trips to Germany and spent years appealing for help from members of Congress and the US State Department.

In August 2018, US authorities, working under a deal cut by the White House, removed former Trawniki man Jakiw Palij from the United States after fourteen years of unsuccessful attempts. He had lived out much of his retirement on a quiet street in Queens, New York, perhaps the last surviving Nazi defendant ordered deported from the United States.

After receiving word that Palij had landed in Dusseldorf, Germany, Rosenbaum emailed Black.

"Hi, Chief," Rosenbaum wrote. "He arrived in Germany a few hours ago."

Black, surprised at the sudden turn of events, quickly responded:

"How in the world did you get the Germans to agree to take him back?"

Rosenbaum also emailed White, who, after twenty-nine years at OSI, began working at the United States Holocaust Memorial Museum, where she became the research director of the Center for the Prevention of Genocide and, later, a historian in the Office of the Senior Historian.

"After so many managed to live out their lives here despite final removal orders," White wrote to Rosenbaum, "this one feels like vindication."

Despite early predictions that the work of the Office of Special Investigations would be finished in a matter of months, the unit was active for three decades. In 2010, OSI was merged with the Domestic Security Section of the US Department of Justice to form a new unit with a broader post–World War II mission. The Human Rights and Special Prosecutions Section prosecutes human-rights violators and other international criminals who participated in genocide, torture, or war crimes abroad.

After spending nearly his entire legal career at OSI, Rosenbaum became a director within the unit, helping to track war criminals who slipped into the United States from new hot spots around the world, including Bosnia, Serbia, Rwanda, and Darfur.

The new unit is as busy as ever.

ACKNOWLEDGMENTS

In February 1989, Simon Wiesenthal told the *Baltimore Jewish Times*, "The history of man is the history of crimes, and history can repeat.... Information is a defense. Through this we can build, we must build, a defense against repetition."

Historians Peter Black and Barry White spent most of their professional careers at the US Department of Justice and, later, the United States Holocaust Memorial Museum, probing some of the darkest moments in human history. This story could not have been told without their wisdom, insight, and steadfast support. They gave generously in ways big and small, with profound patience and perspective, to further the public's understanding of the Holocaust. I am grateful for their somber and objective counsel, and for their dedication to accuracy, from the inception of this project to the very end.

Special thanks to Eli Rosenbaum, the former director of DOJ's Office of Special Investigations and now the Director of Human Rights Enforcement Strategy and Policy at the Human Rights and Special Prosecutions Section. Despite his heavy workload, he offered extensive and ongoing guidance on legal and historical matters with passion and precision. The analysis, memories, photos, and audio and video files he provided were invaluable.

Many other lawyers and historians involved in OSI's work contributed to this project, most notably Neal Sher, Charlie Sydnor, Jonathan Drimmer, Patrick Treanor, David Rich, Allan Ryan, Ellen Chubin, David Marwell, and Todd Huebner, who provided significant historical guidance for the map created for this book.

Though I never knew Michael Bernstein or Ned Stutman, their families made me feel as though I did. Thank you for sharing time and memories. The children of Feliks and Lucyna Wojcik were incredibly supportive as I set about introducing their remarkable parents to a wider audience, and I am sincerely grateful for the guidance, photos, and generosity.

My sincere thanks to the United States Holocaust Memorial Museum and the knowledgeable staff in the archives, particularly Vincent Slatt, Nancy Hartman, and James Gilmore. Thank you to Nicole Navas at the US Department of Justice.

Much help came from experts in Poland, including Tomasz Kranz and the staff at the Majdanek State Museum, the professionals at the Warsaw Museum of the History of the Polish Jews, and the Taube Center for Jewish Studies, particularly Helise Lieberman. Thanks also to guides Joanna Krauze in Lublin and Pawel Szczerkowski in Warsaw. In the Czech Republic, Michaela Jiroutova skillfully helped me retrace the steps of OSI historians when they mined the archives in Prague in 1990.

The painstaking and important work of other journalists also must be acknowledged, including stories, photos, and video that appeared in the *New York Times*, the *Washington Post*, and the *Chicago Tribune*. Several books about OSI also provided compelling and detailed roadmaps, including *Quiet Neighbors*, by Allan A. Ryan, and *The Right Wrong Man*, by Lawrence Douglas.

The talented and persistent group of research assistants from George Washington University who spent many months reporting and fact checking deserve special acknowledgment: Colleen

Grablick, Julia Goldman, Audrey Hickcox, Kendrick S. Chang, Kelly Del Percio, Elise Zaidi, and Nicholas Jepson.

Thank you, Joelle Delbourgo, my astute and passionate literary agent, who knew this story needed to be told. Her absolute commitment to the world of books was, as always, a great inspiration.

Every writer needs a steadfast team of editors and supporters. I am fortunate to have a stellar team at Hachette Books, which supported this writing project from day one. Paul Whitlatch's deft editing skills were as invaluable as his guidance, wisdom, and knowledge of world history. Thank you also to gracious and talented assistant editor Mollie Weisenfeld, who stepped in to provide extensive editorial insight during production, and to managing editor Monica Oluwek, publicity manager Michael Giarratano, marketing manager Quinn Fariel, senior marketing director Michael Barrs, copy editor Kelley Blewster, and associate publisher Michelle Aielli. Mauro DiPreta greenlit the book, and Mary Ann Naples provided guidance and inspiration as it neared publication.

I am deeply indebted to my friends and colleagues, including those at the *Washington Post,* the George Washington University School of Media and Public Affairs, and Northwestern University's Medill School of Journalism. Journalist Michael Sallah as well as Michael and Pam Rubin, provided important feedback over many months. I am profoundly grateful to my mother, Renee Cenziper, the ruthless reader of rough drafts, and my husband, Jeffrey Rohrlick, the most wonderful man I know. Finally, thank you to my boys, Brett and Zack. Your generation gives me faith every day that perhaps our future won't be as grim as our past.

NOTES

PROLOGUE

Nazi recruit 865 ducked into the US Attorney's Office in the Southern District of New York: Transcript of sworn interview, Jakob Reimer, US Department of Justice, Office of Special Investigations, US Attorney's Office for the Southern District of New York, May 1, 1992.

He was an obliging helper who had come when he was called: Eric C. Steinhart, "The Chameleon of Trawniki: Jack Reimer, Soviet Volksdeutsche, and the Holocaust," *Holocaust and Genocide Studies* 23, no. 2 (2009): 239–262.

Soon, the US Department of Justice would move to expose one of the most trusted and effective Nazi collaborators: Peter Black, "Lease on Life: How the Collapse of the Soviet Union in 1989–1991 Impacted U.S. Investigations of Trawniki-Trained Guards," paper given at the 35th Annual Conference on Holocaust and Genocide: Holocaust and Genocide Trials, April 12, 2018, Millersville University, Millersville, PA.

He had lied with ease for years: Jeffrey Goldberg, "The Nazi Next Door," *New York Magazine*, March 14, 1994.

…1.7 million Jews had been murdered in less than twenty months: "Operation Reinhard," Holocaust Encyclopedia, website of United States Holocaust Memorial Museum.

CHAPTER ONE

Go east, his father had said, since there was no place left to run: Much of Feliks's story comes from videotaped interviews spanning a decade, conversations with family members, and on-the-ground research in Lublin, Warsaw, and Vienna.

Jews had lived in Poland since the Middle Ages: "1,000 Years of Jewish Life in Poland," Taube Foundation for Jewish Life and Culture, 2011, Warsaw, Poland.

...*Hitler directed the German army to carry out a surprise attack against the Soviet Union:* "Invasion of the Soviet Union, June 1941," Holocaust Encyclopedia, website of United States Holocaust Memorial Museum.

The mobs forced Feliks into a sprawling labor camp set up in a factory on the outskirts of the city: "Janowka," Holocaust Encyclopedia, website of United States Holocaust Memorial Museum.

CHAPTER TWO

War had come to Lublin from an angry night sky: Much of Lucyna's story comes from videotaped interviews spanning a decade, conversations with family members, and on-the-ground research in Lublin, Warsaw, and Vienna.

...*both of Lublin's Yiddish newspapers, the* Lublin Daily *and the* Lublin Voice, *had stopped publishing:* "Lublin, Occupation and the Ghetto," Holocaust Education and Archive Research Team, Holocaust Research Project, www.HolocaustResearchProject.org.

The place was filthy, tens of thousands of bodies squeezed onto streets covered with a thick layer of mud: Joanna Krauze, guide, Rootka Tours, Lublin, Poland, 2017.

...*past the miserable houses packed tight with miserable people:* Various photos, Grodzka Gate NN Theater Centre, an activity of the NN Theater, Lublin, Poland.

The men in black uniforms and black caps seemed to appear out of nowhere: US District Court Southern District of New York, United States v. Jack Reimer, 92 Civ. 4638.

The Jewish doctors and dentists had been taken to the camp down the road, the terrifying place called Majdanek: Tomasz Kranz, "They Arrived at the Ghetto and Went into the Unknown: The Extermination of Jews in the Government General," introduction to exhibition catalogue by Robert Kuwalek, Dariusz Libionka, State Museum at Majdanek, Lublin, Poland, 2012.

CHAPTER THREE

The Warsaw ghetto sat behind ten-foot walls topped with barbed wire and broken glass: "Conditions in the Warsaw Ghetto," Holocaust Encyclopedia, website of United States Holocaust Memorial Museum.

After Warsaw's four hundred thousand Jews were forced into the ghetto: Pawel Szczerkowski, guide, Warsaw, Poland, 2017.

In the frigid early months of 1943, the ghetto's young Jewish leaders were forging plans to fight back: "Warsaw Ghetto Uprising," Holocaust Encyclopedia, website of United States Holocaust Memorial Museum.

The German commander in charge of the operation would soon send a detailed report to SS chief Heinrich Himmler: "The Stroop Collection," Yad Vashem, World Holocaust Remembrance Center, Jerusalem, Israel.

CHAPTER FOUR

"Are you Peter Black?" the voice on the other end of the line inquired: Peter Black, conversation recounted in an interview with author, 2017.

In 1942, Maikovskis, a police precinct commander in German-occupied Latvia, had carried out orders: Robert McG. Thomas Jr., "Boleslavs Maikovskis, 92; Fled War-Crimes Investigation," *New York Times,* May 8, 1996.

Black had heard whispers for years about Nazi perpetrators who had made their way to the United States: Allan A. Ryan Jr., *Quiet Neighbors: Prosecuting Nazi War Criminals in America,* San Diego: Harcourt, Brace, Jovanovich, 1984.

...a housewife in Queens who had used the soles of her jackboots to beat and torment prisoners: Douglas Martin, "A Nazi Past, a Queens Home Life, an Overlooked Death," *New York Times,* December 2, 2005.

A Cleveland autoworker stood accused of terrorizing and torturing doomed prisoners: "John Demjanjuk: Prosecution of Nazi Collaborator," Holocaust Encyclopedia, website of United States Holocaust Memorial Museum.

"Half-hearted, dilatory investigations," berated Brooklyn congresswoman Elizabeth Holtzman: "INS Accused of Conducting Dilatory Probe of More than 60 War Criminals," Daily News Bulletin, Jewish Telegraphic Agency, May 21, 1974.

...Holtzman had helped pass legislation: Joseph Polakoff, "U.S. Immigration Agency Lists 37 in Inquiry on Nazi War Crimes," *New York Times,* December 2, 2005.

She had also pushed to create a new unit within INS singularly focused: Theresa M. Beiner, "Due Process for All: Due Process, the Eighth Amendment and Nazi War Criminals," *Journal of Criminal Law and Criminology* 90, no. 1 (1989).

Despite the nature of the work ahead, OSI had opened with little fanfare: A. O. Sulzberger Jr., "Agency Studying Nazis Is Upgraded," *New York Times,* March 29, 1979.

It seemed a scolding, not a question, and Black hesitated: Peter Black, conversation recounted in interviews with author, 2017, 2018.

Tens of thousands of German documents were stashed behind the Iron Curtain: Elizabeth B. White, "History in the Courthouse: The Presentation of World

War II Crimes in U.S. Courts Sixty Years Later," in *Nazi Crimes and the Law,* eds. Nathan Stoltzfus and Henry Friedlander, New York: Cambridge University Press, 2008.

History needed to have a place in the deliberations: Benjamin Guterman, "The History Professional: An Interview with Elizabeth B. White," *Federal History* 8 (2016): 14–25.

"Don't be nervous," Marwell quipped, flashing his Department of Justice credentials: Charles Sydnor, conversation recounted in interview with author, 2017.

CHAPTER FIVE

...when he had been a prominent leader of the Romanian Iron Guard: Peter Black, "Viorel Trifa and the Iron Guard," Office of Special Investigations, 1982, Peter Black files, United States Holocaust Memorial Museum, Washington, DC.

...the federal government eventually filed a complaint against him, repeatedly pressed by a Jewish Holocaust survivor from Romania: Ralph Blumenthal, "Dr. Charles Kremer, 89, Dies; Pressed Trifa War Crime Case," *New York Times,* May 28, 1987.

The deportation hearing for an archbishop: Ari L. Goldman, "Valerian Trifa, an Archbishop with a Fascist Past, Dies at 72," *New York Times,* January 29, 1987.

Immigration judge Bellino D'Ambrosio called the Trifa hearing to order: Trial transcript, United States of America in the Matter of Valerian Trifa, 1982, US Department of Justice Immigration and Naturalization Service, United States Holocaust Memorial Museum.

He gradually reduced the number of criminal investigators and hired more historians: Ryan, *Quiet Neighbors.*

The archbishop, Ryan said, would admit that he had been a member of the Iron Guard: Thomas O'Toole, "U.S. Deports Romanian as War Criminal," *Washington Post,* August 15, 1984.

The next morning, the Chicago Tribune *reported:* "Archbishop in Nazi Case Will Leave," *Chicago Tribune,* October 1982.

Years earlier, an article in a Soviet Lithuanian newspaper had alerted the Justice Department to a sixty-two-year-old Chicago man: United States v. Liudas Kairys, United States District Court for the Northern District of Illinois, Eastern Division, CA 80 C 4302.

He found work at the Cracker Jack Company, married another Lithuanian immigrant: Andrew Gottesman, "U.S. Still Pressing Fight on War Criminals," *Chicago Tribune,* February 8, 1993.

On his visa application, Kairys claimed that he had worked on his father's farm:

Cameron McWhiter, "Accused Nazi Guard Loses Court Bid," *Chicago Tribune,* April 6, 1993.

But in less than twenty months, the Germans had wiped out 1.7 million Jews: "Operation Reinhard," Holocaust Encyclopedia, website of United States Holocaust Memorial Museum.

Back in the 1970s, federal prosecutors in Florida had pursued another man: Feodor Fedorenko, record of sworn statement, United States v. Fedorenko, District Court Southern District of Florida, Fort Lauderdale Division, Immigration and Naturalization Services, 1976, 77-2668-Civ-NCR.

CHAPTER SIX

...Main Commission for the Investigation of Nazi Crimes in Poland, headquartered in a sprawling behemoth of stone and brick: Aleksandra M. Sajdak, senior program manager and genealogist, Taube Center for the Renewal of Jewish Life in Poland Foundation, Warsaw, Poland.

...Czeslaw Pilichowski, a noted scholar and author: "Czeslaw Pilichowski," *New York Times,* October 25, 1984.

...fought in the Polish Communist underground during the war: Czeslaw Pilichowski, oral history, 1981, United States Holocaust Memorial Museum.

The sixty-nine-year-old director was in no mood for pleasantries: Peter Black, conversation recounted in interviews with author, 2017, 2018.

Few other countries, Black knew, suffered more: Museum of the History of the Polish Jews, Warsaw, Poland; "The Invasion and Occupation of Poland," United States Holocaust Memorial Museum.

...wiped out a people and a culture that had influenced Polish life for nearly six hundred years: "Polish Victims," Holocaust Encyclopedia, website of United States Holocaust Memorial Museum.

He was looking forward to working again with Danuta, who had written to him over Christmas: Letters, Peter Black, donated files, United States Holocaust Memorial Museum.

Please undress. Go the bath area. Shower. Relax on the straw: Robert Kuwalek, testimony of a Polish resident of the town of Belzec, *Das Vernichtungslager Belżec.*

...a one-time hothead in the Austrian Nazi Party: Peter Black, "Odilo Globocnik, Nazi Eastern Policy, and the Implementation of the Final Solution," in *Forschungen zum Nationalsozialismus und dessen Nachwirkungen in Österreich. Festschrift für Brigitte Bailer,* ed. Dokumentationsarchiv des österreichischen Widerstandes, Vienna: Plöchl Druck, 2012, 91–129.

...had enjoyed the confidence of top Nazi officials: Peter Black, "Rehearsal for

Reinhard? Odilo Globocnik and the Lublin Selbstschutz," *Central European History* 25, no. 2: 204–226.

Lublin was a blood-stained city: "Lublin: Occupation and the Ghetto," Holocaust Education and Archive Research Team, Holocaust Research Project, www.HolocaustResearchProject.org.

...with a picture of the twenty-three-year-old ethnic Ukrainian dressed in an earth-brown uniform: John Demjanjuk, Trawniki Identification Card, United States Department of Justice, United States v. John Demjanjuk, United States District Court for the Northern District of Ohio, Eastern Division 1:99CV1193.

Black leaned over in his seat: Peter Black, conversation recounted in interviews with author, 2017, 2018.

CHAPTER SEVEN

One of them was a sixty-seven-year-old land surveyor: "Washington Talk: Justice Department; Lobbying the Office That Hunts Nazi Suspects," *New York Times*, March 3, 1987.

Sher had read the court's damning assessment so often that he had committed key passages to memory: Karl Linnas, Petitioner v. Immigration and Naturalization Service, Respondent, 790 F. 2d 1024 (2d Cir. 1986).

...where a court in 1962 had tried him in absentia and found him a traitor and a murderer: Arnold Lubasch, "Deportation of L.I. Man Is Approved," *New York Times*, April 2, 1987.

...Sher had scoffed when Buchanan criticized OSI: Glen Elsasser, "Buchanan Hunts the Nazi Hunters," *Chicago Tribune*, November 6, 1986.

...its pull had reached the most powerful law enforcement agent in the country: Glen Elsasser, "Panama Reversal Bars Suspected Nazi," *Chicago Tribune*, April 16, 1987.

...and in this case the decision was Panama: "Striving for Accountability in the Aftermath of the Holocaust," draft report, Judy Feigin, Office of Special Investigations, United States Department of Justice Criminal Division, December 2008.

Sher needed support, a political powerhouse with strong ties to the Jewish community: Neal Sher, conversation recounted in interviews with author, 2017, 2018.

...Buchanan, who several years later would argue that the diesel engines that pumped carbon monoxide into the gas chambers: Pat Buchanan, "Dividing Line," *New York Post*, March 17, 1990.

...young Jewish girl murdered by a high-ranking member of a Ukrainian militia group: United States v. Kowalchuk, 571 F. Supp. 72 (E.D. Pa. 1983).

...he had often wondered why Pat Buchanan and others had taken such a contemptuous,

public stance against OSI: Bernard Weinraub, "Buchanan Takes on an Influential Role in the White House," *New York Times,* April 11, 1985.

But Buchanan, who had once chastised the Justice Department: "Conservatism Gets Soiled," George F. Will, *Newsweek,* March 3, 1996.

…the lyrical voice of WQXR-FM classical-radio host: "Duncan Pirnie, 70, WQXR Announcer," *New York Times,* November 16, 1993.

…NASA scientist Arthur L. H. Rudolph, who was accused of overseeing slave laborers: Wolfgang Saxon, "Arthur Rudolph, 89, Developer of Rocket in First Apollo Flight," *New York Times,* January 3, 1996.

…Holtzman and Rosenbaum caught a flight to Washington: Eric Lichtblau, *The Nazis Next Door: How America Became a Safe Haven for Hitler's Men,* New York: Harcourt, 2015.

Panama was withdrawing its offer: Jay Mathews, "Agreement to Send Linnas to Panama Is Canceled," *Washington Post,* April 16, 1987.

The aide shook his head, glancing outside: Eli Rosenbaum, conversation recounted in interviews with author, 2017, 2018.

He was about to be double-teamed: Crossfire, CNN, April 15, 1987, video courtesy of Eli Rosenbaum.

The Supreme Court had declined to hear the final appeal: Al Kamen and Mary Thornton, "Accused War Criminal Deported to Soviet Union," *Washington Post,* April 21, 1987.

Linnas struggled at the door of the aircraft: John J. Goldman, "Appeal Fails: Nazi Suspect Deported," *Los Angeles Times,* April 21, 1987.

CHAPTER EIGHT

…where he had taped an adage from a fortune cookie to the door: David Margolick, "The Law: At the Bar, Colleagues Bid Farewell to a Nazi-Hunter, His Quest Ended by Modern Murderers," *New York Times,* December 30, 1988.

Bernstein and Peter Black had worked on investigations of former guards: "Mauthausen," Holocaust Encyclopedia, website of United States Holocaust Memorial Museum.

The only massive concentration camp on Austrian territory: Mauthausen Memorial, Mauthausen Memorial Federal Institution, Mauthausen and Vienna, Austria.

In Bonn in 1954, the Foreign Office of West Germany had signed a critical commitment: Memo, Foreign Office of West Germany, Bonn, Germany, 1954.

American diplomats also secured a nearly identical guarantee from neighboring Austria: "Declaration of Readmissibility to Austria," United States Department of State, 1954.

. . . where they could step off the plane, renounce their American citizenship, and potentially continue to receive Social Security benefits: David Rising, Randy Herschaft, and Richard Lardner, "Millions in Social Security for Expelled Nazis," Associated Press, October 20, 2014.

Rosenbaum also proposed sending defendants to the US occupation sector of West Berlin: Eli Rosenbaum, conversation recounted in interviews with author, 2017, 2018.

. . . the US State Department balked at the idea of agitating the Germans: "Unclassified Action Memorandum," New Department of Justice Program on World War II War Criminals, United States Department of State, 1984.

. . . they had worked on the high-profile Nazi war-crimes investigation: "In the Matter of Kurt Waldheim," Office of Special Investigations, United States Department of Justice Criminal Division, 1987.

Pan Am flight 103, just thirty-eight minutes into its route from London to New York: "Air Accidents Investigation Branch Final Report," National Transportation Safety Board, National Transportation Safety Board Aviation Investigations, London, 1990.

Richard asked a question that Rosenbaum would remember years later: Eli Rosenbaum, conversation recounted in interviews with author, 2017, 2018.

He would deliver remarks at the memorial service on behalf of the Department of Justice: Eli Rosenbaum, remarks during memorial service for Michael S. Bernstein, 1988, courtesy of Eli Rosenbaum.

He would help write the Justice Department announcement, three months later, declaring that a California man who was once an armed SS guard at Auschwitz had been deported to his native Austria: United States Department of Justice press advisory, 1989.

. . . a plane with a bomb wrapped in baby clothes and tucked inside a suitcase: Auslan Cramb, "Charred Baby Suit Traced to Malta," *The Telegraph,* July 12, 2000.

CHAPTER NINE

In the mid-1980s, two members of the Estonian émigré community secretly arranged to collect the trash from a dumpster used by the Office of Special Investigations in downtown Washington: Lawrence Douglas, *The Right Wrong Man: John Demjanjuk and the Last Great Nazi War Crimes Trial,* Princeton, NJ: Princeton University Press, 2016.

. . . they took heaping bags of garbage to a local garage and dumped the contents onto the floor for sorting: Tamar Lewin, "Family of War Crimes Suspect Recounts Its Trial by Ordeal," *New York Times,* June 15, 1992.

Inside the packages, which were sent anonymously, the Demjanjuk family found material that appeared to undermine OSI's case: "Striving for Accountability in the Aftermath of the Holocaust," draft report, Office of Special Investigations, US Department of Justice.

Demjanjuk's family accused the government of withholding critical evidence: "Demjanjuk Family Request Denied by Federal Judge," Jewish Telegraphic Agency, February 7, 1990.

Black was lost in thought when OSI attorney Bruce Einhorn knocked on the door, clutching a slip of paper: Peter Black, conversation recounted in interview with author, 2017.

Black had read an infamous 1944 report about the murder of Poland's Jews: Peter Black, "Odilo Globocnik, Nazi Eastern Policy, and the Implementation of the Final Solution"; Odilo Globocnik, report to Himmler on the results of the Reinhardt Action in Poland, 1944, Nuremberg Trials Project, Harvard Law School Library, Cambridge, MA.

"The evacuation of Jews," Globocnik reported, "has been carried out and completed": Report of Odilo Globocnik to Heinrich Himmler, January 1944, United States Holocaust Memorial Museum.

...in the thousands of demonstrators who had lined the city's grandest boulevard to greet Mikhail Gorbachev: Walter Mayr, "Cutting the Fence and Changing History," *Spiegel Online*, May 29, 2009.

OSI historians had for years dug through the archives in the West and in Poland: Peter Black, "Lease on Life."

A photo of a young Reimer, with cropped black hair, an oval face, and a smile that could have passed for a scowl: Jakob Reimer's Trawniki identification card, United States v. Jack Reimer.

But Reimer had said nothing about the camp: Jakob Reimer, visa application, US Immigration and Naturalization Service, 1951, US Department of Justice.

...investigators from the US Army Counterintelligence Corps found that Reimer had been granted citizenship in Nazi Germany: Investigative file, Jakob Reimer, United States Army Counterintelligence Corps, 1952, US Department of Justice.

CHAPTER TEN

"Fleisch," MacQueen remarked late in the day: Elizabeth "Barry" White, conversation recounted in interviews with author, 2017, 2018.

The documents were thin, faded, and sheared at the edges: Streibel Battalion Files, batches 114-242-6, 114-242-7, Central State Archives, Prague, Czech Republic.

He studied the first page, scanning dozens of names and Erkennungsmarken, *German military identification numbers:* Elizabeth B. White, "History in the Courthouse."

CHAPTER ELEVEN

In May 1945, a British armored cavalry unit had found Odilo Globocnik: "Odilo Globocnik: The Worst Man in the World," Holocaust Education and Archive Research Team.

…Streibel had been born at the turn of the century in southern Poland: Peter Black, "Foot Soldiers of the Final Solution: The Trawniki Training Camp and Operation Reinhard," *Holocaust and Genocide Studies* 25, no. 1 (Spring 2011): 1–99.

Streibel worked for Globocnik in Lublin as early as 1939, mustering and training ethnic German auxiliaries: Peter Black, "Odilo Globocnik, Nazi Eastern Policy, and the Implementation of the Final Solution."

The criminal justice system in West Germany had largely gone soft on Nazi offenders by the 1970s: Bradley Graham, "Eight Are Sentenced for Nazi Crimes," *Washington Post,* July 1, 1981.

The prosecutor offered Black the criminal indictment: Karl Streibel indictment, 1970, United States Holocaust Memorial Museum.

Black was particularly intrigued by the work of historian Mike MacQueen: Peter Black, conversation recounted in interviews with author, 2017, 2018.

One was the protocol of an interview with Streibel himself: Karl Streibel interview, Hamburg, West Germany, United States Holocaust Memorial Museum.

Streibel had also described one of the most dreadful events of the Holocaust: "Trawniki," Holocaust Encyclopedia, website of United States Holocaust Memorial Museum.

Black found a statement from a second guard: Peter Black, donated files, United States Holocaust Memorial Museum.

"What was Trawniki?" a prosecutor had once asked a witness in the Liudas Kairys case: United States v. Liudas Kairys.

Black found the statements and interrogations of former Trawniki men particularly helpful: Peter Black, donated files, United States Holocaust Memorial Museum.

CHAPTER TWELVE

A California jury had acquitted four white police officers: Seth Mydans, "The Police Verdict: Los Angeles Policemen Acquitted in Taped Beating," *New York Times,* April 30, 1982.

He stood up and offered Reimer his hand, an excruciating pleasantry: Transcript of sworn interview, Jakob Reimer.

"There's something about the man who pointed to his head that you haven't told me?" Rosenbaum was fishing again: Transcript of sworn interview, Jakob Reimer; audio of interview excerpts, courtesy of Eli Rosenbaum.

CHAPTER THIRTEEN

Years later, one historian would call Globocnik "the vilest individual in the vilest organization ever known": Gregor Joseph Kranjc, *To Walk with the Devil: Slovene Collaboration and Axis Occupation 1941–1945,* Evanston, IL: Northwestern University Press, 2013.

…he was an intrepid thirty-seven-year-old from Vienna with slicked hair, a long face, and a fanatical devotion to the Nazi Party: Peter Black, "Odilo Globocnik, Nazi Eastern Policy, and the Implementation of the Final Solution."

But Globocnik had soldiered on, focused and fearless, risking prison time to spread Nazi propaganda: Joseph Poprzeczny, *Hitler's Man in the East: Odilo Globocnik,* Jefferson, NC: McFarland and Company, 2004.

In July 1941, Himmler gave Globocnik the go-ahead to build a massive concentration camp on the outskirts of Lublin: Peter Black, "Odilo Globocnik, Nazi Eastern Policy, and the Implementation of the Final Solution"; Tomasz Kranz, "They Arrived at the Ghetto and Went into the Unknown."

"Gentlemen," Globocnik would say later, "if ever a generation will come after us": Paul R. Bartrop, *Resisting the Holocaust: Upstanders, Partisans and Survivors,* Santa Barbara, CA: ABC-CLIO, 2016.

In late summer 1941, Jakob Reimer arrived at Trawniki in a convoy of seventy captured Soviet soldiers: Steinhart, "The Chameleon of Trawniki."

If the Germans discovered his rank, Reimer knew there would be no mercy: United States v. Jack Reimer.

Some received more base pay than junior Reich German Waffen-SS men: Government's post-trial brief, United States v. Jack Reimer.

Early one morning, a company of Trawniki men climbed onto SS trucks: United States v. Jack Reimer.

It was the assembly-line killing that Globocnik had imagined: Peter Black, "Odilo Globocnik, Nazi Eastern Policy, and the Implementation of the Final Solution"; "Odilo Globocnik," Yad Vashem, SHOA Resource Center, the International School for Holocaust Studies.

CHAPTER FOURTEEN

The largest ghetto in German-occupied Poland had once confined more than four hundred thousand people: "Warsaw," Holocaust Encyclopedia, website of United States Holocaust Memorial Museum.

…the inhabitants of the ghetto had fled to a labyrinth of dugouts: Marci Shore, "The Jewish Hero History Forgot," *New York Times,* April 18, 2013.

The inhabitants of the ghetto, with some support from Polish resistance fighters, attacked: Alexandra Richie, "The Jews Who Fought Back: The Story of the Warsaw Ghetto Uprising," History Extra, April 19, 2019, www.historyextra.com.

Jakob Reimer needed a break: Peter Black, "Lease on Life."

…in July 1943, his commanders gave him two weeks off with pay: Transcript of sworn interview, Jakob Reimer, 1992.

But Reimer opted to find his sister in the Ukrainian countryside: Government's post-trial brief, United States v. Jack Reimer.

In Trawniki, Reimer started making plans for a new life after the war: United States v. Jack Reimer.

In 1944, he applied for German citizenship and was recommended for immediate naturalization: Jakob Reimer, immigration file, US Department of Justice.

CHAPTER SIXTEEN

From the deck of the USNS General R. M. Blatchford, *she looked across the Halifax harbor:* NavSource Online: Carl R. Jr. Friberg, "USNS General R.M. Blatchford (T-AP-153)," Photograph, NavSource Online: Service Ship Photo Archive.

A conscientious worker whose concern for his job takes priority over personal interest: Jakob Reimer, immigration file.

…he had been only a guard-soldier and interpreter, and later a paymaster in the Trawniki administration: United States v. Jack Reimer.

CHAPTER SEVENTEEN

…a retired machinist living in the suburbs of Chicago: Matt O'Connor, "Hajda Was Nazi Camp Guard, Court Told," *Chicago Tribune*, March 18, 1997; United States v. Haida, 135 F.3d 439 (7th Cir. 1998).

White had also identified Trawniki man Wasyl Lytwyn: "Ex-Nazi SS Officer Leaves the Country," *Chicago Tribune*, December 16, 1995.

One day in the spring of 1942, about twenty to thirty of us SS men were placed into motor vehicles and driven from Lublin: Transcript of eyewitness statement, Nikolai Leon'tev, 1964, United States v. Jack Reimer.

Black picked up another eyewitness statement, also taken by the Soviets in 1964: Transcript of eyewitness statement, M. E. Korzhikov, 1964, United States v. Jack Reimer.

...Reimer had appeared in his bedroom slippers on the front porch of his house in Lake Carmel and complained to a reporter from New York Magazine: Goldberg, "The Nazi Next Door."

Reimer had been deployed to three Jewish ghettos to participate in mass deportation operations: United States v. Jack Reimer.

...Black and Stutman settled into a conference room at the US Attorney's Office: Transcript of deposition of Jakob Reimer, office of the United States District Court Southern District of New York, Office of Special Investigations, US Department of Justice, 1997.

"There comes a time after the most horrible acts when the possibility of reconciliation outweighs any possible need for retribution": David Margolick, "The Long and Lonely Journey of Ramsey Clark," *New York Times,* June 14, 1991.

CHAPTER EIGHTEEN

...a frontier-fortress outpost built in the 1600s to protect Russia from the Crimean Tatars: Dan Moody, "Penza: One of Russia's Most Historic and Fascinating Cities," *Russia Beyond,* December 5, 2012.

Drug traffickers and mob bosses had commandeered much of Russia: Lee Hockstader, "Russia's Criminal Condition," *Washington Post,* February 26, 1995.

...violent criminals known as Vory v Zakone who had murdered bankers and businessmen: Michael Schwirtz, "Vory y Zakone Has Hallowed Place in Russian Criminal Lore," *New York Times,* July 29, 2008.

Tourists had also been targeted, particularly on the Trans-Siberian Railway and other remote routes: Uli Schmetzer, "Gangs Terrorize Famed Siberian Train," *Chicago Tribune,* November 17, 1993.

As the train to Penza rumbled through the Russian countryside: David Rich, conversation recounted in interview with author, 2018.

"I'm with the United States Department of Justice," Stutman began, speaking slowly to give the interpreter time to convert the words to Russian: Transcript of interview, January 5, 1998, Penza, Russia, United States v. Jack Reimer.

...Neal Sher had gone to New York to meet in chambers with the judge and defense attorney: Neal Sher, conversation recounted in interview with author, 2017.

...who had grown up in New York City during the height of the Cold War: Susan Sachs, "Trial Is Over for a Man Accused in War Crimes," *New York Times,* August 20, 1998.

CHAPTER NINETEEN

...an average guy in comfortable American footwear: "Nazi Guard Hides Face at N.Y. Hearing," *New York Post,* August 4, 1998.

"In Operation Reinhard, which lasted from March 1942 until December 1943, the Nazis killed an estimated 1.7 million Jews," Stutman began: Trial transcript, United States v. Jack Reimer.

Stutman had read up on Clark's involvement in the defense of Karl Linnas: Kenneth B. Noble, "U.S. Deports Man Condemned to Die by Soviet Union," *New York Times,* April 21, 1987.

While awaiting trial, Linnas died of natural causes in a prison hospital in Leningrad: Thom Shanker, "Linnas Dies in Soviet Union," *Chicago Tribune,* July 3, 1987.

Clark had defended other high-profile and controversial clients: Jennifer Latson, "A Murder That Shocked the World, at Sea and on Stage," *Time,* October 7, 2015.

After court, Sydnor and Stutman met for dinner at Windows on the World on the top of the World Trade Center: Charlie Sydnor, conversation recounted in interview with author, 2017.

CHAPTER TWENTY

At seventeen, Sophie Degan had been taken to the training camp to sort the belongings of the dead: Ellen Chubin, conversation recounted in interview with author, 2018.

...Chubin stole a glance at Reimer, who had stared straight ahead for much of the morning as the first survivor took the witness stand: "Holocaust Victims Testify to Horrors," *New York Daily News,* August 11, 1998.

Sixty-eight-year-old Samuel Hilton, an accountant from Arizona, had been a boy of thirteen when the SS ordered every remaining Jew in the Warsaw ghetto to report for deportation: Trial transcript, United States v. Jack Reimer.

CHAPTER TWENTY-ONE

Reimer wore a knit tie and striped shirt, a most ordinary American: Saundra Mandel, "Holocaust Survivors Attend Opening of Former Nazi's Trial," Jewish Telegraphic Agency, August 5, 1998.

For more than two days on the witness stand, Reimer had spun a hard-knock story before the judge: Trial transcript, United States v. Jack Reimer.

"You should get an electric chair!" a woman had called out the day before when Reimer stepped down from the stand, carrying a batch of legal folders: "Court Spectators Rip Accused Nazi," *New York Daily News*, August 18, 1998.

...Reimer was nearing eighty, with stooped shoulders and a cough that had developed after hours on the witness stand: Steve Lipman, "Gov't Pokes Holes in Reimer's Story," *New York Jewish Week*, August 21, 1998.

During a break, Suzanne Stutman pulled her husband into an empty corner in the back of the courtroom and touched his hand: Suzanne Stutman, conversation recounted in interview with author, 2018.

CHAPTER TWENTY-TWO

"It seems that there is always some crime, some image, perhaps from our latest case," Rosenbaum had told a Jewish congregation in Richmond, Virginia, just before the start of the Reimer hearing:* Audio of remarks, Temple Beth-El, Richmond, Virginia, April 19, 1998, courtesy of Eli Rosenbaum.

That same year, the Sixth Circuit Court of Appeals in Cincinnati had lambasted OSI for its handling of the case: Stephen Labaton, "Judges Assail U.S. Handling of Demjanjuk," *New York Times*, November 18, 1993.

"Prosecutorial misconduct," a three-judge panel had bluntly declared: John Demjanjuk, Petitioner-appellant, v. Joseph Petorvsky, et al., Respondents-appellees, 10 F. 3d 338 (6th Cir. 1994).

Eli Rosenbaum had picked it up in Tel Aviv and placed it in a waterproof container: Eli Rosenbaum, memorandum, "Subject: Transporting Four Trawniki Cards from Israel to Washington," 2000, John Demjanjuk file, US Department of Justice.

When Rosenbaum reopened the case against Demjanjuk, the editorial board at the Washington Post *had called the move "correct, even courageous":* "Mr. Demjanjuk's Citizenship," editorial, *Washington Post*, May 22, 1999.

But only his son and son-in-law sat at the defense table alongside Tigar: George J. Tanber, "Suspected Nazi Guard Is Prisoner of Past," *Toledo Blade*, June 4, 2001.

Drimmer was eager to hear from Demjanjuk's lawyer: "Oklahoma City Bombing," Famous Cases and Criminals, Federal Bureau of Investigation.

"Good morning, Your Honor," Stutman said, rising: Trial transcript, United States v. John Demjanjuk, United States District Court for the Northern District of Ohio, Eastern Division 1:99CV1193.

But now Stutman's face was ashen: Jonathan Drimmer, conversation recounted in interview with author, 2018.

CHAPTER TWENTY-THREE

...billboard that John Lennon and Yoko Ono put up in cities around the world in December 1969 as the Vietnam War raged: Jon Wiener, "'War Is Over! If You Want It': John and Yoko, 40 Years Later," *The Nation,* December 27, 2009.

Eight months after the hearing in Cleveland: David Johnston, "Demjanjuk Loses Citizenship Again; Judge Cites Lies," *New York Times,* February 22, 2002.

Federal judge Paul Matia had called the government's evidence "devastating": United States v. John Demjanjuk.

Trawniki became the training ground, command center, and supply depot: Expert report of Charlie Sydnor, September 2000, United States v. John Demjanjuk.

There was silence on the line after Rosenbaum delivered the news: Eli Rosenbaum, conversation recounted in interview with author, 2018.

"Our efforts," Rosenbaum said at the press conference, "were inspired by the courage of the survivors": Audio of prepared remarks, US Department of Justice press conference, 2002, courtesy of Eli Rosenbaum.

Federal judge Lawrence McKenna had ruled for the government, stripping Reimer of his citizenship: Ruling, United States v. Jack Reimer.

In New York, US Attorney James Comey, who would go on to become the seventh director of the Federal Bureau of Investigation, told the New York Times: Benjamin Weiser, "Judge Revokes Citizenship of Man Linked to Nazi War Crimes," *New York Times,* September 6, 2002.

...Trawniki man Vladas Zajanckauskas, who had penned a journal: Linda Matchan, "Two Faces of a WWII Case," *Boston Globe,* September 29, 2007.

"To me, among those who've survived": Benjamin Weiser, "Judge Revokes Citizenship of Man Linked to Nazi War Crimes," *New York Times,* September 6, 2002.

CHAPTER TWENTY-FOUR

"To manage the murder of two million Jews": Peter Black, prepared remarks, "Trawniki Men and Operation Reinhard," Conference, Trawniki, Poland, October 24, 2013.

Judge Sonia Sotomayor, who would later accept a seat on the US Supreme Court, had penned the ruling: United States Court of Appeals for the Second Circuit, United States v. Reimer.

...he later took his case to Germany and, in a speech to scholars and prosecutors, pleaded for help: Eli Rosenbaum, speech delivered at conference, 50th anniversary of the Central Office of the State Judicial Authorities for the Investiga-

tion of National-Socialist Crimes, Ludwigsburg, Germany, December 2, 2008.

"Like the cherry blossoms on the Tidal Basin in Washington": Ned Stutman, *Facing Up: Grateful Ned's Guide for Living and Dying with Grace,* Bloomington, IN: iUniverse, 2009.

EPILOGUE

No other country has more rigorously pursued Nazi war criminals: Efraim Zuroff, "Worldwide Investigation and Prosecution of Nazi War Criminals," Simon Wiesenthal Center, Israel office, December 2016.

"To be successful at preventing future genocides": Guterman, "The History Professional: An Interview with Elizabeth B. White."

Though OSI won cases against dozens of Nazi war criminals, eight defendants under deportation orders died on US soil: Debbie Cenziper and Scott Nover, "Former Guard at Nazi Camp Is the Last Remaining War Collaborator Ordered Out of the United States; Authorities Want Him Gone Before He Dies," *Washington Post,* December 16, 2007.

In August 2018, US authorities, working under a deal cut by the White House, removed former Trawniki man Jakiw Palij from the United States: Debbie Cenziper and Justine Coleman, "'Get the Nazi Out of New York': The Secret Operation to Deport the Last Living Nazi Defendant in the U.S. Was a Rare Success," *Washington Post,* September 1, 2018.

INDEX